Out Spoken
A Vito Russo Reader
Reel One

Out Spoken

A Vito Russo Reader
Reel One

Edited by Jeffrey Schwarz

with Bo Young and Mark **Thompson**

White Crane Books
New York, New York

White Crane Institute / White Crane Books
First edition, first printing: July 2012
ISBN-13 978-1-938246-01-2
ISBN-10 1-938246-01-2

Editor: Jeffrey Schwarz
with Bo Young and Mark Thompson
Associate Editor: Delia Avila
Cover Design: Scott Grossman
Book Design and Production: Toby Johnson
Frontispiece: Howard Cruse
Section Introductions: Mark Thompson
Back Cover Photo: Lee Snyder

Library of Congress Control Number: 2012937090

Contents

A Lavender Lens

Russo on Film

A Quarter Century with Vito Russo

By Michael Schiavi

It is September 1987 in Washington, D.C. I'm seventeen-years-old, a brand-new freshman at American University, spending all my time in the library because I have a couple of secrets. First, I'm gay and trying, with little success, to keep the world ignorant of this fact. Second, I'm in lust with my roommate, who's also gay but clearly uninterested, prompting much horny anguish on my part.

At the library, I'm reading everything I can find on homosexuality, about which I had not realized that sympathetic books existed. Suddenly, there it is on the shelves. *The Celluloid Closet*, in its just-released second edition. Wait a minute. A book on homosexuality *and* film, my other obsession? Too good to be true. The author is Vito Russo, a *paisan*, and a hilarious one at that. Within seconds, I'm on the floor greedily clutching the book, hiccupping with glee over Vito's flippant references to some of my favorite films. The Cowardly Lion might be gay? *Dog Day Afternoon* is based on a true story? *The Ritz* is based on an actual gay club in New York, where Bette Midler had performed?! But Vito also analyzes a ton of films in which homosexuality is treated as either an ugly joke or a social disease. He's livid about this injustice. All at once, so am I.

How I longed to meet this brilliant, funny writer who was introducing me to hundreds of films I'd never heard of. I made it my life's mission to watch every one of them. (Twenty-five years later, I'm close to realizing this goal.) And after a dozen bullied years in Pittsburgh public schools, I started to understand that homosexuality isn't a punch line. Vito taught me that even if Hollywood could be as vicious as my peers had been, some gay men were yelling their lungs out to show just how wrong homophobia was.

Three years later, I was devastated to learn that Vito had died of AIDS. By that time, I was a proud member of the gay community, but it took Vito's death to make me feel the grotesquerie of this unchecked virus robbing us of our leaders.

There was some comfort in knowing that Vito's legacy would live on. In 1995, I cheered the release of Rob Epstein and Jeffrey Friedman's exuberant film version of *The Celluloid Closet*, which brought Vito's name and work to a new generation. Then: silence. Followed by hostility. To the next generation of queer film theorists, the *Closet* book seemed too Hollywood-focused, too kneejerk-offended by outmoded stereotypes. I understood these reactions, but they angered me. Where was the appreciation for Vito's achievement, which was nothing less than the invention of gay and lesbian media studies, the very field that these detractors were plowing?

In response, I wrote an article for *Cinema Journal* assessing Vito's impact on queer film theory. While preparing the piece, I interviewed Dr. Larry Mass, one of Vito's dearest friends, as well as a co-founder of Gay Men's Health Crisis and author of the world's first article on AIDS. Larry casually suggested that someone should write a biography of Vito. Just like that, I had the project that would occupy me for the next five years and give me the greatest professional fulfillment I had ever experienced.

Part of the joy in writing *Celluloid Activist: The Life and Times of Vito Russo* (University of Wisconsin Press, 2011), as well as participating in Jeffrey Schwarz' splendid documentary *Vito* (HBO Documentary Films), has been witnessing the resurgence of interest in Vito's life and career. While promoting my book and teaching gay-themed courses at New York Institute of Technology and Pace University, I've come to realize that almost nobody born after 1970 has ever heard of Vito Russo. But upon learning his story, young people can't help but be inspired by his fervor. I love watching students' dawning admiration as they understand that Vito not only wrote *The Celluloid Closet*, not only helped to shape post-Stonewall gay politics through Gay Activists Alliance (GAA), not only was a co-founding member of the Gay and Lesbian Alliance Against Defamation (GLAAD) and the AIDS Coalition to Unleash Power (ACT UP) — but that he achieved all of this by the age of forty-four.

Vito left us a legacy richly worthy of the term "gay pride." He taught us to come out, no matter our fears, and show the world that our lives matter.

In an era when LGBT teens are routinely bullied to the point of suicide, queer visibility and validity couldn't matter more. Vito also taught us that if we don't like the way we're portrayed in the media, it's our responsibility to stand up and scream about it. I'm writing these words after months of watching Republican presidential hopefuls Mitt Romney, Rick Santorum, Newt Gingrich and Michele Bachmann make international headlines by promising to "defend marriage" against perverts like me. What would you give to see a sixty-five-year-old Vito shrieking himself hoarse at a Republican rally? And how many young queer lives might be saved even now through Vito's love of self and community?

I, for one, can't wait to meet Vito's Twenty-First century successor.

— New York City, February 2012

Editor's Note

By Jeffrey Schwarz

After coming out and becoming secure in my identity as a gay man in the early 1990s, I naturally gravitated toward films with LGBT themes. Even though I was a newbie, there was one book that everyone knew was the bible of gay film - *The Celluloid Closet* by Vito Russo. That book was incredibly empowering for me personally because it fused my passion for film with my burgeoning gay identity. Vito introduced me to a whole world of images I had no idea existed, and helped me see films in a new way. He opened my eyes to the ways Hollywood had depicted LGBT characters on film – as either frivolous clowns, twisted and psychotic villains or pathetic victims. As an activist, Vito knew that the key to acceptance was visibility and championed sympathetic and realistic portrayals of our lives.

Around that time, I read an interview in *The Advocate* with Rob Epstein and Jeffrey Freidman about their upcoming documentary adaptation of *The Celluloid Closet* for HBO Documentary Films. I jumped at the chance to be part of it and moved to San Francisco to become an apprentice editor on the film. Working with Rob and Jeffrey on *The Celluloid Closet* film adaptation gave me a chance to help bring Vito's vision to the screen. It also allowed me to get to know Vito Russo, only three years after his death from AIDS. It was his desire during his lifetime that a film be made from his book, and his spirit was very much guiding the making of that film.

During the making of *The Celluloid Closet*, I had access to a treasure trove of Vito's original research – interviews, articles, videotapes, lectures – and best of all, Rob and Jeffrey's extended conversations with Vito himself. Beyond his work as a film scholar, I learned about Vito's life as an activist within the early gay liberation movement, how he integrated his love of movies with his critique of how they represented LGBT people, and of course his personal story of the years he spent battling AIDS. As he watched the world he loved crumble beneath his feet during the AIDS epidemic, he found a way to channel his rage and grief into effective and history-making activism via ACT UP, which he co-founded. Although he didn't live long enough to see much of the progress he had been hoping for, his work forever changed the landscape for those living with the disease.

Vito participated in every significant milestone in the gay liberation movement – from the dark days of pre-Stonewall invisibility, the Stonewall rebellion and its aftermath, the emergence of LGBT critical studies and independent filmmaking, the formation of GLAAD, and of course the AIDS crisis of the 1980s. His story is the story of the LGBT community, and I felt that making a documentary about him could make these struggles personal and relatable. A film could contextualize how he and his gay liberation brothers and sisters were able to begin to overcome homophobia and oppression, and emerge from invisibility to liberation. The resulting documentary, *Vito*, has helped acknowledge Vito Russo as one of the founding fathers of the LGBT civil rights movement. It's my hope that the film will allow his work to once again move and inspire us all as we continue the battles that he once fought.

In the course of making *Vito*, we were able to uncover and catalog the copious amount of writing Vito produced during his lifetime. The work ranged from celebrity interviews, profiles of people he admired, reportage on gay life in its many hues and, of course, news and views about the movies. It became clear that gathering this hard to find material and making it available to the public needed to happen. The book you hold in your hands is the end result.

As supervising editors Mark Thompson and Bo Young and myself embarked on this project, we realized there was too much material, in fact, to include in just one volume. So that is why *Out Spoken: A Vito Russo Reader* has been published in two companion books - Reel One and Reel Two.

Reel One deals with the cinema, starting off with an array of fascinating conversations with performers and filmmakers. Vito wrote widely about the filmmaking process, and these interviews are followed by a selection of the numerous articles he wrote about the movies — the good, bad, and ugly — for various publications. In the late-1980s he was given a regular film review column in *The Advocate,* and those pieces follow in order until the last one he wrote.

Reel Two deals with a wider variety of topics — candid conversations with politicians and recollections about the early days of the gay liberation movement. More personal essays about places he lived in and liked, on working at the baths, the meaning of camp humor and many other colorful subjects follow. And then, finally, some trenchant notes about living with AIDS and how the epidemic affected others.

In just two decades — the 1970s and 1980s — Vito created an invaluable scrapbook of passionate, funny, searing and well-written words. Now, collected here for the first time, they provide a choice vantage to experience the inner life of a wise and much beloved man, and to witness the rapidly evolving world in which he lived.

"Vito was one of the dearest and most adorable friends I ever had. He was also a ferocious truth seeker. I am grateful to have this collection of his writings. Reading Vito's interview with me was a loving and eye-opening visit with my own consciousness—almost four decades later."

—Lily Tomlin

Show People

Film critic Pauline Kael famously declared she "lost it at the movies." Without a doubt, Vito Russo found everything he was looking for — and more — while deeply immersed in film. A gawky kid, precocious and not prone to playground skirmishes, Vito found a natural refuge in the movie theaters of New York City where he grew up. He'd race home after consuming a whole day's worth of flickering images on the silver screen, eager to download in exact detail what he'd just seen to the first captive listener. For Vito the movies were more than a passion, an escape: It was a life, indeed, his life.

Years later, as a committed, young, gay activist, he used his love of the movies as a means to raise funds for the Gay Activists Alliance, one of the city's first gay rights groups. There at the Firehouse, the group's headquarters and hang-out, Vito would screen old classics for a generation that had probably not seen them. Saturday nights were never so much fun when the likes of The Women *and* All About Eve *were viewed through a thick haze of sweet smoke and lusty bonhomie.*

It was only natural, then, for Vito's vast knowledge of film to be transferred into curiosity about the people who made them—the writers, directors and stars. As he began his freelance journalism career in the early 1970s it was inevitable that he made the world of cinema his beat. He wrote reams of reviews, dozens of thoughtful analysis pieces, but his forte was clearly talking with the talents both on and behind the screen.

Vito was personable — always charming and bright — yet a serious student who knew all the right questions to ask. This obvious sincerity was invariably returned. With defenses down, how could anyone dissemble, deflect or just say no? His interviews are perfect models of the form: intimate and warm, yet always direct and at times audacious.

They could be innovative in their writing style, too. Vito's 1976 conversation with actress (and friend) Lily Tomlin takes the reader on a journey literally all over the map — from swapping stories over a kitchen sink to searching for a vintage car in the depths of Orange County. The article is a mash-up of form and content, intellectually probing and hilarious all at once. Played big as an Advocate *cover story, the article was a real game-changer for both the magazine and its author. In another few years, Vito Russo would be as well-known as some of his subjects.*

Some people lose certain key parts of their character when fame happens, but Vito remained untouched by renown. He stayed the wide-eyed boy with the disarming laugh: his vitality, his truth-digging, his sense of wonder open to the world to the very last.

Bette Midler

The Advocate — **April 23, 1975**

Don't let all the recession-obsessed soothsayers fool you. People are still lining up to see a good show. At around midnight of the evening before tickets went on sale at New York's Minskoff Theatre for *Bette Midler's Clams on the Half Shell Revue,* the line began to form for what turned out to be the largest single-day ticket sale in Broadway history. The previous record had been set more than a year ago by Bette Midler at the Palace Theatre. Red Skelton said it when he was told that over 10,000 people had shown up at movie mogul Harry Cohn's funeral: "Give the people something they want to see and they'll come out for it." At a time when people are selling apples on the street corners in Greenwich Village for $1.50 each, I'm convinced that we do indeed "need it now."

It wasn't always so easy to sell tickets to a Bette Midler concert. There was a time when you could take your pick of any one of fifty empty folding chairs in the basement of the Continental Baths on 74th Street. All you had to do was take a breather from the upstairs activity. The rest of the patrons were 100 feet away, splashing in the pool, oblivious to the fact that the little woman with the red hair would someday command the attention of the entire entertainment industry. Bette Midler would complain weekly that the pool activity and "that goddam waterfall" were cramping her act.

Playing the baths was a new and, believe it or not, daring thing for a performer to do in those days. No entertainer with ambition to be anything would consider it. Playing gay-oriented bars and hangouts was the mark of a faltering career. Bette had been knocking around New York since 1965 when she arrived on the money from a bit part in the motion picture *Hawaii.* She auditioned endlessly for *Fiddler on the Roof* and played Tzeitel in it for three years, often spending her late evenings singing in showcase bars and gypsy hangouts in the theater district. She was working at The Improvisation when she heard about the Continental Baths and its owner, Steve Ostrow, who would give her $50 a night to sing for gay men in towels. It proved to be the turning point in her career, garnering the attention of the New York press and eventually an audition for *The Tonight Show*. The publicity she got at the time was due as much to the fact that she was singing in a gay bathhouse as the fact that she was shaping up as the hottest thing in music since Barbra Streisand. Critics compared her to Piaf and Garland and waxed ecstatic about the Jewish girl from a Samoan neighborhood in Hawaii who grew up to be the darling of the beautiful people in a decadent New York bathhouse.

Bette was in her element in those days. It is fair to say that the people who saw her then probably saw the best and most exciting work of her career thus far. Every night she took her audience someplace else, enacting all of her fantasies and the fantasies of the audience. They pushed her to the absolute limits of her daring and gave her the kind of support and confidence which made her a star.

She sang things at the baths which she has not recorded and has seldom, if ever again, done in concert. There were moments during which she taught her audience sides of herself yet to be revealed to the general public. Also, she got away with more than she could later on. The world wasn't watching yet and she could afford to be self-indulgent and try out new things on the spot. Low-down songs like "Fat Stuff" by Seth Allen and "I Need a Little Sugar in My Bowl," a Bessie Smith favorite, have all but disappeared from her repertoire, along with strokes of genius like "Marijuana" from the film *Murder at the Vanities*. She'd wrap a pink towel around her head and stick ten-cents-worth of fake cherries in it and do Carmen Miranda for twenty minutes. She also developed a resiliency at the baths which served her well later on the road. It made her tough.

The folding chairs began to fill up, and it wasn't so easy to get a seat anymore. If you were at the baths for fun and games and wanted to catch the show you had to come downstairs an hour early and wait for the seats to be set up so as not to lose out. Mick Jagger showed up. Rex Reed came in a strictly professional capacity for the first time to check things out. The

Warhol crowd and the beautiful people began to drift down to rub elbows with the young lovers in towels who held hands throughout the performance.

Some of the heterosexual couples didn't know what to make of it all. A new tour guide agency which sponsored "Mystery Tours" began to make the Continental a surprise stop on the agenda, leading housewives from Dubuque and their nervous husbands down into the steamy depths of a subterranean nightclub to be surrounded by men in towels. Incidents were common. A straight woman called a man a drag queen and he threw her in the pool. Fights broke out between straight men and gay men who tossed off their towels and danced nude in front of shocked wives. It was, as we were fond of saying, "a trip."

It also provided Bette with enough comedy material to last her entire career. She went through it in a weekend. Reverend Troy Perry of the Metropolitan Community Churches came one Saturday night to make a speech about the advent of Gay Pride Week. Bette rushed into her dressing room and shouted, "Quick! Gay priest jokes!" Onstage she feigned incredulity.

"Whhhhaaat is this? Bingo on Friday, Bango on Saturday? They oughtta call this dump 'Our Lady of the Vapors.' Tonight he'll walk on the water in the pool, and tomorrow night he'll be walking the third floor. Puhleeese."

It was a happy family in spite of the chic invaders who grew in number each week. Bette, now appearing occasionally on late-night television, could remain fiercely loyal to the Continental and the gay men in her audience. "Lissen, they gave me a big push and that'll always be part of me even after I've moved on. Me and those guys just went somewhere else."

Move on she did, to pack Carnegie Hall on a late June night in 1972 and to draw almost 100,000 people to Central Park for a Schaefer concert. It was the happiest time of her career to date ("I felt like Marilyn Monroe in a newsreel from Korea"). Many changes began to take place. After a farewell performance at the Continental Baths which packed over 1,000 people into a space meant for 500, it was clear that she had outgrown the space. She began to work on her first album, a process which took ten months and three producers due to her unrelenting quest to know every aspect of studio recording. She embarked on a cross-country tour (backing up her material a little) so that the people in Buffalo could catch up on the latest dish on Karen Carpenter's drumming ("It sucks") and Johnny Carson's penchant for wives named JoAnn ("He must've had a sled named JoAnn when he was a kid"). She paused long enough to politely but firmly decline an invitation to sing for Richard Nixon at the White House but found the time to go to a Chicago suburb and sing "Friends" and "Boogie Woogie Bugle Boy" for seventy people at a benefit for George McGovern.

On New Year's Eve, 1973, at midnight, she rose up from beneath the stage at Lincoln Center's Philharmonic Hall in a diaper, singing "Auld Lang Syne."

"My dears, are you ready for this! Philharmonic Hall. Heavy on the Danish Modern. From 74th Street to 65th Street in a single year!"

They loved it, and rock critic Lillian Roxon said the next day, "1973 is *definitely* here."

Once again that year, Bette reminded us that she was loyal and grateful to her gay following by appearing before 17,000 gay men and women in New York's Washington Square Park to help celebrate Gay Pride Week. In jeans and a red work shirt, knotted at the waist, she burst upon the stage and drawled, "Lissen, I heard a little bit of this on the radio and it sounded like you people were beating each other up out here so I came to sing a song." She did two choruses of "Friends" and was carried over the barricades to a waiting car. Her accompanist that day on the piano was Barry Manilow, her longtime musical arranger who heard the proceedings on the radio and decided to join her.

Later that year she was awarded *After Dark*'s Ruby Award and accepted it with a good-natured smirk, hardly recognizing her old friends from the baths in their tuxedos and black ties. She went on the road again, while her manager planned a limited engagement at the Palace Theatre. It promptly sold out and became the theatrical event of the New York concert season, leaving Liza Minnelli and Josephine Baker second and third in the running. For this engagement she was given a special Tony Award. She also received the year's Grammy Award as the Most Promising Newcomer. It was handed to her, appropriately, by Karen Carpenter. Doubled up with giggles, she kissed Carpenter and said, "Oh, my dears, isn't this a hoot? Me and Miss Karen. I'm surprised she didn't hit me over the head with it."

The Palace stint, in spite of all the publicity and the accolades, was more of an emotional and financial success than a musical one. Bette was tired, and her voice was weary from all those nights on the road. On her opening night she raced across the stage in a frantic last bust of energy and effort and tried to make it all work by dint of sheer goodwill. The show was commercial and slick and it showed. When she said, "shit," it was because she knew that the hipsters from northern New Jersey and the young marrieds from Bayside expected it. It was shock and tits all the way. These people had heard about the trashy lady from the baths and she was giving them what they wanted. If she got upset or bored with what the audience asked of her, she put down *last* night's audience. It wasn't Bette Midler, and it wasn't even The Divine Miss M. It was what the press told the people to expect, and they loved it. Suddenly they were decadent and "in."

It wasn't her fault; she was tired and was learning not to give all of herself all the time. In a conversation with her longtime friend and comedy writer, Bill Hennessey, I asked if she'd made a conscious decision not to give all of herself every night.

"Absolutely. You just can't do it. Look at Joplin. She attempted to do it all the time and it burned her out. Of course, she did it with the help of drugs, but that only attests to the fact that it's an impossible thing for a human person to achieve."

I was in the dressing room when Bette would come back dripping wet after playing to ten to fifteen thousand people and say, "Hey, fuck *this*! I was out there giving my ass and tits and my soul and I got nothing back." And she was right. "You just can't keep it up or it'll kill you."

The time had come for a vacation. For the past sixteen months Bette has been traveling, going to the movies, seeing shows and taking classes in anything that interests her or will help her work. She took tap dancing lessons and attended lectures on animation techniques at the School of Visual Arts. She worked briefly as a presenter on the Grammy Awards show and appeared recently on the Cher special, but for the most part has enjoyed herself and stayed out of the public eye.

A few months ago, plans were completed for her return to Broadway. She was been working twelve hours a day with choreographer Joe Layton, readying herself for what promises to be an evening full of surprises. Tony Walton has designed a number of sets which are to form the framework for her different moods and songs, including a barroom scene in which she will perform "Drinking Again." The show's run is limited, but plans have already been made to extend it for another six weeks and to take it to Los Angeles when it closes in New York.

The show opens in Philadelphia, and Bette can see me for a brief session on the day she is preparing to leave. When I arrive at her house in Greenwich Village she is in the kitchen in a green velvet bathrobe, making scrambled eggs. She's just gotten up. I remember that Richard Amsel had jokingly suggested I ask if she slept in the nude.

"No, I sleep in flannel pajamas and two pairs of socks with an electric blanket 'cause there's no heat in this house. How are ya?"

I begin to go through the motions of thanking her for the interview, and she says, "Yeah, I know, Vito," and smiles a little. I know that she's thinking, "*if everybody is so sorry for bothering me, then why doesn't anybody leave me alone?*" Giving my cigarette the evil eye she calls for an ashtray, and we sit at her little dining room table while she inhales her scrambled eggs.

"So, how does it feel to be back on Broadway?"

"Well, I'm not there yet, but I'm excited and looking forward to it."

I asked her what ways she thinks her music has changed after having had a year off.

"It's not so much my music that's changed as my perspective on my work. I think it's changed a little bit. I'm not as frightened as I once was, mostly because I don't have all that much invested in it. I'm not as emotional about it as I once was. I enjoy it a lot more, you know? At least I've certainly enjoyed these rehearsals. Generally when I'm in rehearsal I'm a mess, you know, because last time I mostly did a lot of the work myself, organizing the people.

"Barry Manilow used to do the music and we always had someone come in to do the girls, generally Andre De Shields who came in again this time, but there was organizing the clothes and where we were going to go and what our attitudes were going to be and all that stuff. It used to drive me nuts. This, however, has been a very much easier thing for me to do. It's like a framework, and I come in and I go out of it and don't have to be there all the time. Even if I'm not there, it just chugs along without me and that's terrific."

Trying to get a line on new things in the show, I ask her if her tap dancing lessons will be put to use now.

"No, not me, dear. My girls will do a little dancing and of course I have a few steps as usual, but no heavy dancing."

We talk awhile about what she's been doing for a year and the movies and ballets she's seen. We talk about *Funny Lady*.

"Oh, I thought the first half was quite marvelous. I liked that."

Is Barry Manilow involved in this show?

"You mean *in* it? No. He's done some music for it, but he won't be in it. He's away in Denver now."

Is the smoke from my cigarette bothering her, and how would she like to talk about the possibility of doing a movie soon?

"Yes, the cigarette bothers me, and no, I don't know anything about a film. I do have a script which I think is marvelous but nothing definite."

When I ask her about elaborating on the script she just smiles and shakes her head. Plowing right ahead, I ask her wouldn't she like to play Dorothy Parker or Piaf.

"Oh, I'd love to, sure." Then a quick change. "Vito, what is the meaning of the earring you wear in your right ear as opposed to the left?"

I tell her that it means absolutely nothing, and that it's only jewelry, which I am getting tired of because it attracts more attention that it's worth. I also tell her that in case she's wondering, it's not an S&M thing with me.

"Yeah. Vito, that's what they all say."

So much for our discussion of her film career. What about television, then? Does she plan a special?

"Oh, well, I loved doing the Cher show, but no. I have no plans for a special. Last year ABC wanted to do a television thing with the show at the Palace, live, but I was so tired and when I thought of all those lights and cameras… oh, I just don't think I could have borne it. It was too much for me. I barely got through as it was.

"The Cher show was really wonderful, though. I had a good time doing that. You know, I hadn't worked for a solid year and here were all these people fetching and carrying and patting you and plumping you up and teaching you dance steps and laughing at you and saying 'Oh, aren't you just the most wonderful thing that ever walked' and oh, it was wonderful. I mean it's a whole other world, you know. It has nothing to do with real life."

I reminded her about the old-age skit where she and Cher and Flip Wilson and Elton John played aging rock stars in an old folks' home.

"That was Elton's skit all the way. Wow, it was fun. He stole that skit. We were hysterical at Elton absolutely all the time. He was brilliant. I really adore him, first of all because he's an incredibly funny human being. He loves to laugh. And he puns all the time. He loves puns. Yeah, he's very much a down-to-earth person and I really love him."

Wasn't she cutting a single with Paul Simon?

"Oh, sure, that's still around. Paul works on it once in a while. He's a very meticulous person. It's called 'Gone At Last,' and I'll be doing it in the show. I'll be doing it with my choir. We're working with the Michael Powell Ensemble, a gospel group from Harlem. On the record we did it with Jesse Dickson's group, three women and a man. They're friends of Paul's. It has a gospel feel to it, and it's a terrific song. Paul wants to work on it until he makes it mind-boggling. He's a perfectionist that way."

What about the third album she's cutting now?

"Well, I go in and I cut when I feel like it, but I haven't really started putting it together yet. Mostly I'm just learning my way around the studio and the producers."

Will it be on the same label or a new one?

"Oh, same label, dear. My dear, I owe them a hundred and fifty-two albums! Well, I owe them two albums a year and I've been with them for three years, so there's just a little bit of backlog. But they don't bother me. They go along their merry way. You know, I'm tempted to record this next show live because there are so many good voices in it with Lionel Hampton and all. It would really make a great album."

The room is beginning to fill with the sounds of departure noises, with people arriving to help pack and Bette's secretary, Patrick Merla, taking calls and messages.

"Is there anything you'd like to say about your musical base? Has it changed? Is it more serious in any way?"

Bette is scrunched up in her chair now, massaging a bruised knee where she hurt herself doing a step the other day.

"I think my musical base has broadened. I try not to take anything too seriously. I still have what people would call my camp business. My singing has gotten a little better, but I still find myself getting hoarse. I've had a little time to listen to new things in the past year and explore different forms. Music is music, you know? And if it enlivens your life it's fine. All kinds of music is wonderful to me — always has been. Saw a great jazz singer the other night at The Cookery. Helen Humes. You ever see her? You should really go. She's sixty-one years old and has a crystal clear voice that's real high and she doesn't sing anything past 1945. She sings in exactly that idiom and she has the most incredible phrasing. I've heard a lot of dames and guys on record and who could do that but not live like she did."

She remembers suddenly that a mutual friend of ours is back in town from San Francisco and I tell her that he's doing research for a project on Judy Garland.

"Christ, him and everybody else. He's only one of about a hundred people. A friend of mind has all her old TV shows and we watched a lot of them one night. She had a huge following: I guess a lot of people know a lot of things about her. It's interesting to see the TV things like that because you can see the way she worked. It's amazing. Some of the stuff, like the classic songs she does, are just wonderful, but she was singing real garbage, like the things people wrote especially for her, I mean it was just such real garbage and she just sailed right through it as if it didn't matter at all."

I read an interesting interview with Barbra Streisand the other day and I ask Bette's opinion about Streisand saying that she's done everything and doesn't have the ambition she used to have. She's thinking of retiring.

"Well, I haven't achieved what I set out to do yet. But I *like* to work. I am a fairly ambitious person, and I think I have the talent to create something of lasting value. I haven't finished up yet. There are all areas of the theatrical arts in my life. I like the theater and I love movies and dance. I love it all. In terms of 'making it,' I'm not the biggest thing that ever was. That doesn't bother me. I like the fact that I can draw an audience. I like that people will pay to see me and be pleased or whatever; it makes me very happy. When I'm finished doing what I have to do in this area I will move on to another related form. It's the *doing* that's fun. The work is fun. It's the going, not the getting there."

I point out that the world is changing rapidly and that some people can't cope with it.

"But it's the way of the world, though, Vito. We're not the first people to have to go through traumas or crises. You wouldn't have wanted to be around during the Black Plague now, Vito, would you? There are always the best of times and the worst of times all the time. It's part of being on the planet. We haven't learned everything yet. I just wish somebody would contact another planet. There'd be so much more to talk about. You know, I take the *Smithsonian Magazine* and there's this article in it about this old civilization that's just been found. I tell this to everybody. It's on the Danube in Yugoslavia and it's 7,000 years older than the oldest caveman drawings. It's intelligently laid out in little trapezoidal areas. (She is drawing little areas on the table with her fingers and is really getting into describing the city in a very fascinating way.) One day these people who lived there just up and left or disappeared. Imagine? So there's a lot going on we don't know about."

Her face is puzzled for a minute and then she says:

"You know, I said something last night to Claudia Dryfus from Newsday about *After Dark* magazine being a gay magazine. It didn't even occur to me that it wasn't the right thing to say."

I tell her that if it was a natural comment, it's okay because there must be something to it.

"Well, you know, Vito, their editorial policy just kills me! *Everything* is wonderful."

Now I think about her comments in *Gay* magazine two years ago when asked what she thought of gay liberation. She told Leo Skir, "For Christ's sake, open your mouths; don't you people get tired of being stepped on?"

"You know, Bette, I'm sort of involved in the gay issue."

"Involved, Vito? *Involved?*" Her eyes are wide in disbelief of my understatement. Then she smiles and says:

"Really, it's nice. I absolutely think you should be."

I ask if she thinks there's a gay audience any more than there's a straight audience.

"I don't know about that, Vito. I really don't. I know that there are individuals, but I don't know if there's a group of people who call each other up and say 'Let's all meet tonight and we'll go to see, uh, Shirley Bassey.' I just don't think it happens. It's not the way it is."

I feel obligated to point out the issue is that performers should let their gay fans know that it's all right to be whoever you are. I do *not* point out to her that after a recent screening of *Sunday, Bloody Sunday* Shirley Bassey said that she had to leave the theater because seeing two men kiss made her sick to her stomach.

"Oh, hell, Vito, listen. It's all right for *anybody* to be who they are. Just as long as they don't let their dogs shit on the street. Just so they don't make your life miserable. I don't think there's enough time to fritter your life away thinking bad things or venomous thoughts about other people and how they live."

She is tired from sitting and has to go to Philadelphia in a few hours. My final question is how does Bette Midler want to end up? What happens much later?

"I think I would like wind up my days in repertory. I would, really, and I'm sort of looking forward to it. You see, I do a lot of studying on my own. Each morning I get up and learn a new little voice or character. I'd like to end up in London, maybe, doing Shakespeare, God forbid…truly…because I have this great fascination with it and a great love for it at the same time. I think that it's a good way to die. It's a good way to end up. I think that people should never stop working no matter how old they are. I think there should be no such thing as retirement. Retirement is the pathway to an early grave. When you lose your work and what interests you, you lose your will to live, and I'm not that kind of person."

A slow and famous smile creeps across her face. It's evident she's thought all these things before.

"I think there are so many paths to take, so many things to learn in this world. I just hope the world is around long enough for me to see as much as I want."

She is positively preoccupied now by the sense that it is getting late and she has a bus to catch. I make ready to leave, and we chat about the show and Philadelphia and Arthur Bell and the *Village Voice* and it's time to leave.

"Take care of yourself, Vito. Love to Bruce. See you here in a few weeks."

In a few weeks Bette Midler will be back doing what she does best: making her music and doing things that people dream of doing all their lives — what she wants, what she loves. Few people have that in this world.

Hell, you could sell tickets to something like that.

Ronee Blakely

Nashville, Her Career, Her Gay Brother, and
Views on Gay Liberation

The Advocate — December 17, 1975

Ronee Sue Blakely, born in Nampa, Idaho. Studied ballet, piano and sewing. Belonged to Girl Scouts, girl's quartet and was a cheerleader. After having a nervous breakdown in the sixth grade, she dropped Girl Scouts. When she was eighteen she took up with a Hungarian gambler and went over the hill. She likes champagne, Faulkner, O'Neill, Oldenberg, Joyce and Drurer. She comes from a girl's school, a university, a conservatory and Hollywood. She studied five languages and speaks none of them. She is for the freedom of all oppressed peoples, especially men. She is fascinated by duplicity but intolerant of it. The most important thing is her honor. The way she sees it, her mother always wanted to be Judy Garland and her father, John Wayne. She has always wanted to be Ronee Blakely, and that seems harder than the fantasies and illusions built on dreams.

Most of that information comes from a biography of Ronee Blakely included in a promotional copy of her Elektra album, released three years ago. It was called, simply, *Ronee Blakely* and featured ten songs she wrote herself. Three of them, "Dues," "Bluebird" and "Down to the River," were used in Robert Altman's *Nashville*, the film which made Ronee Blakely a star. It has also turned her life slightly upside down. One day she could walk down the street in perfect privacy, and the next, her picture graced the cover of *Newsweek* and articles in her hometown paper in Idaho were doing the hometown-girl-makes-good routine.

"It's really strange to actually *say*, 'I'm an actress, a singer and a songwriter' you know, It's such a trip to try to be professional. This is what I've been doing all my life! But it takes a lot of nerve to say it because then all your friends are saying, 'Oh, she thinks she's better than us' or something. You just have to learn to define yourself as what you really are and have courage about it."

We are sitting in her fifth floor, New York-style apartment overlooking Sunset Boulevard, the sounds of traffic wafting up through the open windows. We are drinking champagne, which I brought with me after reading her bio, and eating macadamia nuts and munchies.

Is all this attention suddenly made your life crazy?

No, I'm pretty solitary anyway and it will stay that way. I did do something I thought I'd never do, though. I had my number changed today to an unlisted one. It was absolutely necessary because I can't get any work done at all with the phone ringing all the time.

Are you aware that it's pretty unusual for a performer to talk about a member of their family being gay, as you have about your brother?

No, but then I'm not the one who's gay. Steve's just very upfront about who he is as a person, and it's not that he stands on Hollywood Boulevard with a sign or speaks from a podium about gay liberation. Being a gay liberationist is just person-to-person, being who you are wherever you go. I was very pleased to see that they described him in *People* magazine as "artist, poet and gay liberationist" …it was totally satisfying.

What's the next step?

The next step is that people who are gay are just going to have to go ahead and talk about it. The problem is really labels. It's amazing that we only have a limited amount of words to cover who we are in the advanced age of the world. We have one word "love" and one word "like" and then "straight," "bi" and "gay" to cover the totality of emotions which are *so* complex and enormous. The fact that these labels have any effect and that they are capable of ruining careers is absolutely frightening! And the guilt they give you! It's a way to put people in a box, like saying, "What's your major?"

How does your family feel about it?

Oh, you have no idea how good it's been. Steve sent our parents a beautifully written letter saying he was gay, and he did it so well that there was really no problem. Do you know that he went home to Idaho with his lover for Christmas and they got to sleep together and everything? But I can't go home with *my* lover because we're not married! Can you dig *that*? It's like they don't *really* know too much about gayness, and they figure Steve is their son and they'll always love him, but heterosexuality is something they know about and they just don't approve of certain lifestyles like not getting married and such. Plus I'm the girl, you know, and they expect certain things.

I had a talk with my father recently and I told him that I didn't feel he really loved me because he really loved an image he had of me. I felt he disapproved of my lifestyle and that really hurt me to where I can't tell you. It was really painful to have to talk to someone who disapproved so much of what I was doing. If someone loves you, they love you for what you *are*, not what they would like you to be. Otherwise it isn't love at all.

How do you handle fag jokes and stuff?

Well, my brother doesn't sit around in a room and take any insults, and neither do I, especially about "queers" or things like that. The only thing that bugs me is that we're gonna have "token" gay friends now. You know, like people will say, "Don't say that because I have a gay friend." I'm glad it's my brother so I can say, "Look, you're all wrong and I *know*."

Do you think it's ready to happen in show-business?

I think it's ready to happen for the first person willing to take it on. It's very tough, though. Remember when Joan Baez did it? Afterwards she had to go to great lengths to cover her tracks, so she really must have gotten some flack about it. And she's a very brave woman, you know.

Have you had any trouble because of it?

Not really, but you know there's a place up in San Francisco called The Wild Side West, where I used to sing all the time. It really kept me alive. It's a very homey, creative club where they pay you they do it with love and wish it were more, you know. So it's a gay women's club and *People* magazine said that I'd played everywhere from college concerts to a San Francisco lesbian bar. That was great, except that I felt it might have been a down for my friends at the club. It was like a downward comparison, like saying from the best to the worst, and that bothered me a bit for my friends who have done nothing but good for me.

My trip is total non-discrimination, and I won't play anywhere where men aren't allowed. When I play Wild Side West, men are allowed in. I've been hassled here in Los Angeles at Studio One when I've gone with my brother. The whole trip is that people start to come out, and they get a certain amount of pride, and then inherent in their assertion of themselves is the putting down of someone else. They always have to keep others out to insure their freedom.

Which is okay when straight men are coming into "beat up the queers," but I see the whole movement as more than just a means to an end. I can no longer tolerate groups of gay people who won't accept people who aren't gay any more than I can tolerate it the other way around.

Sure, it's that gay people are now looking down on other gay people who don't conform to their idea of what people should be like.

Yeah, like transvestites. I don't think they should be discriminated against, either. They have a right to do and be whatever they want. Listen gang, there's nothing like solidarity. As a matter of fact, that's something that's bothered me about *The Advocate*. If anything, I've always thought that it was totally sexist. I support it totally because I believe it is good, but it *must* expand to include all people, right?

There are more women beginning to work on it now and hopefully that's one of the things which will change about it.

Well, I'm glad to hear that, just as I'm glad that there are more men coming to the club I work in San Francisco. You know, I was in the White House a couple of weeks ago and I was talking to Ron Nessen, and I told him that I was running for President in 1976 on a platform based on massage parlors and houses of prostitution for women to go to. If there's any example of male supremacy in this world, it's that for centuries a man could go to any town in the country and get laid but a woman can't.

[Steve Blakely arrives. He is handsome, quiet and soft-spoken. He reads some of his poetry, which is beautiful, and we send out for another bottle of champagne. Ronee has missed an appointment, and I've noticed that the sun is sinking.]

Tell me something…

Yes, yes, what do you want to know?

In your bio you said that your mother wanted to be Judy Garland and your father John Wayne, and then in "Bluebird" there's a line that goes "If bluebirds fly then why can't I?" and in your breakdown scene in Nashville *you talk about liking* The Wizard of Oz *and talking like a munchkin…*

My, my, my…aren't you observant, though? Nobody ever picked up on that stuff before.

Tell me about it.

Well, you just told *me* about it. It's just *there*, that's all. My mother sang in talent contests in Kansas when she was little, and she won singing "Over the Rainbow" in Smith County and I remember when she took me to see *The Wizard of Oz* and it turned to color. I screamed bloody murder at the witch's green face and had to be taken from the theater.

How much of that breakdown scene in the hospital was jealousy between you and Connie White?

None, really. I thought Barbara Jean was jealous of the fact that Connie White was on the Opry stage, but not of her as a person. The breakdown scene was to show that Barbara Jean wasn't all sweetness and light, that there was a jungle side to her as well. Barbara Jean's only contact with friendship was her fans, and that's why she was jealous. Outside of Haven Hamilton and her husband and Lady Pearl, she had no friends.

Is it true that the actors would get together and decide on scenes between themselves?

Yeah, all the time, and I think we went too far sometimes. Like we thought that since Lady Pearl and Barbara Jean were friends, she would come to visit me in the hospital even though it wasn't in the script. So Barbara Baxley went out and bought a fifty-dollar doll to bring out, and then she went and showed it to Altman and he said, "Wait a minute! That's real nice, but we've got 18 hours of film. What the hell's going on here?" She had to return the doll.

Why do you think the assassin pulled the trigger when he did? Why you?

Well, I thought that's one question they'll never ask me because I'm dead, right? Ha! Oh, I think it could have happened at any time. I thought he came there to kill Hal Philip Walker and there was so much emotion going on. Barbara Jean was up there, and the flag was waving, and it almost brought tears to *her* to sing "Idaho Home" and maybe he felt his own wretched life more pronounced. I would never put it into all these words if I didn't *have* to. He went there to kill somebody and I have never gone anywhere to kill someone but I imagine that your state of mind, once you get there, is such that it doesn't matter who you kill as long as they're important.

Was there a lot of discussion about it?

Well, we had to do it in two takes because I only had two dresses and they exploded. They were wired for the shots, you know. So I asked Altman should I die right away because I'd had a few words prepared...ha-*ha*...and he said, "I'll tell you later," and just before the scene he said, "Die instantly." In some ways I feel it doesn't need to be explained because there are such things as irrational acts.

I remember reading that Altman used the word "fag" in reference to a character in one of his films recently.

Yeah, well I'm not too sure about him anyway. He's great but a little... well, we just have to change the language, that's all. For everyone.

What now?

Now I start to work again on my music. I'll be playing clubs and looking at scripts and things, but mostly it's my music. I have a lot of work to do. You may get to see me at Reno Sweeney in New York yet. Just hang in there.

Lily Tomlin

**With Edith Ann and Ernestine, co-starring Boogie Woman, the
Fame Fairy, a 1956 Corvette, 24 Tourists From Connecticut, and
Several Very Perplexed Busboys, Waiters, Parking Lot Attendants
and Passers-By**

The Advocate — **January 14, 1976**

> *Oh, I'm a clown*
> *and I'm proud to be.*
> *Big shoes and red noses,*
> *bright faces and free...*

Lily Tomlin is an original and demands to be studied. Her career is
unlike that of any other American entertainer in that she shows us ourselves
by showing us parts of who she is through her diverse characters. For those
of you who do not read, go to nightclubs or concerts, listen to radio, watch
television, buy record albums or, more recently, go to the movies, Lily Tomlin
is the funniest group of people in the business.

Her film debut in Robert Altman's *Nashville* drew unanimous raves.
Her sarcastic, irrepressible telephone operator, Ernestine, became the hit of
Rowan and Martin's *Laugh-In* in the late 1960s and was the subject of the
Grammy Award-winning album, *This Is A Recording*. Her five-and-a-half-
year-old Edith Ann, funny and sad, wise and theatrical, has a best-selling
album of her own called *And That's The Truth*, which Tomlin buffs claim is
the first comedy album which is consistently revealing and funny even after
years of playing. Lily Tomlin has won two Emmys for her television specials,
which have been hailed for their singular perception and thoughtful humor,

and will release a single for the Bicentennial, consisting of a tribute to her hometown — Detroit — and Edith's storytelling monologue from her last TV show.

She radiates a refreshing, foot-loose diversity which is as present in her daily life as it is in her work. Her characters are not "taken from life"; they are simply borrowed, shown and left intact. Each of them lives out in the world somewhere. Edith Ann is a bittersweet remnant of her childhood, haunting the streets of her neighborhood world, looking for someone to talk to, to entertain with the latest gossip, to complain to that she "had a terrible day at school today" and who sometimes needs an Alka-Seltzer. There is Lupe, the world's oldest beauty expert; Bobbi-Janene, the cocktail organist who listens to people's troubles with a smile and a song; the 1950s teenager at the dance and Susie Sorority fighting for the squares of the world, by golly. And, of course, Ernestine, commenting on everyone with a deadpan directness and a sharp ear for trouble.

Interviewing Lily Tomlin, therefore, is a little like sharing a lifeboat with Eve White, Eve Black and Jane with Sybil at the oars. *They* are there at all times, and one is almost never unaware of them. If Lily says something with which Ernestine disagrees, a snort somehow works itself into the conversation. Edith Ann comments occasionally upon the way of things and promptly disappears, leaving a smiling Lily Tomlin.

Her two Emmy Awards are used as doorstops in her just-this-side of Beverly Hills home, which is filled with eye-catchers like the picture over the mantle of her uncle, dressed like Josephine Hull in *Arsenic and Old Lace*. The genuine Wurlitzer juke-box plays Al Jolson 78s, and the statues surrounding the pool wear Dynel wigs and sunglasses.

Not all of what came to be known at this interview took place there. Other locations included various restaurants, a visit to Ports O'Call in San Pedro, a recording session for her aforementioned single, and a drive to Torrance, California, in my rented Vega, to look at a '56 Corvette she considered buying.

Only a few of these occasions yielded actual interviewing as we have come to know it in the civilized world. She interviewed me, I interviewed her, and sometimes everyone talked at once, including Edith and Ernestine. Mostly, though, they appeared only when I asked to speak with them, and gave us a little trouble. This is not always the case. As Lily says of Ernestine, "I just hang up her clothes and try to stay out of her way."

We are at a small restaurant on Santa Monica Boulevard, having dinner on our first evening together. A middle-aged man stares at us throughout dinner and finally comes over to ask, tentatively, "Excuse me, but did I hear you mention *Nashville*?"

Lily looks up at him a little blankly. "No. We didn't."

Plowing right on, he says, "You were in *Nashville*, weren't you?"

A little smile appears on Lily's face. "Well, yes. I was."

"I knew it! My daughter will be so happy. She just loves you. Wait until I tell her I met Christina Raines."

We finish dinner, swipe the sugar bowl, and leave.

The evening ends at Studio One, where a gay male singing group is appearing. Lily is besieged by people who want her to play the club as her friend Ruth Buzzi did a few weeks before. She is polite and later indicates that she has heard that women are hassled at the door there.

The following night we are at a small restaurant outside of Beverly Hills. Lily tells me that they have the best chicken soup in town. Sitting next to us are fourteen tourists from Fairfield, Connecticut, although at the time we couldn't possibly have known that. The waiter brings the soup, and it is the best chicken soup in town. Edith Ann looks up and says to the waiter, "Oh, thank you. This is just the way I *like* my soup."

Later the same waiter offers us strawberry shortcake for dessert. Lily wants to know where they get the whipped cream. It is from a can.

"I'm sorry," Ernestine says crisply. "I cannot support the use of aerosols. I'll have it plain."

The fourteen people from the next table are on their way out and gather around our table. A woman says that they'd like to have her autograph because they "came all the way from Fairfield" and that she's the only "movie star they've ever seen." A twelve-year-old girl holds out a scrap of paper, and Lily, saying "I don't sign autographs," writes:

"I'm a 32-year-old actress, and I'm trying to find some meaning to my life. Love, Lily."

They exchange enormous smiles.

"Why don't you make up questions and have me respond and it's really Edith from the album?'"

We are at Lily's house, sitting near the pool, and it is nighttime. It looks as though we are getting somewhere, and Lily looks like she was just asked to order her last meal.

"Like, just ask me a whole bunch of questions and use answers from the album, but pretend that it's me saying it."

I had wanted to talk about her beginnings in Detroit and her work before *Laugh-In*.

"That's such old stuff. It's been printed a million times. Meanwhile, I started out in Detroit and I worked in coffeehouses and made up characters. Do you really wanna hear all this?"

I assure her that I do.

"At the coffeehouse I worked at, called The Unstabled, we would do plays which very few people would come to see, so after the plays we would put on little improvisations and poetry readings. Maybe we should go into the house. I feel like bugs are getting on me out here."

We stay outside, however, and continue. It has occurred to me that Edith can say things that an adult cannot, and using her characters is one way for Lily to make important statements.

"Yeah? So what?"

Well, in the summer of 1966 she got her first job in New York. She had been working out at The Improvisation on 44th Street and Madeline Kahn saw her and gave her Rod Warren's number. Warren was producing the show at The Upstairs at The Downstairs, where Madeline was working, and pretty soon Lily was in it too. That fall, she got on *The Garry Moore Show*.

"But I bombed. Don't use that expression. I mean, the show was cancelled in mid-season and replaced with the Smothers Brothers. I went back to working for a marketing research firm which operated out of a suite at the Plaza Hotel. Then the following summer I went up to Provincetown to work and did essentially culture types. I was also emcee of the cocktail show."

Although it was almost three years before she got on *Laugh-In*, she had done six or seven Merv Griffin spots and a Vicks Vapo-Rub commercial, which put her in demand in advertising circles. Ernestine was one of her characters way back with Merv Griffin, but Lily wasn't doing her in drag at the time. I wondered when Edith was born?

"Well, I didn't do Edith until I'd been on *Laugh-In* a while. I went on the show on December 29, 1969, and I did twelve shows. We introduced Ernestine, the Tasteful Lady and the Fast Talker. When the show closed down in February, I had taped six or eight shows, and I had no idea what a sensation I was going to create. I mean, I knew they liked it around the studio because grips would come up to me and snort, you know, like Ernestine, but the first time she was seen on the air she made a *huge* sensation. But *I* didn't know that, and I felt sort of uncomfortable because people would stare at me in the street and whisper. Then I came home, and I was living out in Malibu, and I was pushing my cart in the supermarket one day and this woman passed me in the aisle and said, knowingly, 'You're that new *star*, aren't you?' and I said, 'Oh, *no* I'm not.' And she was *so* disappointed. She said, 'You *know* who I'm talking about don't you? That new girl on *Laugh-In*? The one who does that telephone operator? Well, we have never laughed so much...'

"And then I was *really* embarrassed. She was so disappointed that it wasn't me. I can't remember now whether I told her or not, because I was so embarrassed. It took a little while for me to stop being self-conscious about it and respond, okay? Then I got over it and began to enjoy it, because I knew the people enjoyed it. They were so crestfallen if you said it wasn't you."

Ernestine smiles crookedly and says, "Oh, but don't worry. They'll take their chances on getting a few shots at you, too."

Lily is back, laughing. "Ha! I was in Phoenix once in an organ cocktail lounge...just hanging around, sort of...cause I like 'em, you know. And this man came up to me and said, 'Can I kiss you?' and I said, 'Heck, no! Are you kidding?' Well, I wasn't even too mean about it at first. Like I said, 'What if I kissed everyone who came up to me? I don't know *you*.' I mean, I was pleasant about it. Semi-pleasant. And he said, 'Every time you come on TV, my wife says, 'I can't stand her' and I wanna go home and tell her I kissed you,' and I said, 'Well, fuck you.' I was *so* mad. People can treat you so low..."

I had been noticing that people don't always recognize her on the streets in Los Angeles.

"Most of the time you don't *have* to be recognized if you don't want to. I mean, depending upon the way you're deporting yourself, people may know that it's you, but they'll kind of lay back. Or they'll do one of these..."

She mouths the words *I know who you are.*

"But they're going to keep your secret, you know. And then they do it for about ten minutes, and pretty soon they're whispering, 'Look over there' without moving their lips."

It's hard to imagine someone really trying to hurt her with a remark.

"Yeah, well you don't imagine it. That's why it was such a surprise. One time I was doing *The Bill Cosby Show*, and it was lunchtime and we were sitting out on the steps. There was a journalist upstairs interviewing Lola Falana, and on his way downstairs he stopped and said, 'Hi, Lily. I'm Bill so-and-so from *The San Mateo Chronicle* or something. And I smiled at him and said, 'How do ya do' and he says, 'Your manager didn't like what I said about you when you played at the Palladium for the Queen' and I said, 'Yeah?' and he said, 'Yeah, she wrote me a letter. She really didn't like what I said' – just really bating me, you know? So finally I just smiled and said, 'Yeah, well I didn't see it.' Hah! And he just sort of kept on and kept on with this Al Capp kind of laugh, '*yeh-heh-heh*, she really didn't like what I said,' and finally I said, 'Well, fuck you' -– real pleasant -– and he and his friend were so startled -– because it was such a true act -– that they left, poor things. There was no thought behind it at all. It was totally pure. He just kept it up so it was a natural retort. There aren't many times in your life when you get a real pure act like that."

I reminded her that she committed another pure act when she walked off *The Dick Cavett Show* three years ago.

"Yeah, that *was* a really pure act. But first I have to go back and give Cavett a little something. I was on the show talking about my Edith album, and the Ernestine album had just won a Grammy. So since Irene Pinn had been the producer of the Ernestine album, I said, 'It's the first time a comedy album produced by a woman has won a Grammy.' He says, 'Why not? Women are getting funnier and funnier.'

"Now this goes back three years, so people were still laughing it up over Women's Lib. And I didn't say anything. I just gave him one of my looks, and then pretty soon I moved down and Chad Everett came out. Ha! Chad's a case anyway. He's from Detroit as well. We went to the same college, but I didn't know him. He was a big star. His name was Crampton. Anyway, Cavett says to him, 'I understand you have a lot of animals' and Chad says, 'Yes, I have three horses, three dogs and a wife.' Then Cavett, with this *limited* consciousness, says, 'Would you like to change the billing?' and Chad says,' Oh, I was only kidding. My wife is the most valuable animal I own.' Ha! Ha! But I wasn't mad, though, see. I said, 'You *own*? I gotta go.' And I just got up and left. I sashayed off.

"Then when I got backstage I was sorta grinning and...I *do* remember thinking to myself, 'Shit. What am I doin' back here?' And Irene rushed out of the green room, where she'd been having a fight with W. H. Auden. He'd been real rude. He'd been watching me and Chad Everett and saying stuff like, 'Whooo arrrrr theezzze diz-guzding peeepole?' But then they started grabbing me by the arm and said, 'Who do you think you are? You'd better go back out there. Chad's a great guy,' and I gave him the old arm yank, you know, and I said, 'Don't you put this bullshit on *me.*' Because then I was mad, see?

"Meanwhile out onstage they were saying things like 'Lily?...Lily? Is she coming back? She *was* kidding, wasn't she?' and then pretty soon Chad Everett got tears in his eyes and started reading poems he'd written for his wife in *Pageant Magazine*.

"Yeah, and then later I was sitting in my dressing room and I heard Chad go by with a friend or something, and he said, 'Well, I thought she was kidding, but if ya ask me she stabbed herself right inna back.' He had to be talking about me, see? I'm not positive but it would be my guess."

Her smile grows up slowly.

Lily obviously did not stab herself "inna" back because this past summer Cavett called her day and night, trying to get her on his summer show. Some people say that if you're good enough you can get away with anything, but Lily has always had troubles with people in charge. Networks sometimes just don't understand her work, and even without hi-jinks, she battles constantly.

"I would always have to go in and pitch stuff to them. A lot of things didn't get on *Laugh-In* because they couldn't relate to the characters I had created. They hated Edith. They thought she was a brat, they wanted her to have Shirley Temple curls; they didn't know why she had to have a dirty face

—— they just didn't like her. So I went in that fall season to pitch her. You know, you go into a room with writers and producers and talk. I wanted to do Edith really bad and they just weren't responding.

"So finally out of desperation I said, 'I've got this other character,' and I didn't really have one at all, just an idea. It was Susie Sorority, but I had done no work on her at all. Well, they picked up the tag line 'from the silent majority,' and they loved her. So I said, 'Well, okay, but I gotta do Edith,' because she was the one I was struggling my life for. And they said, 'Yeah, yeah, okay'—like I'd forget or something. Well, Susie was a bomb. She's real good now 'cause I've worked on her, but then she was just sort of weak and Edith was a smash. People would be tuning in to the show for just twenty seconds to catch Edith. All those early weeks, they went around bad-mouthing Edith, and I'd walk around the studio being her and saying to executives, 'Yes. And your head is bald, too.' It was my only defense."

I ask Edith what she thought of people calling her a brat.

"I think they would be fooling. If I knew they could think those things I would think they was just pretendin'. They wouldn't say that about me. Really."

Lily lowers her voice and muses somewhat confidentially, "Do you suppose she really knows? I don't want her to. She gets hurt enough as it is."

I hear that the telephone company has asked Ernestine to do commercials for them.

"Yes, in the beginning they asked her, but she said no."

I ask Ernestine why she turned down the offer.

"It was an insult, that's why! Listen, you: I'm nobody's fool. Just because they have all the money in the world doesn't mean they can buy into anything, you know." Snort.

She talks to them on the phone, of course, and if Lily has to give her name, operators will ask, "Have I reached the party to whom I am speaking?" Fans send her telephones and statues of Ernestine at the switchboard. She also gets a lot of photos of men and women in Ernestine and Edith drag.

"Didn't I show you that dial I've got inside? Some guy at the airport in Las Vegas, a short order cook, ripped the dial off a pay phone and served it to me between a hamburger bun."

We get on the subject of Ernestine imitations, and I'm curious to know if she's seen any of them and what she thinks.

"Well, one time I was doing a concert and I came out on stage and there in the first row was Jan Russell in Ernestine drag. I loved it. Also, I hear there's a midget in Chicago who does Ernestine, and he's even got a little switchboard and all. I'd like to see him sometime. But I don't think anything about it. It's like it's not me. It's like watching someone imitate Bette Davis. Ernestine is just a person in the culture and people imitate her because she's so funny."

Once she was on *The Tonight Show*; first Ernestine came out and talked for a while, and then Lily came out later on. Johnny Carson asked what Ernestine's plans were and Lily, looking offstage, worried that Ernestine might be listening, said, "Oh, she has an offer to do Vegas, but I don't know if she'll ever leave the telephone company." A few weeks later in Phoenix, a woman approached her and said, "You seemed to know that telephone operator real well. What is she really like?" The woman was totally serious.

People fight over Lily's characters all the time. While some people think she's being sympathetic to her people, others think they're just devastatingly satiric. Actually, they're both right and wrong at the same time. There is no judgment in Lily's work except that which comes from her audience's own perceptions of the life she recreates. Her country-western singer and her black woman, Opal, which she played in a diner with Richard Pryor two specials back, have both been the subject of much disagreement. While some people love them and look upon them tenderly, others think she had a lot of nerve doing them in the first place.

"I don't think I have any judgment about them whatsoever. People always think it has to mean something. The country-western thing was like a poem to me. All I ever want to do is what *is*."

I tell her that a lot of what makes people uneasy about *Nashville* are that they don't like to be shown who they are at times.

"Well, I don't want to get into *that*, but I don't think there's anything contemptuous in the characters I do. It's satire with feeling."

There are things she will not do. When *Laugh-In* had John Wayne as a special guest, Lily refused to appear in the same shot with him or do any routines centered around his presence on the show.

"Oh, well, that was while the [Viet Nam] war was going on, remember. I don't really like talking about this sort of thing because you almost always have to hurt someone in order to do it. I always find it very painful to say that other performers are full of shit. Besides, it's so dreary because then they come after you…

"But there's almost no integrity anymore. For instance, how can I appear on a television show for which the sponsor has cut down half a forest to do the commercials and not comment on that on the show? My mind is too satiric; I'd *have* to. You really have to watch it, though, or they'll rope you into all sorts of things. The only reason anybody is interested in you in this business is because if handled properly, you can make millions of dollars."

This leads to a discussion of the Academy Awards as a forum for political beliefs and whether or not Jane Fonda should have taken her opportunity to say something.

"Oh, I think anything is the proper forum, but there's no black and white about it. Sometimes you take your opportunities and sometimes it's more visceral, like with me on the Cavett show. It just happens. Jane Fonda made her choice then for whatever reasons she had at the time."

I suggest that Fonda's silence was out of respect for Charlie Chaplin, who got a special award that year.

"Yeah, sure. But then there's Chaplin singing 'Smile,' and they're rolling the credits over his face for Exxon and Kotex and all sorts of repulsive things. So you don't win. The thing is that nothing is going to stop me from saying what I believe. You can't pander to those who say they won't like you because of your politics. It's only a matter of self-esteem.

"It doesn't hurt to have a little compassion for people either, you know. There's just too much going on, and I can't be rigid about anything. I could never understand someone who could adopt a doctrine and just live by it. How can anybody of thought answer all our questions?"

We discuss how television and movies are or are not changing with respect to stereotypes. Lily doesn't see many movies and is shocked to hear that words like "faggot" and "pansy" are still in use on the screen. She asks me for examples, and I mention that recently in *Funny Lady* James Caan calls Roddy McDowall a pansy. Richard Amsel (who is photographing Lily for the interview) points out that the film was supposed to be a period piece.

"Oh, I don't buy that! You've got to have an intelligence behind anything you do. I look at Marx Brothers films, which are very sexist, but I don't condone it. If you can perceive a point of view behind it that elevates it and gives it some insight, then there's a consciousness there. If someone is behaving in a certain way on the screen, it's put there so that we can perceive something about the character.

"I'm very offended when that isn't present. I was recently sent a script for a television movie which was supposed to have a slightly elevated consciousness. It's just so corny I can't believe it. I mean, their idea of an elevated consciousness is when the woman considers getting a part-time job."

What does she do about it?

"Well, I just sent it back with a note and I said, 'Thank you for thinking of me for this, but I cannot participate in it because of my own personal views. It simply isn't radical enough from a feminist viewpoint.' Which is no big deal, but you have to do it or how will they know why you're turning it down? Gee, this piece is getting awfully dull. Isn't it?"

Okay, then, would you like to win the Oscar for *Nashville*?

"Oh, gee, I don't know. Wow. What if such a thing should happen? If I get nominated I'm going to have my hairdresser and my makeup man on either side of me, and when the camera pans the audience, they'll be constantly fussing with me, keeping me perfect. And then if I win, I could have my dresser follow me up the aisle with a needle and thread, sewing on a last sequin. Don't use any of this in case I decide to do it. Oh, hell, you can use it. But what if it turns out to be a really lousy interview? Could we just forget the whole thing? I'm tired of being humiliated by pieces."

Settle down, Lily. Would you like to answer the question seriously?

"You mean, do I want to win the Oscar? I think it would be fun, yeah. Except they're in such bad taste these days that you almost don't want to go."

I point out to her that there's a good possibility that some of the other stars of *Nashville* will be nominated as well.

"*Oh*. I hadn't thought about that. Well, then I'm not going. It's such a drag to be in competition with your friends. Plus when they put the nominees' faces in little boxes to announce the winner, my expression will show if I'm disappointed. I'm staying home. Maybe."

Smile.

The next morning the phone rings at 10:00 a.m. Lily is at a recording studio on La Cienega and wants to know if we feel like hanging out. She is recording her new single, "Detroit," which she sang on her last TV special, and will use her Edith Ann monologue on the other side of the record.

It's an interesting day. Rick, the sound man, knows something about cars, and it's a good thing, because Lily is scanning the car ads in the *Los Aneles Times* and needs some advice.

"Oh, here's a 1955 DeSoto Firedome. What's that?"

"That's just an old DeSoto."

"Oh."

She finally decides to call about a 1956 Corvette, ninety-percent restored, six cylinders.

"Hi, is the Corvette sold yet? What color is it? What kind of interior? And it's real nice? And it's got a rebuilt engine? How many miles on it? When can I come and see it? Torrance? Is that on the way to Disneyland?"

We are going to Torrance the following day, and if Lily can find a wig we are also going to try Disneyland. After the recording session (which takes six hours), we adjourn to a fancy restaurant called Ma Maison, which is literally not ready for us. They haven't had their bread delivered yet and don't start serving food for an hour. We are starving.

"I'm dying to eat, you guys. What time is it? I think we should pay for these drinks and move on. Better still, we should *not* pay for these drinks and move on. Perhaps we can even turn over the table as we leave."

She turns to the table across the garden and sees people eating soup. No one told us that soup was ready. Irene Pinn and I decide to find out how the soup is, and after counting to three yell, "Hey, how's the soup over there?"

The soup is fine, but we are not fun people, and why don't you mind your own business. We reconsider turning over *all* the tables as we leave, including the occupied one with the soup. Lily has the solution.

"Listen, you guys. I've got a great idea. Let's have something different in each restaurant. We can go to Au Petit and have the mushroom salad and then move on."

Wrong. Two people disagree.

"Oh, come on. This can be great fun."

Ernestine takes over, sensing we need organizing:

"Now listen. We'll go to Por Favor and have guacamole and…no listen, listen, nobody is paying attention. Settle down."

Ernestine, overwrought, decides to let Lily handle the unruly gathering.

"Okay, now where are we going to do the bulk of our eating here tonight? Let's plan it. We can use the phone here to call ahead and make reservations at other places. Then we can go to see *Bambi*, but we've got everything to do now, so let's get organized. You guys are starting to get on my nerves.

"Now what's the greatest thing they have at Au Petit Cafe? How late is Duke's open? All night? We can go to *Bambi* and…listen, I have this fabulous idea! There's an Italian restaurant over by CBS where they have singing waiters and we can get espresso…

The waiter is standing over us, smiling, ready to take our order. We quietly order a full dinner, and stay at Ma Maison for the rest of the evening.

After dinner, we stop at a Rexall drugstore on Beverly and La Cienega to get some film for Lily's camera. It turns out to be $6.40 a roll. Lily looks at the price, lets out a piercing scream and hits the floor like a ton of bricks. She lies completely motionless, and a crowd of late-evening shoppers begins to gather around her in a circle. The saleswoman shakes her head sympathetically and asks, "Does this happen to her often?" All the time, I assure her.

Back at Lily's house, we are preparing for a photography session, and Lily is dressed as Edith, complete with dirty face. Richard Amsel is busily setting up a camera and wondering out loud if Walt Disney used to sit up nights in the garage, painting animation cells.

Lily considers this for a moment and retorts, "Yeah, but did he freeze her, too? Nooooway!"

It's true. Walt had himself frozen when he died, but Mrs. Disney didn't even get air conditioning.

Sometimes, when it's late at night like this, Lily has Ernestine call strangers from the phone book in the interests of comedy research. At two in the morning, Ernestine will inform a dozen people that their number has been changed. She illustrates:

"A gracious hello. As per your work order dated October 3rd, number 267034820, I am calling to inform you that your number *has* been changed."

Usually, people will get slightly upset and rant for a while, after which Ernestine will repeat the exact same speech in exactly the same tone of voice. Finally, they will ask for their new number, at which point they will be informed,

"I'm sorry, but that number *is* unlisted."

The possibilities are endless.

We are driving to Torrance. Lily and I are in the front seat with the tape recorder between us. I am driving, and Richard is in the back seat, taking pictures. Lily has the microphone and is controlling the off-on switch. She asks me to print whatever I find on the tape. She is interviewing me about the corduroy jumpsuit I'm wearing:

"I don't know, Vito. This is going to be real duddy. That's why I stopped doing interviews. Where did you get the jumpsuit?"

At Stone Free in New York.

"Do you wash it or have it dry-cleaned?"

Dry-cleaned.

"Is it new?"

Yes.

"Did you have it dry-cleaned between wearings?"

Yes, every time.

"Oh, well, that's quite expensive, see, because I imagine a garment like that would cost in the neighborhood of three to five dollars to clean."

Yeah, it'll cost me about $4,000 in the long run.

"Have you actually calculated that? Because I know that the average person in their lifetime spends four hours out of 569,400 hours experiencing orgasm. And I for one spend nine hours a month conditioning my hair."

Lily, can we talk about Nashville?

"Someone told me that I resembled Greta Garbo in *Nashville.*"

Greta Garbo was in Nashville?

"Ha! No, I mean…Ha ha, that I made them think of Garbo. Cut it out."

What were you thinking of in that scene in the nightclub when you were listening to Keith Carradine sing "I'm Easy," and the camera was moving in on your face?

"I was thinking of going to Taco Bell for an enchilada."

I can't print that: it's not true.

"Actually, I was thinking of something very profound but you couldn't be less interested. Does profundity make good press? Never."

Mamoulian, who directed Queen Christina, *told Garbo to keep her face blank during the last scene and it would take on a character for each member of the audience.*

"That's absolutely true of film, but you'd better get over to the right if we're getting on the Harbor Freeway."

If I print that you were thinking of Taco Bell in that sequence it won't be pure — it'll be made up.

"It's never pure with this stuff. You're a naive imbecile if you think it's pure. What are you, kidding me or something?"

Lily, who would know how to kid you?

"Do you have your stud earring in your ear today? No. You changed from stud to circle. I saw that in your ear the other day, and I had just read that S&M piece in the *Village Voice*, and I thought that you were demonstrating that you were submissive by wearing your jewelry to the right."

It's just jewelry.

"I was glad to learn that, because I haven't yet been able to adjust to that concept of…Awwww, but I guess it's just lack of…experience…Don't print that."

[There are beginning to be gaps in the tape where Lily manipulated the mike. She continues.]

"You know, I could try to think up some stories with celebrities, but I don't know that I can, because I always behave in such a wholesome manner…Did you hear that Cher got divorced the other day? When *was* that? See, you guys think I know all this good stuff but I just sit in my house and get amazed…I can't say that I have…Oh, let's go to Ports O'Call…Let's do it; absolutely…John Paul Hudson's sister lives in Torrance…she used to.

"I can tell you a good story. See if you like this story. When I was in college I had this zoology teacher named Dr. Schooley, spelled like school with an "e-y" at the end, and we had almost a full term fetus in a jar. And this girl came in one day and said, "Oh, this is horrible…this is grotesque. Why don't you take this baby and baptize it and bury it?" And Dr. Schooley looked up from his microscope and said, 'Is there any hurry?' See, this is no good. I can't do anything…my life is a series of…"

[I suggest to Lily that perhaps the Fame Fairy would like to tell us a few stories about the people she made famous. The Fame Fairy is a brassy lady who never shrinks from taking the credit. She is a huckster, emerging swiftly and loudly.]

"Frank Sinatra! Comes out, sings a song, finishes it, throws his coat over his shoulder and walks off. In the old days I hadda take him aside. I said, 'Frank, just the coat. Forget the shoes and socks.'" Mitch Miller! A huge sensation. He went on television and everybody sang along with Mitch. In the old days he used to go door to door. I said, 'Mitch, you'll exhaust yourself.' Walt Disney! Had a great idea. Wanted to build a park for children of all ages. I said, 'It's a good idea! You've got your parking lots, you've got your cotton candy; your little animals singin'. *Don't call it Waltland.*'"

[Lily is back and serious.]

"Listen, Vito, this is *The Advocate*. It's going to look funny if we don't discuss the gay issue."

Yeah?

"Well, what did Bette Midler say about it?"

She said that it's okay to be anything you want as long as you don't let your dog shit on the street.

"Oh, see? Bette is wittier than I am."

Yeah, she is.

"Fuck you, you commie queer."

Let me talk to Edith for a minute.

"Edith: Yes, all right."

We're going to play a word game. Just say anything you think of. Money.

"Money is good for things to buy…you could buy an ice cream and you could have new shoes and you don't have to worry that the bills don't get paid."

Nixon.

"Is he go to Crossbin School?"

Lily: "Nixon's not so good. Please don't ask her about him."

Ford.

Edith: Ford is not too good, either. How is a five-year-old s'posed to know about everything in the President's house?"

Doris Day.

"I like Doris because first she is named the same as my doll and next she likes animals and treats them kindly and if a cat does not have a home she will let it come and move in…"

[Lily takes over.]

"Okay, let's get down to business. Shut up, Edith, we're doing an interview here. Vito, do you think that there's a good reason why gay performers don't come out of the closet?"

Sure. People don't come out for all kinds of reasons. Some people have families that they're considering and their state of mind.

"Yeah, but that doesn't mean any of that is justified or right even though on a professional level it's still not safe to do. You know, I've been associated with people who consider themselves very hip, and I've sat in a room with them, and when someone overtly homosexual leaves the room, they will acknowledge among themselves that the person who has just left is homosexual and they are not. And men are the worst offenders. Very simply it can be summed up…how *can* it be summed up? It cannot be summed up, simply. And trade this Vega in as soon as possible."

What has the entertainment industry taught about gay people? Have they reflected the reality of gay life?

"I think they very rarely reflect the reality of anything. If it's TV it has to be terribly watered down and made palatable, and movies seem to me to be getting more and more like TV all the time."

You mentioned that Dick Cavett would never make an anti-woman statement today, yet he did three years ago. Why has that changed?

"Well, the women just didn't give up, that's all. Plus, I hate to say something like this, but things happen when the time is right. For lots of reasons the time for the Women's Movement had come, because culturally it was necessary. I swear that this great big lump of humanity doesn't let anything happen it just doesn't *have* to let happen."

Is there anything you don't understand about what gay people are doing now?

"Oh, I understand everything."

You said you had some questions…

"Oh, that just had to do with being male in the culture. It was about the S&M thing. You know, there's a place here in L. A. called the House of Dominance, where you can tour their dungeons. The ad on the radio is great. You can get a half and half, which is fifteen minutes of dominance and fifteen minutes of submission, for $40. They have the very finest in dungeon equipment. But then I can't be sure of that because I've not compared it with any other. Now I'll get a rep as an S&M freak, right? I don't believe in...Well, I won't say that...Okay, I don't believe in pain and humiliation, but Vito says it's okay. Not to believe in it."

The Bicentennial is coming. What are your wishes for it?

"Oh, can I work on that? That's good. What did Bella say when you asked her about that?"

She said she wants a tri-centennial.

"Oh, wow. Bella's so hip! Here's what I want to do for Bella. We were on *The Mike Douglas Show* together, you know, and I thought, 'How can I contribute to Bella the most?' Because I'm just so glad she's out there. And I looked down, and she was wearing pumps. Now I know how uncomfortable store-bought pumps can be, and one of the things I did when I made it was to start having my shoes made. I've been meaning to convey this message to Bella. Perhaps we can do it via *The Advocate*. I would like to pay for Bella's shoes for the rest of her life. I would like her to come to L.A. and go to DeFabrizio the shoemaker, and he would make molds of her feet, and anytime she wanted a shoe he could copy it for her and they'd be real supportive plus comfortable, because she has to do all that stomping about. I'm just so glad she's out there."

What about Martha Mitchell?

Unlike most people, I did like Martha. When she was abducted after the Watergate break-in and all the dudes were going around saying it was a menopause breakdown, I was just furious. At least she was out there, too. I'm for all those people who are out there."

We are in Torrance and the car is a disaster. When Lily tries to open the door it won't open and the steering wheel comes loose in her hands. The car has no grille and someone has painted a sloppy white stripe around the body. After saying "Are you kidding?" as politely as possible, we are on our way to San Pedro to have lunch at Ports O'Call.

Ports O'Call is swarming with tourists and Lily listens intently to all conversations. The ladies having lunch at the next table are all Ida Morgenstern look-alikes and we pretend to be taking pictures of each other in order to snap away at them, but they catch us and glare. Near the main gate, an old man with a white beard is lecturing a young man seated next to him. We take some pictures of Lily standing in front of him so that she can eavesdrop. On the way to the car she becomes Boogie Woman and loudly asks unwary tourists if they've ever put Jell-O in their shoes.

On her last special, Lily Tomlin did a little sketch about a clown born to "normal" parents in Dull City, USA. The clown had no friends and the doctor pronounced to the distraught parents, "In my opinion, your daughter is a clown." One day she met another clown who took her to a place unknown to the residents of Dull City, where clowns could have fun. It was raided and she was taken to prison to be "de-clowned." Stripped of her abnormal ways, she emerged from prison an ex-clown. Her friends were waiting for her, saddened by the change. As she shook hands with one of them, though, her hand came off in his, and she smiled broadly. Once a clown, always a clown.

The next day my mother called and said, "I saw the Lily Tomlin show last night. That clown sequence was about gay people, wasn't it?"

It was about people who are different, I told her.

"Well, it was really beautiful."

A few hours later, Lily calls from Los Angeles. She doesn't even say hello:

"Listen. Don't you think our parents should all support their children's lifestyle and that it's our job to teach them the truth of a situation if they've been lied to?"

I tell her yes. I believe that it is.

"That's what I thought. I can't stay on the phone all day. I've got work to do."

Lily's clown sequence is becoming a classic. High schools and colleges are requesting its use in minority problems classes. She is working.

Her new album, *Modern Scream*, discusses gay stereotypes from a novel and myth-exploding viewpoint. She is working.

She works at change, always with an eye toward being a little gentle with those who don't understand. She is in the business of exploration, and she's taking everyone with her. It's going to be an interesting trip. When you're as good as she is you can get away with anything. There's no telling how far a proud clown can go.

Valerie Harper

The Advocate — February 11, 1976

Valerie Harper laughs a lot, and I was glad. I'd always gotten a very clear message from her that said, "Hey, loosen up, kid; you'll live longer." I was right. We first met at the Children of Paradise Theatre on Santa Monica Blvd. where her husband, Dick Shaal, directed a very free and funny series of sexual vignettes called *Bawdy Tales*. It's been a decided hit and may be winging its way to New York to take up residence at the Plaza. I hope so. It could only help. New York hasn't had a show as fast moving and full of fun and surprises since *Story Theatre*, in which Valerie played Henny Penny.

After the show, we found our way upstairs to a bar which I must describe as early Ramada Inn. I don't suppose there's really any connection, but *all* straight bars have red flocked wallpaper and mini-skirted waitresses? Anyway, this one had little cocktail tables with electronic tennis games built into them, and we fell up on them at once. I won consistently, having had lots of practice at Studio One, where that's all there is to do, but eventually Valerie got the ball past me. She broke out in a yell immediately.

"Yay! I beat Vito from New York."

Valerie was okay. It was like being back home. As I walked to my car, I heard her yell to someone, "Hey, you in the yellow shirt! Looking for a permanent relationship?"

It was a very New York thing to do. But Valerie can't be pinned down. She was born in Suffern, New York, but moved to Southern California when she was five and has lived in Michigan, where she attended St. Mary's Academy, Oregon, where her sister became an usherette at the Shakespeare Festival. ("It didn't get to me yet, though. I wanted to be a ballerina. What can I tell you? I'd seen *The Red Shoes* and never got over it.") Then her family moved back East to New Jersey from which she commuted into New York in order to be a dancer. She never got to be a Ballerina, but she did get to be a dancer on Broadway, and when I think of her tearing around the theater district, it seems to me that the real Valerie Harper lives on Bleeker and Perry and runs through Shubert Alley ever day.

I tell her this, finally, on the day we meet in her manager's Beverly Hills apartment.

Yeah, I know what you mean, but I don't think there is such a thing as New York type person. You are where your body is located geographically. As an actor, you're either here or in New York, because that's where the work is. If I weren't doing *Rhoda*? Well, maybe Majorca or Italy! Ha!

Does she miss doing theater?

Well, I got back, you know. I just did it. I was in Seattle doing repertory. Two Leonard Melfi plays, *Lunchtime* and *Halloween*. I played a twenty-five-year-old in the first and a woman of fifty in the second. It was really great. I do miss *seeing* theater, though. Like I keep hearing about *A Chorus Line*, and Michael Bennett is such a good friend of mine, and I still haven't seen *Equus*. But I take little trips all the time.

Valerie has been involved in causes – a word she and I hate – for a long time.

It's a hard thing to describe – about that work – it sounds so…I don't know. But the reality is that I've been concerned about things and therefore have been involved in so-called movements because I was getting something out of it. It was mainly for me as a person. It did start with all that Sixties stuff from when Rosa Parks refused to get up. And King…King will go down as one of the great world leaders; not just black leaders, I mean like Ghandi. But I guess a lot of people know that, don't they? So he really captured my admiration and what he was trying to do slipped into my belief system--that if we're in America, let's not live the lie.

But we're so *full* of lies. In a way it's really kinda good because somebody is always shouting "Live up to this!" If America was saying there's no freedom to yell, there wouldn't be any movement. I was at a point in my life when I was dancing in shows in the chorus and was thinking about going back to college or the Peace Corps. And then Kennedy was shot, and I said to myself, "Peace Corps, my ass. There's a lot to do right here." I started working to integrate all non-white performers into shows; commercials and industrials, which are a real staple for young actors. So that period was James Farmer and

CORE, Seven Arts CORE, which I helped to start. A lot really happened. Real physical change. They did begin to hire Orientals and blacks. I did this stuff not because I was into causes. It was a real personal insult to me when these people were denied jobs.

I was surprised at how much of Valerie's warmth and humor is intact when you meet her. It's easy to see why people identify with Rhoda on television. I wondered how she thought people see her.

Well, as many people as there are, see me in as many ways. I do think that young women identify with Rhoda because she doesn't have that absolute perfection of a movie star. It looks *possible*, you know. Like Rhoda is somebody they could be. It's not a worship sort of thing. I feel that people think that Rhoda is very approachable, and she's a friend.

Does this cause any problems in public?

Not really. Only once, in New York. I was coming out of *Over Here* one night, and somebody said, "There's Rhoda," and it got a little tight, and I had to duck into a stage door.

How strong is your sense of loyalty to your beliefs? Are there things you will not do?

Yes. There are things you don't do. On the engagement show, for instance. They had me begging Joe to marry me, saying "Please, please, I know it will work." And I said to them, "You're saying two things here. First, it's the famous men-don't-want-to-get-married routine." Well, everybody gets what they want because they *have* it, right? Hah! I mean, men get married because the woman wants to. The begging was just proliferating 1950s stuff about the man chasing the woman until she catches him. Second, I said, "You make him the schmuck of the world if he says no and she says 'I know it'll work' and he says okay. I mean what is *that?*" So they changed that.

There's a problem of reflecting life and also showing what life can be. Sometimes the humor comes out of the very mistakes we make, the neurotic fears, the uptight angers. There's this funny story. I won't say who it is but somebody who works at the studio, a woman, came up to me the other day and referred to one of our producers, Charlotte Brown. She said, "You know, this girl came up to me and said something about me coming in late, and she told me she was the producer," and I said, "Charlotte Brown?" and she said, "Yeah, that's her. Well she *said* she was the producer." And I said, "Yeah, she's the producer." And she said, "Charlotte — she's a woman, right?" And finally I said, "Look. *Get* this, please. She is a woman who is the producer." Then I talked to Charlotte, and she said, "I told her *three* times 'I am the producer.'" It's marvelous.

While Valerie is enjoying this story she is also thinking of how much her writers have supported new ideas on the show.

Our writers will cut a joke in order to get to the point of a scene. In order not to sacrifice it, I mean. And they're extremely sensitive to the gay issue. They'll never do jokes which are even bordering on offensive.

This brings up the Mary Tyler Moore Show *episode in which Rhoda dated Chloris Leachman's brother, who turned out to be gay.*

That was an interesting thing because there was some discussion about how that line should be delivered, and it was changed. When I have to tell Chloris that her brother is gay, they had me whispering it, [with her hand to her mouth]. Like they said, "You should say *he's gay!*" And I *laughed*! I said, "Oh no, no, no. Not at all!" It was like Chloris was saying "What's the matter with my brother? He's charming, he's witty, he's tall…" and I say, "He's gay," and it *had* to be that. It had to be like, "Are you going to the beach?" "No, he's sunburned." Or you didn't have a joke. And it was the longest sustained laugh we ever had on the show.

I remember we stayed afterwards that night, and Chloris tried the last line ten different ways until we got it. First they had her saying, "He's what?" And I'd say, "He's gay--we're not gonna get married." And she says, "Oh, Rhoda. I'm *so* relieved." But if she doesn't know what gay means then we haven't got a line, right? Because actually what she was saying was, "Better he's gay than he marries you, you…you Jewish woman, you." Ha, ha. You see, *that* was the joke. We never did *that* thing, but it was implicit in the WASP character Chloris played. It was part of the reason she didn't like me. Plus I was loud, and I had Mary's ear, and so forth.

But that's using the situation instead of laughing at it. At the beginning of that episode he wasn't supposed to be gay at all. The producers said, "Here's a chance — let's do something." Jim Brooks and Allan Burns wrote that with Triva Silverman.

We were obviously off and running. When you're talking to Valerie Harper, you don't have to ask the questions. She just gives you the answers.

You know what I'd like to see, Vito? I'd like to see some of the myths swept aside. Like this child molesting thing. If you look at the statistics, it's not the homosexual at all. It's your heterosexual, or crazo, who are doing these things. And yet that's the issue with teaching and jobs like that.

I tell her the story of a call I one got when I appeared on a live radio show. I got a woman who said that she resented her son being approached by men asking him to go home with them. I asked her how she'd feel if it was her daughter, and she replied that that would be okay because at least it would be normal.

Ohhhh…you see! Because it's a crazo that's calling. I'm just appalled, though. I don't know what the *fear* is. I have a very close friend who is a gay man, and he said to me recently, "You know, I meet a guy, and he feels superior to me because he fucks girls." That's an incredible thing. It's a way to dominate, see. Because he's not only gay. He's my friend, he's an uncle, a son, the best tenor on Broadway--he's fifty things. His gayness is just a life choice that's part of his humanness.

Well, Valerie. I have a question to ask if you don't mind.

Am I gay? Ha, ha, ha ahhh…go ahead. Ask me anything you want. Clitoral or vaginal? Both darling. I'll take anything I can get. Hah! No, what sweetheart, what is it?

The question is, if you were a lesbian, would you come out in public?

Oh. Gee. I don't know. That *is* hard. See, I don't talk about my sex life anyway, and that's just a personal choice, so I don't know if…it's funny…

I point out to her that her heterosexuality is not her "sex life."

What, darling?

Well, I tell her, if you were to go on a talk show and refer to your husband, it wouldn't be discussing your sex life.

What are you saying? Wait. When you say, "I am a lesbian," it means you sleep with women, does it not? Or isn't that what you're talking about?

No, I mean, if you allow the world to know that you're married to a man, you are actually saying that you're heterosexual, but that says a lot more than what you do in bed.

Ahhhh…I see. Well, I went right to sex because that's where the bugaboo is. Do you know that in the heterosexual world, it's the same thing? If I'm having lunch with a guy and he's not gay, the word gets around and they go right to, "Oh, she's cheating on Dick." Immediately. It's the sexual thing they're all worried about; they see us and they say, "Oh! What is that?" We are *having* a hamburger, that's what it is!

So when you say, "I am a lesbian," they don't think, "Oh, she's having a life relationship with a woman for twenty years." They think, "Ohhhh, they do some strange thing…and they *hug* and their breasts touch…" You know, all the pictures which have been programmed into them. Which are really nobody's business but the two people involved. It's such a joke…but maybe there would be value in saying it. Hell, maybe it's around the corner because of people like you… [a bright smile comes across her face] Maybe because of you, single-handedly, darling. Ha! No, I mean it would help where people wouldn't be hiding in a closet like they do…it leads to such self-hatred, see, and it backs it all up. When blacks stopped straightening their hair, it was the most significant thing of the century…when Dixie Peach started dropping off in sales. So what we're saying, I guess, is start taking some responsibility for who you are.

I suggest to her that the reason gay performers don't come out is because, deep down, they are ashamed. They are not proud of the people they love.

Oh, don't say that, darling. That hurts my heart. Lemme say something though, because now we're right into it. It wasn't until very recently that I've seen heterosexuals who would admit to living together without being married, so I think we're coming around to it. I just think that more people are getting hip to letting the dreams die. It used to be that movie stars were not even supposed to let the public know that they were married because then the women couldn't fantasize with Clark Gable, you know, that it was actually them, or could be them. Now we all know that Robert Redford raises horses on a farm in Utah with a beautiful woman and doesn't fool around. So the truth about gay is due. Anyway, screw 'em if they don't accept it!

Talking about how much things have changed, I mention to her that ten years ago she probably couldn't have done an interview like this.

What? You mean talk to *The Advocate*? Why not?

Marlboro cigarettes, I tell her, refuse to advertise in The Advocate because of their image.

WHAT? Are you kidding? Come on. Their whole appeal is to rough trade.

Valerie has a way of cutting through all the rhetoric and finding the heart of an issue, its humanity, and she says slowly, as if lost in thought….

I don't know a lot about it, Vito. You read books and they say it's genetic, it's a sickness, it's this, it's that. All I know is I have friends who've suffered. All I know is closing gay bars and throwing men and women on the streets. All I know is there is entrapment…all kinds of incredible stuff. I know first-hand about a teacher who was accused of trying to involve himself with a student. He was gay, and so was the student, and he wasn't interested, because he's basically interested in guys his own age. This student said, "Either I come to your apartment, or I tell my parents you tried something." I know this first-hand, see. If there only wasn't so much negative energy…

Valerie is doing something very important. She's had the courage to stand up for her friends. We talked about the issue of advocacy from one's friends and she told me a little story which I think typifies her attitude.

In a cab in New York, ten years ago, you would get in, you know, and it would be the famous New York cabdriver, saying "These niggers…they keep this up and they'll lose my support!" I would lean forward and say, "Listen, you. Don't think you're talking to your friend. You're talking to the enemy. Because when the fire next time occurs, I'll be uptown in blackface. *You* are the enemy. You are the enemy of America, and you're my enemy. Be careful who you talk to!" And he would swallow hard. You *have* to do it. Because a lot of gays are like Uncle Toms, you know. It's house nigger time. They'll laugh at fag jokes and all. Gee. There's just gotta be a new language.

After we disposed of a few hundred other vital issues, Valerie, late for an appointment with a friend, rushed off with an admonition.

I think the ultimate humor is a human being thinking that we are all significant. You're only significant to the point that you realize how insignificant we all are.

Half and hour later, the phone rings, and it's Valerie, who asks to speak to me.

I thought about your question all the way home in the car. I think that the thing that scares people about coming out is that, heretofore, it has not been proven that it's safe; that it has worked. Therefore, I would do all I could to work for the day when such a statement would be possible and then unnecessary. Like it is for heterosexuals. You only have to say it so that it will be understood, you know.

Gay people, it seems to me, *are* doing it for themselves, and things *are* getting to that point. In defense of those people who are afraid to do it, I think of myself having to admit certain things which I know are right but are frowned up on by society. Like if I'd had an abortion, I don't think I would let people know but I don't think it's wrong to do that. What it boils down to is that gays themselves have to *get* that it's good to be who they are. And at first, we all have to applaud them for it a little so they'll know.

I couldn't agree more, Valerie. You are living proof that the world is changing for the better.

Martin Sheen

In Touch — May, 1976

Martin Sheen looks at you when he talks to you. He's not counting the leaves in the drapes and explaining detente at the same time. In fact, Martin Sheen couldn't care less about detente. What he cares about is acting and how to communicate both his art and his feelings with truth instead of bullshit. He is sometimes vehement about this. But not always. Most of the time we spent together he was relaxed, ready to laugh and very interested in things beyond the chit-chat of most interviews.

Sheen has played, in the last few years, some of the most controversial and thoughtful roles on television and film. Known to television audiences for his compelling portrait of the young emissary priest from Rome in *Catholics* and his stunning portrayal in the title role of *The Execution of Private Slovik*, he is also the actor who played Hal Holbrooks' lover in ABC's *That Certain Summer* a few seasons back.

"How was the show received in the gay community?" he asks. I tell him that although many people considered it a breakthrough for television, some gays thought that it was ultimately a cop-out which came off as timid and weak because the lovers did not share any physical exchanges whatever.

"That's a bunch of shit. They don't know who they're dealing with. You know yourself how many of the top echelon people at the networks are gay, right? These people are all fucked up. Everything is misinterpreted by them, even Shakespeare. There is no good or bad except thinking makes it so, don't you agree? There's nothing but dirt in these people's minds."

It becomes clear to me slowly that Sheen's way of dealing with issues like this one is to deny them any credence within his own spirit. I ask him how he thinks attitudes like those can be fought.

"There is no fighting to be done. If you fight something you create tension. There is no defense for love. It just is. For example, I don't play to please anyone. I really don't. I don't give a shit what anyone thinks of my work or of me personally. I play because I hear the music inside me; because it pleases me. And I hear the music best by acting. You hear it, I hope, by writing. But one must hear it or what good is doing anything?"

Would this mean that he was not conscious of the fact that a number of actors shunned that role in *Certain Summer* because they didn't have the courage to play a homosexual?

"It took no courage to play that part. They called me and they said, 'We've got a fascinating script about two gay guys.' And I said, 'Who's playing the other   guy?' and they said, 'Hal Holbrook' and I said, 'I'm in.' You see, I knew they were serious. That's all I ask. If they were a couple of clowns trying to make fun of a relationship--gay or straight--I would have said 'fuck it'."

If it was so easy for Sheen to accept it, why are so many men in the industry still scared to play a gay person?

"Because we all have the macho image - 'feel that arm' – you know? We're all fucked up with images. All over the place. And we never get to the core of the reality! All of us are poor fucking lost slobs and we've given ourselves an image which is confirmed in the press and in the roles we play. It's all bullshit. Every one of us is lonely. We wouldn't be acting if we weren't. You suddenly realize that when you get in touch with the hurt that goes on inside you."

I mention the name of a world famous actor who is gay and ask why he should have reason to fear public disapproval of his sexuality.

"Okay. Do you know what it really is? I'll tell you. I used to approach a role and say, 'Well, this guy is white, he's thirty years old, he's from Indianapolis' and then I'd put on that mask. You know what acting really is?" Martin Sheen leans forward and looking into his eyes you know that he has learned what he is saying through pain and experience.

"It's taking off the masks. And that's the pain. You see, he can't face the pain and its tragedy. I understand the pain of living with dishonesty. It's very tragic. Do you know why people identify with us as actors? Because we do publicly what they can only do privately. Who likes to cry in public? It's embarrassing because we're taught not to; we should, of course, we should cry and touch all the time. But it isn't manly, it's not the image. So we cry into our pillows. But the actor has to break down in front of forty technicians on cue so he can't have that luxury. In some fashion, the public lives vicariously through us in this way."

I tell Sheen that I feel cheated because there are no gay heroes on the screen--only straight ones and I resent this.

"So! You need heroes and images too, see. You want a hero! You don't need a hero."

Well, what about black children? Don't they need black heroes?

"No because you're only given that image that you need a hero. Hank Aaron. Every black child in the ghetto should identify with Hank Aaron? How the hell can they identify with a multi-millionaire who happens to be strong enough to hit a ball out of the park? They can identify with a construction worker who makes $4.50 an hour. That's a hero. Or a teacher who's teaching in the ghetto instead of a University. That's a hero. You see. Our images are screwed up. More so than our society. It's our misconception of each other. And when you get rid of all that shit and see how much you have to do, then you're the hero. I don't want a hero. You listen to your own music. If you have to accept the image of a hero then you're accepting something they give you. Get rid of it and you begin to see your own spirit. When people settle down and look at themselves, they'll never hear a louder scream than the one coming from inside themselves. That prisoner we've kept in because of the images. It doesn't make any difference whether someone is gay or straight. It's the people. It's the feeling."

I can't resist saying that if only gays had images of good teachers and simple construction workers, we might not have to look for phony heroes but we don't even have those although I get the feeling Sheen has said his piece. I also bring up constant lies on television and talk show insults.

"If you're gonna tune in Johnny Carson and listen to that noise, you won't be able to hear yourself. It doesn't make any difference what they're saying. You know what is really true. We've been listening to that shit all our lives. The time comes when you have to shut it out. When I did *The Execution of Private Slovik* I had never done a talk show and they asked me to go on Johnny Carson. John Denver was the guest host and since I'd met him and liked him I asked if I could be on with him. Well, it turned out that his list was full so they said they'd put me on with, uh…what's his name? That clown from Vegas?"

Don Rickles?

"Don Rickles! They said okay so you'll go on with him and I said no. They said, 'Why? He loves you. Very funny guy!' I said, 'He doesn't love me. He doesn't even know me or understand me. Do you want me to embarrass him? Because that's what I'll do. I'll ask him why he's so terrified. Why he feels he has to shout and insult people.' He's really apologizing. Love me. Forgive me. That's what he's all about. And I would have said that to him on national television. I would have said, 'Why do you hurt so much? Why do you feel afraid of people? They don't need you to make them laugh. They've got a President who makes them laugh.' And when I told them this they said 'take a walk.' See, they don't want people to really talk on these things. It's all pizazz. They're selling dog food. They're selling automobiles. They're selling beer. They're selling, selling, selling. And they're selling ideas. And you can buy the dog food and the cars but the ideas are fucked! Every one of 'em. They're not gonna be worth a dime to you when you wake up in the morning. So why do you give a damn what they say on television? Their moral frame of reference is all bullshit."

I ask why he thinks his film *Badlands* didn't receive any real attention in Hollywood despite critical acclaim. He laughs while he answers.

"Because they didn't understand it, that's why. Are you kidding? Did they understand Orson Welles? They got rid of him because he was dangerous and then I watched them six hundred and fifty strong at The Century Plaza Hotel talking about how great he was and then he got up and asked for money and they turned him down! Because they can't trust him. He might deviate from the script. He thinks. Hollywood ain't doing shit and they'll never be ahead of the game because all they're interested in is money, not ideas. All the tears ever shed at the Academy Awards are all bullshit. This town has never done one fucking thing as far as portraying the reality of a situation. They did it to their own people in the 1950s when it happened here with blacklisting. They were the first to castrate their own heroes. You can't trust the bastards and don't trust their films."

He mentions to me that he's going out for Tom Hayden for the Senate and that he thinks Hayden can make it. I wonder if he is aware that audiences will see his politics and judge them whether he likes it or not.

"For me as an actor, I couldn't give a fuck less about the public's opinion of my choices."

This obviously extends to his professional life as well. I wondered if he'd do a script he disagreed with politically because it happened to be a good script.

"I have such a script coming into focus right now. It's the story of a professional killer, *Joey the Hit Man*. I don't care about stuff like that. I just want to play everything. I want to do it all. I want to work with John Wayne and the hell with his politics. I don't seek any identification with the public. All that has nothing to do with art. If you can't have a good time, quit."

I believe Martin Sheen means what he says. He has a singular vision; he wants to act. And he's smart enough to know that you can't have the smell of the greasepaint without the roar of the crowd. Since he isn't particularly interested in the roar of the crowd, he's also taking off the greasepaint and the symbols and false images which go with it. What's underneath is an actor.

Debbie Reynolds

Christopher Street — **November 1976**

"I was shocked by the nudity in Hair. *I couldn't believe it. No wonder the children in the country are all mixed up."* —Debbie Reynolds, 1968

You can imagine my misgivings. I mean, Debbie Reynolds has been saying stuff like that since 1949. Not to mention that, in boning up for my interview with her, I had spent several hours at the library reading old *Photoplay* stories with headlines like "My Fans Only Like Me in Nice Girl Roles," and — my favorite — "Eddie and Debbie: The Marriage the Whole World Waited For."

Now it is a dark, rainy day in New York and I'm on the subway to the Minskoff Theater to interview Tammy of the pigtails and Molly Brown of the brass bed. My umbrella is dripping on somebody's open-toed shoe, and from the cover story of my new *People* magazine Paul Lynde is telling me that his audience is straight and gay people killed Judy Garland.

She looks terrific, laughs a lot, and although she hasn't seen *Christopher Street* magazine, she says she finds the idea interesting. I have to turn on my tape recorder immediately, because she isn't waiting for questions:

I'm glad to see this magazine, really, because creatively, I think, people who are of an open mind are understanding homosexuality and realizing that some of their friends who they never knew were gay, *are* and that doesn't make them less of a person. You know, a lot of older people really have a terrible prejudice in their minds and it's amazing. I can remember when my father said, "You're not gonna bring that girl/guy home, are you?" and I said, "Daddy, you told me that all my friends are welcome home. You didn't give me any kind of category. You just said all my friends. Well, he's my friend." And he would say, "Well, it's silly. How'd he ever get that way?" and

I said "Well, he took out an ad…." It's so infuriating. After all, everyone I know who is really creative in the sense of decorating or choreography… well, creatively, like artists and sculptors…not that you have to be gay to be creative…but most of my friends and associates *are* gay and they are very creative.

When I was a young girl all the guys I liked to date were gay. Of course I didn't know that then because in those days you didn't dare admit you were homosexual. But I liked them because they were gentlemen. I didn't realize that they found me *totally* unattractive. Ha! In the sense of man to woman, I mean. So talk about being in the closet, the whole subject was in the closet. I said to a friend of mine recently, "Gee, you know, that I never *knew* you were really attracted to guys, and he said, "Well, Debbie, in those days you couldn't talk about it." Gays were not accepted then. They were accepted everywhere on an unrealistic level, sort of a social…surface….

You mean a silent conspiracy where everyone knew but nobody talked about it?

It was never talked about. And if you were a movie star, like if a girl — a movie star lady — was promiscuous, it was always hushed up. So if you were a guy and went for guys, nobody ever knew because he was supposed to be this big stud leading man. It was all very hush-hush. I *like* that the intelligence of everyone seems to be able to accept people today for what they really are whether it be religion or politics or their own sexual…um….

Preference?

Yes, I guess preference would be the best word.

A few weeks ago Carleton Carpenter discussed being gay in The Advocate.

I would have thought that he'd have done it years ago. Now I never knew that Carleton was gay because I never knew anybody…well, first of all, I mean, I was sixteen and my life was *very* Middle American. In our area they wouldn't sell houses to Negroes or Jews. It was just ridiculous. You weren't even aware of it as you grew up because you were just living in the neighborhood where everyone was white and just the same as your family. And then finally this revolution of a sort has happened and it's wonderful. Carleton and I were partners and he was like my big brother. When he was sick and we were on the road, my mother would nurse him like he was her baby. Carleton always had ulcers and stomach problems and he's very high-strung. I just thought he was more of a mama's boy in that sense, you know. I never saw him dating girls but I never saw him dating guys either. I was *truly* innocent. I was raised in a Nazarene religious home where girls didn't go to bed with guys unless they were married. That was just *shocking*.

When I was about nineteen years old, I was dating Hugh O'Brian and one night he had a fist fight with some guy in a bar over me. There was this guy who used to work at MGM and when you'd walk by he'd whistle and stuff like that. He was real fresh and I just thought he was a big jerk. And he just kept hounding me to go out with him and I didn't want to. I was just really into my career with singing lessons and dancing lessons, bowling. I was really a busy girl. And one night Hugh was in this bar down in Santa Monica and this guy at the other end of the bar is saying to the bartender, "Oh, yeah, I've been out with Debbie Reynolds. You know *she's* a dyke." And the bartender says, "You're kidding! Tammy's a *dyke?*" So Hugh goes over and says, "Excuse me, Johnny, have you ever been out with Debbie?" and the guy says, "Yeah, sure, once." "And what happened?" Hugh asked him. "Well, she's *gotta* be a dyke, because I took her home and she didn't wanna kiss me or do anything…." And Hugh said, "Just because she found you unattractive, that makes her a lesbian? That makes you an idiot, and I'd like you to step outside." And they had a fist-fight. So the next day I called this guy on the phone. I'm a very direct person. I go right to the source. I said, "Hello, Johnny? This is Debbie Reynolds calling. Where do you get off calling me a dyke? The reason I didn't want to kiss you is number one you wear braces, number two you have halitosis, and number three you're totally unattractive to me, and never talk to me again." And to this day, twenty-three years later, I have not spoken to him.

Johnny who?

Oh, I'm not…no. We were young and we both grew up and it's over. He just wanted to lay every girl he could get his hands on.

It's the old macho thing of any woman who won't come across must be a lesbian because otherwise she would?

Sure, he's probably a closet queen himself for all I know. Those are the kinds of stories that exist, though. I'm glad that there are gay bars now where gay people can go. I'm still a little startled at seeing women together, I must say.

Really?

Yes, but I am *really* old fashioned so.... I mean, I know it and I understand it and it's the same thing as the guys, but it does just shake me up a tad. *Only* because I guess I really dig men in the sense that I want to be a woman. That's lucky for me that I was, uh, since I was born my attractive yearnings went to men. And so I never really had to face that tremendous turmoil my friends had to face trying to cover it up. I had a very good friend who married and had a little girl and he was gay and he finally got a divorce about seven years ago and has *never* been happier. His wife took it amazingly well and understands and the child will have to understand later. See, that's the thing. Those are the problems when you're forced into a marriage and it hurts the children. The child has to grow up and introduce them and the father is dressed better than the mother.

Do you think the attitudes in the film and entertainment community have changed with respect to role playing and men having to prove their masculinity?

Well, it's really how the man handles it, isn't it? Now if a fellow acts really butch...take the English actors on the overall. They are trained in the legit theater and generally their voice and attitude are very masculine. Now they have ten guys or two guys or one boyfriend or whatever, but their life is a gay life. Their work and their presentation on stage, however, are very masculine. So, for me, what you are personally should not affect what you are professionally. The boys in *my* show are like half and half and they all get along great, they have a wonderful relationship. I always say to my boys, "*I'm* the girl onstage. I don't care if you're the girl offstage, but onstage you have to come across as a very strong guy because most of the girls out there really want to see those attractive young boys up there dancing and think maybe they can get a date with them." I prefer that look for my act. If a show is specifically written around a situation that shows the gay life, like *Applause* or *A Chorus Line*, then that's different. But I'm happy to have lived through all the change. And it's interesting that you say that about Carleton because he was raised a very strict New Englander and I can't imagine Carleton would finally come out and say it.

Well, he didn't do anything strident. He just quietly talked about his feelings. You have an extraordinary vision, being one of the last people hired by L. B. Mayer at MGM, the end of the studio star system. It was you and Pier Angeli and...

Leslie Caron and Rod Taylor. Speaking of butch guys.

That vision gives you a view of the changes which have taken place....

I've lived through a lot of changes in this business. And in the world, too. My best friend happens to be col...uh...black. I always say colored. He does too, by the way. In fact, I went to a memorial concert for Dr. Martin Luther King at the Hollywood Bowl with my dear friend Shirley Bassey and on the way home in the car she said, "Isn't it extraordinary? Every time I come to this country..." (she's Australian, you know)..."I find that I'm black. I always thought I was colored, and I can't figure out what the difference is...."

Well, I have a black woman friend who wonders what color they're talking about.

Yeah. Ha! What is it, green? Fuchsia? Puce? Well, it *is* a silly line, colored, it's an old-fashioned line. I think when you're raised, as I was, in Texas, and you heard colored for such a long time you just say it. It doesn't mean you're putting anybody down by saying it. But 'black' is a better word to describe an actual color of black. But then Shirley is not black. She's a gorgeous copper. I'd love to imitate her in my show. But your magazine...I haven't read it, but I'll take this copy if I may. I'd enjoy seeing it. In fact, I've never discussed this subject. Well, nobody ever asked me to.

Until recently, people didn't discuss the subject at all.

Well, I had an interview here in New York. I wish I could remember his name because I found him to be a very prejudiced person against being normal. It was right after a dear friend of mine, Agnes Moorehead, had passed away. I've never discussed this, but it made me so angry. I hope he reads this. Agnes was married twice before and they never worked out or something. I never discussed those marriages. She never talked about her private life, ever. She was a brilliant actress and very, very religious and very straight-laced. *Very.* And I certainly never heard a rumor about Aunt Agnes being gay. Which, by the way, now I understand the word "gay" applies to both men and women.

I think lesbians would prefer "lesbian" because when one says "gay," people think of men but never women.

Well, I have two girlfriends who live in New York and they call themselves gay.

It's queer and dyke we're not crazy about.

Well, this man in the interview says to me, "I understand that you and Agnes Moorehead were more than just friends." So I said, "What is more than friends?" He goes, "Well, you know, *more* than friends." So I said, "Well, why don't you come right out and say what you have to say since you're being so rude." He said, "Well, I hear Agnes was gay." I said, "Yes, she was a very happy person." And he goes, "No, no, I mean...ah..." and I was *not* going to help him. It wasn't that I would have minded if she *were*, which she wasn't, but I hated him doing that to her memory, to talk about her in that direction. He could call me anything he wanted to...I have no reason to... ah...I am *not* gay, Agnes was not gay, but he was intimating we were because we were friends. Women aren't supposed to be friends and be straight. I just think that people should be what they are and have true friends and have their loves if they want them, which I don't, and everyone should do whatever they want as long as they don't hurt anybody.

Why do you suppose married women don't have men friends the same way they have women friends?

Well, because they'd have to be lovers. But I have many male friends and my *best* friend is color...uh...black. He was my accompanist twenty years ago and we'd go dancing at the Mocambo. Now he's teaching school because he wants to do his own thing. But he happens to be a straight guy, and Harrison Carrol the columnist, who is dead now, called my mother and said, "I wanna know who this new lover of your daughter is. You now, he's black and it's just shocking!" My mother told me and I said, "Well, mother, I don't care what they say because they're going to make more of it whether he's my friend or not." So I have never gone with convention in that sense. And Carleton will tell you...we used to go out dancing and I'd dance with Carleton's boyfriend and then they'd dance. There were no gay bars then, but we'd all go out dancing and have a great time. As a matter of fact, Carleton's boyfriend was a great jitterbugger. Now Carleton and I have been friends since 1949. That's a long time. We still keep in contact. He sends me his books and they scare me to death. I really enjoy his books. Everyone has to create his own work. It's so important. Like I'm doing with my show. I'm putting it together and producing it because nobody is going to do it for me. You can't sit around and wait for the world to come to you because the phone is never going to ring.

I don't know whether it's because there was a restriction on your behavior at the studio, but there seemed to be a point in your life when you just broke out of the Tammy image.

That's because people don't know me personally. While I *am* a lot of Molly Brown, Debbie Reynolds is actually very outspoken and very direct. I love fun and I love people. I'm not prejudiced or a putter-downer. I think everything is possible at all times and I hate the word "can't."

You were once asked by John Springer what your most gratifying role had been and you said you've never been gratified on film.

In *The Unsinkable Molly Brown*, yes. I also liked *Goodbye Charley*. I didn't like how the picture turned out eventually, but I liked the role. Also, I liked a picture I did with Shelly Winters called *What's The Matter with Helen?* The others I enjoyed but...I am a *woman*. I am not a child and I am not a young girl. I am a mature woman and I hope I've learned something by now because if I haven't, at forty-four, I should go downtown and jump off one of those twin towers.

You once said that your fans only like you in nice girl roles. Is there still that relationship where fans can dictate?

I think they like me in anything that doesn't break their image of me. But actually there's nothing to worry about because I would never take a role which is contradictory to my own beliefs. Because I *am* square when it comes to moral issues. I really also don't like watching people go to the bathroom in the movies. I have to do it, but I don't have to watch it. Or people throwing up on the screen. That's a thrill a minute, isn't it? I wouldn't do anything, for instance where lovemaking required any kind of nudity. I think something should be left to the imagination, I really do. I think we've gone *too* far but it's my opinion and that's one of the reasons I don't do films.

You've talked a lot about so-called "clean pictures." Could a story about a gay woman or a gay man be a clean picture?

Of course. What's dirty about it? Unless they're gonna take off all their clothes and have a daisy chain. I don't want to see that with straight people. Anyway, the world is not ready to see me strip because they'd lose money on that one.

Gay people have never really felt that their lifestyle was presented on the screen because all the people in films are supposed to be heterosexual. It's like we don't exist.

Yes, but I think you have to realize, really now, that the majority of people are *not* gay and that mass audience is out there. If you're a producer and you want to make money, you make pictures to appeal to what we call the norm or the straight audience. Unless a producer had a wonderful story and produced an understanding and poignant interesting film, but they haven't done it, have they?

Sunday Bloody Sunday is about the best so far.

I didn't see that picture. But usually they're portrayed as something of buffoons, aren't they?

Yes, we are.

It's like they're the biggest queens in the whole world. Well, that can be amusing but it's not the average gay man or woman. At all. At *all.*

That's what we've been hollering about.

Didn't Tab Hunter come out recently and say that he was both or something...? Well, I dated Tab and he was not seemingly gay. He was probably nineteen then. I thought he'd recently said in an interview that he was for both or something, but I think what he wants more than anything is to find someone who really loves him. You know, he really did a super thing. His brother was killed in the war and he went and raised his brother's children with his sister-in-law and gave up his career for eight years to do it. That's why he found it so difficult to come back. My hat's off to him. Gay or straight or whatever...he's my friend and I couldn't care less.

There's a song in Molly Brown *called "He's My Friend."*

(Sings) "Doesn't matter what the other people say.... He's my friend and he'll stay my friend...." I like that song. It should be a slogan, really, for all gays. Let's have a march to that! You know, though, Paul Lynde, who's a great friend of mine....

(Pulling my copy of *People* out of my bag) *This week he says his audience is straight and that gay people killed Judy Garland.*

Oh, I *don't* think he *meant* that exactly. I'm sorry if the writer misquoted him. Let me tell you that Paul is a very special human being. I think what he meant was that the people around Judy at the time, and they *were* gay, didn't protect her. But that was one gay person. And it's not true that his following is all straight. How does he know that? Do people have it on their birth certificate? I know I have a lot of gay following and I'm delighted because they're so funny. Although I have found that very few gay women follow me perhaps because I'm not gay and I guess I don't appeal to them very much. I can't say that, though, because I have some really special friends who are lesbians. But you know? They don't push their lifestyle on you. It's what you want to accept, isn't it? I'm certainly not embarrassed to go out with gay women. I'm not worried that people will think I'm gay. I know what I am and I couldn't care less. These are my friends. I don't know why explanations are due. We should just *be*.

Look at Bobby Short. He was a pacesetter with an open shirt and jewelry and shoes with no socks before anybody. Everybody accepted Bobby at a time when they didn't accept anyone in what we call the rich society. Bobby went to Europe, Bobby went to Jamaica, royalty loved Bobby. Nothing has changed, we're all just breaking out a little bit again. I only know that my family in Texas was as square as can be and they're no longer prejudiced about gays, blacks or Jewish people. When I married Eddie Fisher they had a heart attack because he was Jewish, and his family equally had an attack because I was a gentile. How stupid can that be? I just think the whole revolution of understanding has helped everybody. *If* you listen. But if you're just gonna stay steeped in your old prejudices-- that because I'm straight, I'm the only perfect person — well, I just don't think that's very intelligent. It's sad and narrow-minded. I don't think you can really experience the fun in life that you can if you can't keep an open mind.

I know you don't usually talk about the Eddie and Elizabeth affair, but do you think it would have caused so much fuss today?

Well, I talk about it. I just think it's yesterday's news. It wouldn't have caused a fuss today at all. Nor Ingrid Bergman having Rossellini's baby. As far as Eddie and Elizabeth and myself? It would still be a headline today because all the people are names, particularly Elizabeth, but it certainly wouldn't have been the scandal it was. I think *I* would take it just as hard. What can I say? The man left, the man didn't want to stay He found somebody he loved more. It happens every day.

You seem to revel in the star system and have a great time at openings and premieres. Do you love all that show biz?

Once I get there I have a good time, but I really hate it all. I hate getting dressed up and putting on makeup and I curse it every minute. But I think I owe it to my business. After all, that's what makes our business happen. The lights and the dazzle and the fantasy are what it's all about and I think we have a responsibility, if we're in it, to put a little chicken in the pot.

Is it true that you didn't want to be called Debbie but Jack Warner gave it to you anyway?

He gave me that name and I didn't answer to it for about three years. Finally, I gave in and I realize now that Debbie is me and Mary Frances was left in Burbank. If I said Deborah now it would seem pretentious. Years ago it would have been better to do something about it, but it's too late now. (Sings) "Too late now...to change your name my dear...." (She looks at Paul Lynde's face on the cover of *People* and taps it with her finger.) You shouldn't have saaaid thaaat! And I'll tell him, too.

Did the studio tell you what to do and how to live?

Not with me they didn't because I was really what they were selling. They did have to teach me how to dress and not to be such a tomboy. Also not to have such a big mouth. I had a violent temper and had to learn to calm down. I had a lot of growing up to do. I was only sixteen and do you know how young that is? I wasn't afraid of anybody and you *were* supposed to be afraid of your boss. I'd go up to L.B. Mayer and slap him on the back. I didn't know you weren't supposed to do that. But he liked it. Then there was Howard Hughes. I had a meeting with him one day about a picture I was supposed to do and he asked me out to dinner. I laughed and said, "Oh, come on, Mistah Hughes. I'm seventeen years old! I'm not your type. You like those girls with the big boobs and all.... I would never know what to talk to you about. I have two hundred dollars in the bank." So I told him he could come to Texas and be my Uncle Howard for the day and my mother would cook us Mexican food. He loved that. He never wanted to be Howard Hughes in the sense of being hunted and haunted by people. He had a very unhappy life. He was married to one of the great women of all time, Jean Peters. She gave a lot of years to him and if she couldn't make him happy, nobody could. People should write about *her*. Well, she won't do stories and she shouldn't. But I mean people should acknowledge what a great lady she was to a great man who should have been left alone.

What about a star's right to privacy? Some performers simply won't see the press.

Oh yeah? Who is it?

Hepburn, Garbo, Bancroft…

Garbo is retired. She's not working now and should have her private life. Hepburn has been abused by the press. Remember, she lived a life of today forty years ago and that's an extraordinary thing. Hepburn had a way of life in the Thirties that was not acceptable to the public at that time. It was to her, though. They would have printed things she didn't want discussed so she stopped doing interviews. She and Spencer Tracy wanted their private life kept private. There are still enough people who are legends who will still give interviews. Bette Davis will still speak to you, Cary Grant, Greer Garson, Ava Gardner…we always pick the ones who won't because we want the unattainable.

Do you suppose that it's about time that women are taking production into their own hands?

They're really taking a step forward and taking a chance. I read that Lee Grant is going to produce a film with Goldie Hawn. Bravo! I think Ida Lupino is one of the best directors in the business. Why didn't she direct more movies? She should have and she could have. There are a lot of talented women who don't get the opportunities they should.

Because they're women?

Yes, because they're women. Men in the industry from the stagehands to the unions just don't want to deal with them.

Recently, in a book by Charles Higham, it was revealed that Charles Laughton was gay and it tormented him because he couldn't share that. Do you think it would be better if people came out?

I think it's very hard for the old school to do that. I know many stars that are gay who will never come out and say that they are gay. For years they have denied it and that would cause even more pain now, having to admit they've lied all these years. But the younger stars are admitting it. A brilliant actor like Montgomery Clift was tormented to death. That's part of the reason he died. What a tragedy that is. I really don't have the answer to that. It's up to the individual. Just because it now happens to be the thing to have magazines for gay guys and gay girls, fine, but I don't think that everybody who's gay should need to come out and say they're gay unless they want to.

What do you think you'd have done if you hadn't gone into show business?

I'd have been a gym teacher. That was the only thing I knew to do. I was so athletic; I guess that's what I would have done. I'd probably have killed a hundred students by now or they me. But that's what I wanted to be and the training has helped me to be disciplined and have the strength you need in this business.

She thinks we've "done it" and so do I. As I pack up my things she tells me she's been noticing my earring and thinks it's cute. As I go out the door she yells, "Just don't get one in your nose. That shakes me up." I promise Debbie Reynolds that I will never have a ring put through my nose and leave.

Tennessee Williams

The Advocate — April 20, 1977

"Actually, we'll only have about forty-five minutes with him. He's leaving for Palm Beach at 2:30." My heart sank. It was already past noon, and we weren't even there yet. I was riding in an elevator at the Elysee Hotel with Arthur Seidelman, who is directing Tennessee Williams's new play *Vieux Carré*. He has persuaded Williams to see me in spite of imminent departure.

Vieux Carré, which I'd read the night before, opens soon on Broadway. It is a very gentle, very funny and surprisingly loving play-within-a-play about the rooming house in the Old Quarter of New Orleans where a twenty-eight-year-old Williams once lived and starved for his art among the craziest collection of people ever assembled. Williams' landlady is Mrs. Wire in *Vieux Carré*, to be played onstage by Sylvia Sidney. It is difficult to think of a more outrageously funny character in Williams' work, and one feels that Mrs. Wire will join the gallery of Williams' women destined for theatrical immortality. In addition to its humor, *Vieux Carré* has an illusory, timeless quality that distinguishes it from other recent works by Williams and recalls in many ways the soft, dreamlike qualities of *The Glass Menagerie*, to which it is sure to be compared. The play shines.

In Tennessee's suite there is controlled bedlam. The playwright is preoccupied with a swollen toe and the diabetes his doctor finally told him about after "drawing blood every two hours and having me piss every hour." He can't find his brown belt that goes with the brown pantsuit and is choosing a pair of dark socks as he sits firmly on the sofa next to me. He complains to Seidelman that gossip columnist Doris Lily reported on television that *Vieux Carré* had opened in London to bad notices. In fact, the play has not opened in London.

"Well, she's a friend of Truman Capote's. That would explain it. Heh-heh-heh." Nice smile. Williams has, in fact, a winning smile. I tell him that his play is very funny, and he doesn't find that unusual.

"I'm a very funny man, you know. I think I'm funnier than Neil Simon. Don't you think I'm funnier than Neil Simon, Arthur?"

He turns to me and is serious about being funny. "You know, you've got to turn into a clown in your later years. People talk about my cackle laugh! Heh-heh-heh. I guess I feel as though I've gone through everything there is to go through, and there's a certain relief that comes with that. I'm free of a lot of pressure."

Could this have anything to do with his coming out in his recently published *Memoirs*?

"I don't think so. I'd never thought there was any question about *me*. *Time* magazine had been saying I was homosexual for *years*. But I would never have used anyone else's name unless I had permission. You know, especially for actors, it's still dangerous because they can suffer."

One of the actors he does not mention by name in *Memoirs* who has since discussed his bisexuality is Tab Hunter, and I tell him this. There is a pause and then the cackle. "Heh-heh-heh. Nice boy, heh-heh. But was there *ever* any question? Heh-heh-heh."

One thing is for sure. The two gay characters in *Vieux Carré*, the Painter and the Writer, are a far cry from the horrors and self-hatred of a Sebastian Venable. There seems to be in these characters a free and honest attitude that comes natural to them as people. Williams agrees. "Yes, there does seem to be, doesn't there? There's a kind of freedom, and they seem natural and human. Well, I've never spent any time hiding my sexuality--I just never thought about it. I was always too busy to think about it. Do you know what offended me most? A review of *Memoirs* in a gay magazine called *Gay Sunshine*, which said that all of my long plays were lies. This infuriated me! They said that I had written love stories that were really between two men but had disguised them as being between a man and a woman. Well, that's ridiculous! Such a thing would never occur to me. Every person has in him two genders, and if he's a writer, he can draw upon one gender to create women and the other gender to create men. It just so happened that, being a Southerner, I found it easier to express myself in the rather poetic style of the Southern woman, in most cases."

Seidelman, sitting across the room, says that Williams' gallery of male characters is as impressive as the women he has created. Williams thinks about this and decides there may be a little of both sexes in his men.

"Well, you take Val in *The Fugitive Kind*. There's something about his sensibility, about how he talks to the birds, you know, which is very poetic. Maybe poetry is more natural in a feminine character, I don't know. It sure didn't seem to embarrass Brando. In hindsight, perhaps there's a feminine sensibility to my male characters. And visa versa."

Seidelman says that Serafina in *The Rose Tattoo* was a "ball buster." Williams chuckles: "Heh-heh. Well, Anna Magnani was a ball buster and all woman and a yard wide too."

Magnani and Brando didn't fare too well in *The Fugitive Kind*, an experience Williams remembers with some relish. "I only saw the film once and thought it was very good considering the difficult conditions under which it was made. At first Magnani was in love with Brando, and she'd send him love notes, which her secretary and then *I* would have to correct for English. She had three of us working on those letters. She *had* to have her cues, of course, or she made mistakes, and Brando would never give her the cues. Poor thing would have gotten an Oscar if Brando hadn't sabotaged her performance like that. She wound up hating him, of course."

The film version of *Cat on a Hot Tin Roof* had been shown on television the previous day, and Williams had tuned in to see what it looked like. "It was really much better than I'd remembered. They did ruin my plays on film, though, pretty much. They cut everything. When most of my films were made, they censored the endings, and I used to tell people to leave before the last five minutes. Even in *Streetcar Named Desire* they intimated that Stella wouldn't resume her relationship with Stanley at the end. This, of course, was exactly the opposite of the truth, which was, heh-heh-heh, that she would jump back into bed with him as soon as they had finished carting off Blanche. Other than that it was done beautifully. I did have to walk out on *Suddenly Last Summer*, though. It was so completely mangled. I never did have any kind of approval over screenwriters or anything, although it was sort of understood that Kazan would do *Streetcar*. Katherine Hepburn did steal *Suddenly Last Summer*, though, I thought."

I mention that Hepburn has been quoted often as saying *Suddenly Last Summer* was a film she didn't want to make because of the "distasteful" subject matter.

"Well, she *can* be rather provincial at times, I gather. I've never heard her say anything like that, and in fact, I'm shocked that she would, because I must say that her attitude is anything but feminine. Heh-heh. In *The Glass Menagerie*, when she was discouraged she would sit with her shoulders hunched over like a man. I've never seen *any* woman posture the way she does. Of course, she *can* be very feminine. After all, she's a great actress. You know, though, the louder people are against it, the more suspicious they are. I saw a photograph yesterday of Helmut Berger dancing the fox-trot with Ryan O'Neal. It was quite amusing." Suddenly Williams seems uncomfortable with the subject.

"You know, I really don't like to talk much about sexual deviation because it makes it seem as though I were obsessed with the subject, and I am not. I am obsessed with work and with the meaning of a play, not the sexual orientation of the characters. And whenever I am interviewed, I am always guided toward that subject, which is really rather peripheral, you know?"

Yes, I know, but *Memoirs*, after all, *was* rather explicit and did cause quite a stir.

"Frankly, I'm sorry I wrote *Memoirs*. I was assured I'd make a great deal of money out of it, not because of any sexual aspect of my nature, about which I am quite unsure anyway, but because I was just assured I would make a lot of money. Well, I didn't." He seems to be really upset by this and has a rather wild idea that the book is being suppressed.

"I never see it on the racks in airports alongside other books, even though it's in paperback now. It seems that it's being repressed for some reason. When I wrote it I had the delusion, the fear, that I would be destitute someday and that this book would protect me from that, heh-heh-heh."

It begins to look as if the interview is over. Williams is on his feet, complaining to Seidelman that Clive Barnes is being replaced as drama critic of the *New York Times*. "At least he always gave me good, serious notices. He's *never* said, 'Run, do not walk to the box office,' which is the *sine qua non*, almost, for a *musical* hit. I wish he *had* said it. Heh-heh-heh. But he's always been good. His review of *Out Cry* was not that good, but then I saw a rave he wrote about it in a magazine put out by American Airlines. He obviously felt free to express himself later with more enthusiasm than he had originally in the *Times*, heh-heh. I am very hopeful for *Vieux Carré*, though. The play has a little more of the old magic I used to put in my plays." The bags are now packed and lined up around the room. I'm wondering if *Vieux Carré* is as autobiographical as it seems.

"It is not, heh-heh, an autobiographical play because I have *never* looked as beautiful as Richard Alfieri, who plays the Writer, even on my good days. Heh-heh-heh. When I met him I said, 'Oh, you're *much* too beautiful, but never mind.' Heh-heh-heh."

Suddenly Williams's agent, Billy Barnes, bursts through the door in a neat three-piece suit with the news that he knows who is replacing Clive Barnes at the *Times*. Since I am a journalist, I must promise not to tell anyone that it is film critic Richard Eder.

The interview is over. Williams hands Seidelman two typewritten pages of what looks like dialogue with a lot of crossing out and rewrites. It is a scene he's been working on. "Here, see what you think of this."

We exchange good-byes, and Williams says he'll be back from Florida in a week to sit in on rehearsals. In the elevator, Seidelman looks over the scene in his hands with amazement. "He writes all the time, Vito. It's an obsession. He's really amazing. He just can't stop writing."

On my way downtown on the subway, I run into an old friend who is reading *Memoirs* in paperback, and I ask him where he bought it. He says that he found it on the rack at the Orlando airport in Florida.

Peter Allen

The Advocate — **July 13, 1977**

By his own definition, Peter Allen is fabulous. In fact, he thinks being fabulous is more important than being important, an attitude that hasn't helped to make him a household word. But as I watch the thirty-three-year-old singer/songwriter streak across the stage of The Roxy in Los Angeles, he seems destined for stardom despite his reluctance to conform. He has no rules, no commitment to his audience except to be real. He expresses open distaste for "safe" performers who dole out "TV dinner shows" and has said, "I am paid to be fabulous."

His songs are personal, sometimes autobiographical, mixing bored sophistication with a fresh-faced eagerness about life. A cross between the Wicked Queen and Snow White, Allen sings about having "been through it all" while smiling nicely for us. One moment he sits almost motionless at the piano, quietly understating his own "I Honestly Love You." Next, it's Carmen Miranda time as he takes an already half-gone audience all the way to "Rio," throwing off a blinding Hawaiian shirt to reveal black sequins, flowing white trousers kicking the air, hands working the maracas furiously, lips blasting away on a silver whistle between clenched teeth.

He is total self-acceptance onstage, his actions and vitality seeming to spring from something primal. He forsakes affectation or "show-biz" for a sometimes blatant reality. Sitting at the piano, sweating, he smiles wickedly at his audience before launching into another song. "I know that about now you're all asking yourselves, 'Is he or isn't he?' Right? Well, I'm gonna tell you. I *am*. Yes, I'm Australian and I knew you could tell…" The audience exhales and roars approval.

The *Village Voice* recently blurted out that he is "a naughty pansexual gigolo…on the verge of becoming the first male pop star of the 1970s with a flamboyantly gay style." His credentials for this reputation are impeccable. Consider the facts.

Onstage at the age of ten, playing piano and singing in pubs in his native Australia, Allen was a war baby raised by five women and hundreds of Hollywood movies. The Technicolor dreams he swallowed whole are partly responsible for his contention that "fabulous" is all. Illusions are his frame of reference. "That's why I don't like it when people come directly backstage after a show," he has said. "Onstage I'm fabulous, and then they come back and they think, 'Who is this short, sweaty person?'" The sense of glamour is easily traced. Leaving his Tenterfield home at fourteen, he went to Sydney, where he teamed with singer Chris Bell as The Allen Brothers. They played supper clubs and appeared regularly on Australian television along with people like Helen Reddy and Olivia Newton-John, both of whom would years later record the songs of Peter Allen.

Both in their late teens, The Allen Brothers were touring the Orient when Judy Garland, recovering from a disastrous Australian tour, caught their act at the Hong Kong Hilton. She took a wicked shine to Peter and asked them both to travel with her as an opening act. A year later, Garland introduced Peter to her daughter, Liza Minnelli, and in 1967 the two were married. The marriage lasted three years, the separation lasted three years and the divorce has been final for three years. In that decade Allen partied forever and became the man who "went everywhere twice, did everyone and saw everything." His introduction to America was a sea of nightclubs, openings and all-night bashes at which he was seen but seldom heard as Mr. Liza Minnelli and Judy Garland's son-in-law.

When he broke up with his "brother" Chris and his wife Liza at the same time, he suddenly found himself writing lyrics on napkins. What emerged was an astonishingly real, surprisingly vulnerable style couched in the sassy, smart attitude of a world-weary satyr. His first two albums, *Tenterfield Saddler* and *Peter Allen*, contain some of his best work but are unavailable due to the demise of Metromedia Records. He captured the period, though, in the title song of his third album, for A&M Records, "Continental American." Suddenly people began to see that the unique reality of Peter Allen was matched in excitement only by his clear willingness to reveal it in his music. He became the first male performer to have a cult following on New York's notoriously female cabaret circuit; and his fourth album, *Taught by Experts*, confirmed his growing diversity by opening up the ranks of his followers to every stripe. His sold-out concerts at Lincoln Center and The Bottom Line in New York are the basis for a new, live album being released soon by A&M, a record company seemingly dedicated to go with Allen as he is and allowing him to continue to be daring and explore his own self through music.

He has been compared to Bette Midler and Errol Flynn, to Noel Coward and Jerry Lee Lewis. He has been lionized by the hangers-on in New York society and praised by the critics, but he continues to move into different spaces. His *Taught by Experts* has been viewed as a farewell to New York, and indeed he has retreated to a quieter life in a house on a cliff near La Jolla, California. He says he fell in love with it the minute he saw it because "it reminded me immediately of Joan Crawford in *Female on the Beach*. I had to have it."

The Chateau Marmont is fabulous. That's where Allen stays when in Los Angeles, and when I arrive at his door the day after his Roxy opening he is neither sweaty nor particularly short. Neither is he any of the things attributed to him by journalists overeager to emphasize his "New York decadence." He's got bright eyes, freckles and a nice smile. His sense of theatrics is heavily lined with irony and a sense of humor. I find this out when I open by asking him how it felt to be a child star.

"A child star? I was never a child star. That was just playing the piano and singing in bars. I've always done that. I wasn't a *star*. I've never been any kind of a *star*!" He groans as I produce a legal pad full of notes. "Oh, I *am* going to be in trouble with the two other people to whom I promised the first *Advocate* interview."

I wonder if he minds talking about what it was like to be eighteen years old, to be discovered by Garland and taken to America.

"The thing was that I was not particularly a fan of Judy's. I *think* that's what saved me. I mean, when I was in Australia I was earning my living singing rock 'n' roll, and when I listened to other stuff I was very heavy into Forties jazz. My idea of a fabulous girl singer was June Christy. And you know, I would go to people's houses and they'd put on Judy and they'd just *fall down*. I mean, these queens were just going ca-ray-*zeee*, and I used to say, 'All I can hear on this record is applause.' I couldn't really get off on it. But I loved her when I saw her in the movies, so when she came in to see us in Hong Kong I thought, 'Oh, a movie star,' you know? And so it was just this American movie star who was coming to see me, not the goddess of the stage or anything. I knew maybe twelve Americans in my life at this point. They scared me to death because I'd worked cruises on the President Lines and all I saw was tourists. I couldn't *believe* them, they were so horrifying! So anyway, Judy took this wild liking to me and it ended up in a series of the looniest days."

There are lots of stories about those loony days that might indicate that Garland was slightly crazy herself. "When she was alone she was quite happy to sit with her glasses on and read a book. All that other stuff was just performance. There *were* some fabulous moments, though. It was endless madness. She and Mark Herron used to fight all the time and it was either my first or second night with her and she made me sing to them in a rowboat because they'd been fighting. And then we took her car to see the sun come up and later she tried to get a drink at a fancy hotel. We were all still in evening clothes, so they wouldn't serve us a drink. So Judy ordered the *whole* breakfast just to get a sherry. I mean it was *so* sickening. And then they ordered us out of the hotel and the car was gone and she and I were sitting in the gutter at nine in the morning with all these people on the way to work, staring at Judy Garland in a sequined gown on the sidewalk.

"So finally Mark turns up and on the way home. He's talking about acting and how you have to be true to yourself and Judy starts yelling that he doesn't know what he's talking about. She rolls down all the windows and starts yelling, '*These* are the people you have to reach! *This* is the audience! *These* are my people!' and thousands of Chinese are staring in the windows." Peter is silent for a moment and then raises an eyebrow. "So I thought, 'Well, she certainly has a sense of the moment.'"

Traveling with Garland meant that Allen got to see the workings of the cult that followed her and the press it engendered concerning gay people. "It was really frightening sometimes because we'd do our set and then the doctor would announce that Miss Garland was too ill to perform. We were *sacrificed* to them. And I got mad at it a lot, because it was only a very frustrated gay section and that was their chance to yell out and be noticed. I watched the audiences and it got to be a real pain in the ass because she would always be real nice to them. She'd just be starting a song and they'd start, 'We love you Judy! Never leave us!' She'd have to say, 'Oh, I love you too, darling.' I guess somebody did it at Carnegie Hall and it became the thing to do for anyone who was the least bit pushy. What was worse, though, was that writers would take it and get really vicious. There was that really evil piece in *Esquire* by Goldman, 'Judy Floats.'"

I have always wondered what Garland thought about gay people and Allen smiles a little.

"She said to me once, 'I don't understand it. I'll call a hairdresser up to do my hair and *all* I'll get is his problems and fights with his boyfriends. Everyone wants to tell me about their most *intimate* sexual thing and I just *don't* understand...' She knew, of course, about her gay audience and she was *so* very accessible to people. She might have given a negative response about it in public, though."

Allen, unlike Garland, lives in an age when things like "gay audiences" are talked about in public, and he appeared on a "CBS Special Report" in New York to talk about this aspect of his cabaret performing, saying that one must reach all people in an audience, not just the majority. I ask him why he agreed to do it.

"But I simply can't *believe* it. Do you know they asked Bette Midler to do it and she said she has *no* gay audience? Her manager Aaron Russo said, 'She doesn't have a gay following; she has no comment on this.' And so I thought, 'That seems *so* stupid,' I mean, you only have to walk into the room and you'll see guys with their arms around each other watching the show...I mean...*well*! My first audience was a gay audience, but *now* it seems that I'm a little "too something" for them. I've tried to play Studio One and gay clubs in Washington, and they don't like me. You know, I think they'd like me better if I was a girl in a gown. See, I'm a little too normal for an outrageous gay audience. In the beginning, gays come to see you and then it broadens out. It's like that with anyone."

Aside from breaking out of the cult mold, Allen has also broken out of the lifestyle that prompted songs like "Glittering Zero" and "Everything Old Is New Again," in which he characterizes nostalgia as "going backward when forward fails." In a lot of ways, this also meant saying goodbye to New York. Does he really think forward has failed, and are all those people out there really glittering zeros?

"Yes, I think so. I'm just thinking that where everyone's going has nothing to do with me. That's where I'm really cynical. People are cutting themselves off from everything. The problem is there's no individuality. You're *this* or you're *that* or you're *this*...so that's why I always try to be purposely different on the stage so that nobody can say, 'Oh yes, well he's bang-bang-bang' and put me in a box. I was in New York for ten years. I just got bored with it. I can write anywhere I'm alone, but it's hard to be alone in New York. You're there and it's just hard to go to bed at night and not go out. And I wasn't having any fun going out. I mean, I'd *done* it. I felt alien in all the crowds and I still feel like that to an extent, but I decided it's all right. I'll just be whoever I want onstage. And you can get away with not belonging much better onstage than in life. I must say, though, I felt a lot better in Europe. It's strange. Even in Tokyo they're much more willing to accept what I do onstage than they are in the Midwest. I don't scare people at all overseas. I think I do sometimes scare people here. My worst audience for a long time was straight men because they were most threatened by what I was doing. And they were even more upset if their girlfriends liked me. They were threatened because I'd wiggle around up onstage."

> *I can't help but feel I'm under*
> *investigation*
> *By the local branch of the women's*
> *and the*
> *gay boys' liberation...*

"Oh, I don't *believe* you know those songs, I never listen to my old songs. Yeah, I remember that line. It was about the pressures of *groups*." He says groups like they should be handled only with a pair of tongs. "I am *the* most apolitical person in the whole, wide world. I have no political thoughts whatsoever."

In "Quiet Please, There's a Lady on the Stage," a song he wrote in tribute to Garland, he writes "...and she's been honest through her songs long before your consciousness was raised/doesn't that deserve a little praise?" I take this as a sarcastic crack at liberation. "Yeah, I guess it is," he shrugs and I tell him that by being who he is he expands the possibilities for people's behavior offstage.

"Yes, okay, but that's not why I'm going out there. It's not done intentionally. People read all kinds of things into what others do. I read that the groupie in the song "Pretty Pretty" is a thinly disguised song about a man instead of a woman. It's amazing what you can learn if you *read*, huh?"

I point out to him that so many performers actively hide who they really are that it's refreshing when someone is real. "Yeah, but to do a good job of hiding your real self you have to be fabulous-looking and have a fabulous voice, etc. The best that I have to give is who I *am*, and then I'm most comfortable on the stage."

Is it easier now to be honest than it was ten years ago? "You know, it's so much easier. *So* much easier," he chuckles. "Of course, it's a lot easier when it looks as though you're going to be successful. Then you can be anything you want."

I ask him if he knows what a "pansexual" is. He says no, but maybe it means that after the show, boys come up and say he's real cute and girls come up and say he's real cute. "I don't know. Sex with goats, maybe."

His sense of freedom was also taught to him by an expert, and I ask him if he'll tell me about Frances Faye.

"Frances Faye was actually a *much* bigger influence on me than anyone else. It's a pity she wasn't better known and was relegated to an almost exclusively gay audience. She was little ahead of her time, I think. In fact, the act I'm doing now is still Frances Faye to an extent.

"She said, '*What* are you doing onstage? What are you *saying* to these people? What are you talking about?' And she did that whole thing with me, Judy would do it unconsciously; she'd never talk to me about it in a specific way, but Frances *drilled* me. She'd say, 'Black music? Black music! That's what you've got to *get*,' because you know we had no black sounds in Australia and she'd send me records and say, 'Listen to this now.' She's truly one of the free people of the world and one of the wildest women I've ever met. When you go to visit her, she doesn't wear any clothes. I mean, she's like sixty-something and she always wants to dance and she's so incredibly animated. She's fabulous. Whatever comic timing I have is from Frances Faye."

His comic timing is pretty flawless. The following night after his first show he tells me that A&M Records president Jerry Moss arrived while *Advocate* photographer Sandy Kaplan was snapping away. "So Jerry comes in and he sees the photographer and he *throws* his arms around me and says, 'Peter!' and I say 'Hi, Jerry. The photographer is from *The Advocate*' and he jumps back six feet and says, 'Oh, really? What's *The Advocate*?' It was fabulous!"

Before I leave, he tells me that he's getting everything he's wanted. "I *loved* being a success in Paris! There's no point in being a success in Des Moines, but there's a fabulous point to being a success in Paris." His visibility is still low, though, and he likes it that way. "People leave me pretty much alone, although now I'm beginning to get some of the crazos. They call me at six in the morning and tell me that they made me and I belong to them. I think, 'Oh please! Are you *serious*? I can't believe this.' I disappear into the crowd offstage and I like it that way. God knows it takes enough to make me look flashy onstage. I like the comforts that celebrity gives, like not having to wait in line for something, but I can do without all the bullshit. I don't even know what to say when people come up and gush at me.

"Listen, I'm just living for life. I have no plans or expectations for the future. I mean, it's like when I was working with Chris and he and his father would make all these elaborate plans for the future and I could never understand." He dismisses them with his hand, "Because you see, I *knew* that the next day I'd meet Judy Garland and be off to America." He smirks. "You can't plan."

Pat Bond

Christopher Street — May 1978

Pat Bond is a fifty-three-year-old ex-WAC from San Francisco who knows about life. She is also a dyke comic who is busily engaged in reviving the lost art of the monologue on the nightclub stages from which she dispenses her life story in episodic flashes of sharp wit and threatening humor. She is currently on view in the new Mariposa Film Group documentary, *Word Is Out*. She flew to New York for the opening this Easter – her first trip to New York in over twenty years. I took her to David's Pot Belly on Christopher Street for a little local color and an introduction to the chocolate egg cream. A gay tourist from Amsterdam sitting two tables away gave her the shirt off his back. Took it off and gave it to her.

"I started out being a little kid. I used to go to the Oriental Theater in Davenport, Iowa, with my grandmother. She wore long cotton socks and it was my job to pull them up for her. The Oriental was one of those huge theaters that had drifting clouds on the ceiling and stars that blinked on and off. And for a dime for me and a quarter for my grandmother we saw three movies and a stage show. And they would have these weird contests where people would rush up on the stage and swallow a goldfish for a quarter. Depression, right? And I would have to restrain grandma from going up to do things like that, so I would threaten not to pull her socks up."

Pat Bond's nightclub act mixes e. e. cummings, Gertrude Stein, and Carson McCullers with some personal reminiscences of a humorous nature.

"I was determined to be an intellectual when I was a child. Come hell or high water. I traded some girl my bicycle for her horn-rimmed glasses once. She couldn't see and neither could I. Her mother had to put her in bed until my grandmother dragged me around the neighborhood to find out who she was and give them back. I was hell on wheels. In high school I had my first crush on one of my teachers. I put the poor woman through hell, you know, riding around following her on my bicycle, calling her and hanging up, sending sweetheart cards unsigned. Of course, she was a French teacher. Nothing so tacky as a gym teacher for me. She was wonderful. In those days they put an ad in the paper: WANTED: TEACHER *Must not smoke, drink, be Jewish, Negro or Italian. Or ever have heard of sex.* And my French teacher answered the ad. I picked up on lots of things. I'd scare my little cousin with what little I knew about menstruation. I hated her. I used to say, ominously, 'Some day you will bleed from your peepee,' and she'd run home screaming. I could never figure out the Modess ads. *MODESS...BECAUSE.* Because why? Do you know? I never did."

She also has the lowdown on Carmelita Pope. Almost too good to be true.

"Yeah, old Carmelita Pope went to our school and *she* was popular. She sang a cappella and played the harp and was in all the school plays even though she couldn't act very well. And we all hated her guts, she was such a cow. And then thirty years later I'm minding my own business in my apartment and this voice comes off the tube. 'Hello, I'm Carmelita Pope.'" And I wrote to the pam people and said, 'Who the fuck is Carmelita Pope? Why won't she announce herself?' Ha! We'd gone to a Catholic girls finishing school and when Carmelita left she joined the road company of *Tobacco Road.* Well, we were just delighted. We got one of those huge posters which showed her lying on the ground with her blouse all torn off and some man straddling her and we put it right up in Mother Geraldine's office. Can you imagine the innocence of those times?"

Bond's innocence was left behind when she joined the Women's Army Corps to forget a woman who obviously was not in love with her.

"Mistake Number 9,998. It *was* incredible, though. It was like a huge gay bar. I'd say ninety percent of the company was gay. Openly. With men's haircuts and everything. And then they had that witch hunt in Tokyo and five hundred women got sent home for dishonorable discharges. And one of our kids killed herself at twenty, they had managed to terrify her so. She jumped from a sixth story window. Then they had the unmitigated fucking gall to have a military funeral for her. Can you imagine the shape we were all in? We were in hysterics, most of us, all of the time for two or three months. They grilled us every day. And you know, talking about this in my act, I finally figured out what happened. Why it happened. When we got there we discovered that there weren't any jobs for us and we soon figured out that MacArthur wanted to show us off to the Japanese women. You know, these are independent American women and this is what they're like. Can you *imagine* his surprise? He got independent women, all right. He got dykes. And of course, that was *it*. As soon as they saw what was happening they wanted us out."

Pat Bond never went back to Davenport. There was a smart post-war gay bar boom in San Francisco and that's where she's stayed ever since. When she hit the City by the Bay in 1944 there were seven gay bars, five of them on Broadway. Not women's bars.

"Mixed, dear. Always mixed in those days. We had nowhere else to go. Except for Mona's, which had male impersonators. And *that* was really wild because they were just marvelous looking dykes. They weren't tacky, you know, they were done up in dinner jackets and they'd sing songs like

> *There goes my gal:*
> *She changed her name*
>   *to Mike.*
> *There goes my gal:*
> *She's turned into a dyke.*
>
> *She used to make men*
>   *stare,*
> *Now she gives the girls*
>   *the eye.*
> *I can't figure out how*
>   *it all began.*
>
> *There goes my gal:*
>   *a lesbian.*

In that era butch and femme were very divided. You were either a butch or a femme. I mean there was no in-between. And the femmes didn't last long because they soon got the word that they had to do all the work. First of all they had to support the butch. Because how could she get a job in that costume, right? And the femmes also had to scrub floors and cook. It was like a heterosexual marriage. Part of the problem I always had with lesbians in those days was that the butch was not allowed to be smart. You see, she had to imitate the male and to her the male drank beer and watched the football game on the tube and was a truck driver. She imitated the worst in men the way female impersonators imitate the worst in women. And there were all kinds of things you never did. If you were a butch and you were walking down the street and you saw someone you knew and she was with people you didn't know, you *never* said hello. Just in case they were people who didn't know she knew such persons. And of course you could always get *killed* for bringing a camera into a gay bar."

She was writing material for female impersonator T. C. Jones. Drags and dykes were often good friends.

"Charles Pierce and I may do something together. You know, he gets a lot of flack for being sexist and we might humorously point out the inherent comedy in the way gay men and women have related over the years. In the old days it was marvelous. The men and the women were very close friends. Lived together. Enjoyed each other. One of my dreams, my fantasies – Ha! – was that I would be a big star like Marlene or Judy or Tallulah – only first names, you know – and all the sad young men would adore me and they would *heap* me with diamonds and drive me around in their used Rolls Royces. But I would have a secret that they must never discover or my following would desert me. And of course it was that *I* was a dyke. But they must never, never know, ha ha. Lesbian and faggot relationships over the years have been extraordinary. I think the men destroyed it, though. It became obvious that they didn't want us in their bars. And since men have more money than women, their money talked. So eventually if a woman walked into a bar they'd ask her for five pieces of I.D. – you know, the old shakedown. It's a shame."

In spite of her girth, Pat Bond is a wisp of smoke. A frail link from an old world to a new one. An endangered species. The chance of bringing her back to New York?

"If someone would send for me it would be darling."

Kaye Ballard

Italian/American Magazine — **July, 1980**

The familiar face, the wide smile, and the clear, bright eyes betray none of the rigors of a life spent working for success. None of it shows. The roller-coaster career spanning thirty years in every medium of entertainment from burlesque to television, the big breaks that never quite broke, and the incessant pressure to stay on top do not seem to have taken a toll on this lady. She is soft and warm. She could be a stylish suburbanite from Tuxedo Park in her Clovis Ruffin original and Mr. Kenneth hairdo. Her words, however, belie the image. She is witty and tough, weary but not bitter. Kaye Ballard has burned in hellfire for her career and has lived to tell the tale.

"Maybe you are destined to be what you are," she says in her borrowed Central Park West apartment. "I have always known what I wanted to do, my whole life. At twelve years old I used to go out and work and bring home money to my mother as if I were paying rent. It was like I was just *staying* there until I got into show business. Hah!" She smiles and remembers. "I used to be an usherette back in Ohio, and I'd perform in the aisles, singing and imitating the stars on the screen."

Years later more than one critic would refer to her as "undaunted," and it seems to be the simple truth. Her performing in the aisles led her to the door of Cleveland agent Dick Jackson, for whom she improvised an "act." It was 1941 and she was fifteen years old. Jackson kept telling her that she was good but should finish school. But Kaye kept coming back every day until she landed a job singing and doing impressions at a local Chinese restaurant for twenty dollars a week. Encouraged by her father and her grandmother, she soon realized that she was not long for Cleveland. She talks expressively about this time in her life.

"They never stopped me. My father is such a beautiful man. He was a cement finisher, and he would never leave Cleveland because he put down sidewalks in every part of that city. Wherever he walks, he feels like it's his. The first time he heard I wanted to go into show business, he bought me a perfume atomizer. That was his idea of glamour and luxury, you know. And when I saw that delicate little bottle in those big callused workingman's hands, I thought, 'What a beautiful father I've got!' He was such a proud man. He never owned a penny in his life, and I'll never forget that he lost his house in the Depression because he didn't have enough money. I used to say, 'Pop, I'm gonna buy you everything someday'--and that was my goal in life. He was Calambrese and so was my mother, but he came from Catanzaro and she was from Cosenza. They'd always argue about which town was classier. How they'd yell! It was a great childhood. We were a very poor family, but you could eat off the floors. And my father fixed up the house like a palace."

She was Catherine Gloria Balotta then, but the independence of Kaye Ballard was already rearing its head. "I'd always be out somewhere instead of hanging around the house. Mostly I'd be over at the Vanucci's because their mother made hot bread and onions and I loved it. My father would work like a dog to bring home meat, and I'd be having onions at the Vanucci's, with their thirteen kids at the table and me on the end."

In spite of growing up around big families and lots of children, Kaye has never married. "When people say to me, 'Oh, I feel sorry for you because you never had kids,' I tell them I was *smart* enough not to have children. It's no big deal to have kids unless you plan to devote your life to raising them properly. I'm grateful that I came from a home with discipline. That's what's missing today. Besides," she says with a laugh, "it prolonged my grandmother's life that I never married. She used to say, 'I'm not gonna die until you get married.' She died at ninety-three. Ha! She got the message, huh?" She shrugs. "No. I don't regret it at all. I just had something else to do."

Something else took her on the road in 1944 with one of the last legit vaudeville runs, the Kemptime circuit, as a straight woman in burlesque skits. In 1945 Spike Jones spotted her at a Detroit nightclub and she joined his loony band, playing the tuba and singing specialty numbers. This, and a tour on the RKO circuit with Vaughn Monroe, led her to New York in 1946 where she began to work in clubs and on the stage. Although her personal reviews were always good, her first stage appearances, in shows like *That's the Ticket* and *Three to Make Ready*, were decided flops. Her biggest boost came in 1954 when she was featured as Helen of Troy in *The Golden Apple* and made the sultry song "Lazy Afternoon" famous. The show landed her on the cover of *Life* Magazine, photographed by Richard Avedon. "Yeah, but there was no story inside! It figures, right? Then I signed with RKO studios, and it folded right after I made *The Girl Most Likely*. I even got kissed by Clark Gable — but on the forehead!" As a pensive smile creeps over her face, I ask her why she's never done straight drama.

"Nobody ever asked me. Once you do nightclubs, you know, people don't think of you in any other terms. When Anna Magnani saw my act at the Bon Soir some years back she told me if they ever did the musical version of *The Rose Tattoo*, I *had* to play the part of Serafina." Her hand is in the air now and her eyes are really shining. "Magnani said that! And recently my agent approached Julie Styne, who is doing it soon, and he said, 'Naaaa, we don't want her. We want somebody like Rita Moreno.' Now Rita Moreno is fantastic, but she's not Serafina. Serafina is a little overweight and *not* a beauty. Ahhh...they're such dummies."

If another imminent disappointment doesn't seem to throw her into despair, it can only be because she's used to comedowns. In 1967 she was signed to play the down-to-earth Italian housewife on "The Mothers-In-Law." For openers, it was scheduled opposite the "Ed Sullivan Show."

"I've had half luck all my life. I loved that show, and it was number seventeen in the ratings when it was cancelled. It was a political move when the show's sponsor was pressured into taking the "Bill Cosby Show" because there were no black shows on the air. They were nervous anyway because Desi Arnaz was very sick, and he was the one who supervised everything. People don't know it, but he was every bit as much a genius as Lucille Ball. A tremendous talent."

She puts on a knowing smile when I ask her how she got along with her co-star, Eve Arden. "Love her and got along with her brilliantly because I always let her have her way. She wanted to be photographed only on a certain side, like Claudette Colbert. Since I never knew if I had a good side or a bad side, I let her have her way. All of these people are wonderful and impersonal. They're not my close friends. I think Doris Day is closer to me than any of them."

And naturally, Kaye is closer to her family. She has realized her dream to give her father a nice life, she's been sending money home for almost thirty years, and her family thinks of her as a star.

"They see me on television and they think I'm rich. They don't understand why Dean Martin doesn't use me on his show. They say, 'Doesn't he know she's Italian?' It's cute. They don't understand that people in this business don't think in those terms. There's more sense of community among Jewish people in entertainment than Italians." She brightens up and begins to laugh. "Oh! I must tell you that Joan Rivers says the only difference between a Jewish mother and an Italian mother is black stockings!" Kaye's spirits rise and fall like her mercurial Italian temper, which flares more in the spirit of passion than anger. Comedy is a rather passionate business, though, and requires a lot of stamina. As a woman in the business, she has often been frustrated by the limited possibilities afforded her.

"First of all, I chose to take the clean route, which is very difficult. Not to be dirty in this business is very hard because people will laugh at anything suggestive. It's a laugh which pays off, though, because the people who do that stuff are making more money than I will ever make in my life. I just can't do it. I can't. Plus, yes it *has* always been more difficult for women than men, even though some of the greatest comics have been women. Look at Martha Raye and Bea Lillie. To me it's tragic that Martha Raye, who is *brilliant*, can't choose whatever she wants to do now. And I am *shocked* that nobody ever asked me to do an Italian album, because every time I do my grandmother's favorite songs I get standing ovations. Italian women would have gone a lot further in the business if they weren't busy being taught how to wash the dishes by their mothers. Orson Welles says that in Italy there are 30,000 great actors and only five hundred are working at their craft. Haaa!"

I ask if she's been to Italy, and she explodes. "Are you kidding? Of course. I even met Pope John XXIII. I have a cousin who is, I think, secretary of state at the Vatican. Benacozzi. You see, my father's cousin, Anthony Balotta, was a famous designer, and his nephew is a man named Benacozzi; so I got to meet the Pope. It was cute. He didn't speak English, but he was learning. He had a translator named Monsignor Kelly, who would translate everything as if he were chanting High Mass. So Pope John said in Italian, 'You know, I never wanted to be Pope,' and Kelly said, 'The Pooooope saaaid henverwantedtobe Poooope!' It was funny. The first thing he wanted to know about was the "Sixty-Four-Thousand-Dollar Question" scandal. He was a fabulous man. And he learned to speak English in three months."

This story about the Pope is told to me while Kaye is having her hair done in preparation for the premiere of her new film *The Ritz*, based on Terrence McNally's Broadway farce about a man hiding out from his mobster brother-in-law at a homosexual bathhouse in New York. Kaye plays his wife, who sneaks into the Ritz in a man's raincoat only to find her lipsticked, mink-coated husband singing an Andrew Sisters song with two gay men. It's a very funny situation with endless possibilities. In keeping with the story of her life, however, the director, Richard Lester, cut most of her part out of the finished film.

"Ahhhh, those dummies! The man who directed *The Ritz* is Jewish and lives in England. It's a story about Italian Catholics and gay people, so where does he come to know about this? Terrence McNally is Catholic, and he wrote such wonderfully funny lines about the Church and how I tell my husband he has to go to a different priest in confession because Father Bonelli knows his voice. It was a scream, and Richard Lester cut all those references because he didn't understand. I have a feeling he previewed the film in England and cut things wherever he didn't get a laugh."

The Ritz is a departure for Kaye in more ways than one. Not only is the subject of a gay bathhouse daring, but she has to shout a four letter word that would give her mother heart failure.

"Oh, please! I told my sister to go to see the movie with her and when I say that word to cough real loud so my mother won't hear it. The gay part doesn't worry me, though. My family is actually very broadminded. Gay people exist, and everybody has to have a sense of humor about himself. After all, great people have been homosexual. Look at Michelangelo and Leonardo da Vinci. Besides, who cares? Everybody is caricatured in the film. It's a farce. Gays should no more be offended by the characterizations than Italians, who are also exaggerated. They're caricatures. All comedy is based on exaggeration of people's traits. That's why I don't understand people who get angry about stereotypes. Butterfly McQueen really *talked* like that! So what?

Italians never just say it's raining; they have to make a whole story. That's the way we are.

"Once my grandmother broke her hip. She had to say, 'Your father was sitting over there, and then I turned around to get the fork…' It's our way. Nobody should get offended by stereotypes. I loved *The Godfather*. It's all so silly! When the syndicate ran Las Vegas you could see a great show for the price of a ginger ale. Now it's a total rip-off. If anyone should be criticized, it's the crooks in the government. How dare they criticize anybody when their house is so dirty."

In any case, the film is causing a stir, and Kaye is getting a lot of attention in spite of her part being reduced to shreds. There were rumors after the film opened that she would be doing a female version of *The Odd Couple* with June Lockhart.

"No. Those are just rumors. What I *would* like to do is something much more exciting. I've talked to Neil Simon about doing a version of *The Sunshine Boys* with me and Martha Raye called *The Sunshine Sisters*. It would be wonderful. Also, we're talking to Twentieth-Century Fox about a special for television called "Kaye and Raye with Feeling." The executives aren't sure, but I'll bet the people would love it. I'd also love to do a movie with Fellini. I'd even do one for Lina Wertmüller — as long as she didn't ask me to take my clothes off! But there will never be another De Sica or Alberto Sordi. They made my favorite films, and they can't be duplicated."

We're riding across Central Park in a taxi, and Ballard is sitting back in her seat, looking out the window. "I love New York. If I had my wish I would have just enough money to keep my house in Palm Springs and have an apartment in New York. And to stay healthy so I can keep working. I've lived my own life and nobody else's. My greatest drawback has always been a lack of confidence, a feeling that I never deserved anything. But a wonderful thing happens with age. A freedom comes with it. You say to yourself, 'What have I got to lose?' and it makes you happier. I have more energy that I ever did. I think I've inherited my grandmother's vitality." She smiles and rests her head on the back of the seat. "I've been very, very lucky."

Allan Carr

The Advocate — June 12, 1984

"Come up! Let me tell you what my life is like today." Allan Carr stands on a small hill near his swimming pool outside his stunning house, which, as everyone knows, was built by MGM for Ingrid Bergman in the late-1930s, when she came from Sweden to do *Intermezzo*. In the driveway are parked maybe seven cars, from a Porsche to a pickup. In the elfin guest house at the foot of the hill toils a small army of aides and secretaries, who answer the constantly ringing telephones with a cheery "Allan Carr Productions!" A young man gestures toward the house and says, "Go on up, he's waiting for you." Just for a second I think of Anne Francis pointing out Ziegfeld to Streisand in *Funny Girl*. "He's up above, honey. Like God."

But Carr doesn't act like God. He acts like Ziegfeld with a sense of humor. The man who manages Ann-Margret's career and gave us The Village People in *Can't Stop the Music* has the artless enthusiasm of a child whose favorite toy is show business. "Let me show you my house. We can't really do an interview today. There are people having meetings in every room. I have to fly to New York to plan the opening of *Where the Boys Are*. I'm doing two hundred benefits of *La Cage aux Folles*. You say yes to one group and it never stops. Claire Luce was right. No good deed goes unpunished."

There really are lawyer types poring over legal papers in virtually every room of the house, and the telephone lines are constantly lit up. I ask Carr how he liked the Grammy Awards the other night. He talks just the way he thinks. "Well, I loved the first hour and a half...the second hour and a half was just...first of all, you have to be there at something like three in the afternoon...it's long...from Donna Summer's opening number I thought it would be fabulous...but then it's just so long...I've been involved in producing the Oscar show and I know how hard it is to do one of those shows...but it was *so* long...listen, we can't do a fun interview in twenty minutes...it's madness today...can you come back on Tuesday?"

On Tuesday the chaos is more controlled. The spacious living room is deserted, but the phones ring regularly, and in about an hour some people are coming to discuss the *La Cage* billboard on Sunset Strip. Carr is finishing a conversation with a publicist. "Don't let her out of your sight for a minute. She's 'My Friend Irma.' She'll end up in San Diego with a sailor." He hangs up and motions me to a chair in front of a huge fireplace. He doesn't wait for questions. "All this craziness is the culmination of *last* year's work," he says. "While we were doing *Grease II* in Florida, I got the idea for *Where the Boys Are*, and we shot that while *La Cage aux Folles* was going into production. The only reason I can do all this is that I'm able to sleep on airplanes. But *Grease* was my high-school fantasy, and *Where the Boys Are* was my college fantasy." He grins. "Now I'm ready for postgraduate work, and I'm very happy."

The forty-one-year-old Carr was raised in Highland Park, Illinois, in a family that encouraged theatergoing. At twenty years old he was a veteran theatrical investor, saving up his money to back shows he found fascinating. One of these was a Tallulah Bankhead vehicle, which closed on the road before he could even see it. His first big project as producer was *The World of Carl Sandburg* at the Chicago Civic Theater, starring Bette Davis and Gary Merrill. Soon afterwards, he met Marlo Thomas and began managing her career, a move that presaged his current reputation as star-maker.

It's one of Carr's dreams come true to have a movie and a Broadway musical playing a few blocks apart at the same time. He's wanted to do *La Cage aux Folles* since 1976, and for several years he kept the project in development with almost one million of his own money. "I saw it on the stage in Paris," he says, "and I envisioned it as a movie for Jack Lemmon and Tony Curtis, sort of *Some Like It Hot* twenty-five years later. But as time went by they made this little movie from it, and I didn't get into that so much. I thought the performances were wonderful, but I *never* thought it would be a big hit. The movie was a sort of breakthrough because the audience could feel that a nice thing was happening between those two men, as silly and outrageous as they were. In the play there was more of a family relationship, and that's what we preserved in the musical. As it's presented on Broadway, people can relate to it in the simplest 'Father Knows Best' way. They have to be either rock hard or have no emotions at all not to come out of that show wanting to call someone to say, 'I'm sorry'— or whatever."

The commercial success of *La Cage aux Folles* was anything but certain in the beginning. "We had all these theater-party ladies over to Jerry Herman's town house in New York to hear the score," says Carr. "And they loved it, but they didn't book it because they weren't sure the theme would go over with their audiences. *Then* came Boston." Many think Carr's decision to open *La Cage* in Boston was a stroke of genius. "Boston is a real serious theater town," he says. "In Washington they love *everything*, but Boston is a real test. I mean, when I saw the first audience, I realized that these were not Katherine Hepburn subscribers...these were Katherine *Cornell* subscribers. And the first matinee in Boston was the real killer. *Old?* Forget Katherine Cornell. These were people who saw Maude Adams in *Peter Pan*. Ruth Gordon came to this theater when she was a little girl. And they went wild. I am telling you, I saw people getting up on their walkers and applauding. You have to know the theater and love the theater to realize what that means."

One thing it has meant is over $2.5 million in theater-party sales and a mini-industry that is planning *La Cage aux Folles* companies two years in advance for Australia, Europe and the Far East. One of those companies may star pop singer Sylvester in the role of Albin. "Sylvester is incredible," says Carr. "I saw him for the first time at the Castro Theater in San Francisco, and he gives Ella Fitzgerald a run for her money. Plus you just *know* from watching him that he'll be able to act."

Carr constantly gets calls from stars who want to step into *La Cage aux Folles*. "Sammy Davis Jr. and Bill Cosby keep asking to do it, but I really don't want to pull a *Hello Dolly!* and make a stunt out of every new person who takes over the show. The play itself is too important. *La Cage aux Folles* is not about a performer putting on a dress and showing off. It's about caring and people and we have to remain true to the material. One of the reasons I was so impressed with Sylvester is that you can tell a lot about a person from how they behave socially. At the party after his show he was a real host, asking if there was enough food and making sure people had a drink. He could have been la diva prima donna, and he just wasn't. There's a niceness about him, and that makes such a difference in a show like *La Cage aux Folles*. The last thing you want is what I call Raquel Welch behavior on or off-stage. So, yes, I loved Sylvester, and we're in touch about him doing the show. I think there's real untapped dramatic talent there."

Carr has strong opinions about what works in show business, mostly having to do with the preservation of glamour. "Show business exists to make people in Cleveland happy," he says, "and I'm a great believer in maintaining the illusion. Some people should never go on talk shows because they really have nothing to say, and they blow their mystique. People like Al Pacino and Robert De Niro are great actors, but they should never appear in public. The difference between the old and the new Hollywood is that in the old days we didn't know too much about the stars. Today they're all interviewed in their homes, and there's nothing we don't know. I see David Steinberg interviewing Burt Reynolds, and Burt says, 'Here I am without my wig.' Now, I respect honesty, but we are still in the business of make-believe. I don't want to see the mechanical shark from *Jaws* on the Universal tour. I want to believe that's a real shark.

"We don't know how lucky we are in this country. I went to Sweden with Ann-Margret and it was closed for the winter. It's Madison, Wisconsin, with Volvos. The people are lovely but no wonder the suicide rate is so high. There's nothing to do. Ann-Margret comes to do a show and they go nuts."

Carr has a well-known facility for packaging talent to maximum effect and exposure. He was responsible for one of the great Academy Awards moments of all time, pairing Barbara Stanwyck and William Holden in a moving presentation a few years ago. He was also behind Ann-Margret's decision to play Blanche DuBois in the television version of *A Streetcar Named Desire*. "I was speechless," he says. "She was incredible. For the first time the play was about Blanche. Stanley is an interesting character blown up out of proportion by Brando's great performance in the past. This time it was about Blanche's problems, and it finally came across in this version that her husband was gay."

In twenty years the only performers he's declined to manage have been Barry Manilow and, until recently, Julio Iglesias. "At first I didn't see Julio's potential in this country, and I was wrong. I'm looking for a film for him now. The thing about someone like him is that you have to tailor a picture to

him the way they did for Robert Taylor in the old days. In a way I *do* wish
it could be like the old days out here because Zanuck and Mayer were able
to push stars to do things they ordinarily would not do, and magic would
happen. Cyd Charisse didn't want to do *Silk Stockings*. It's her best role.
Debbie Reynolds didn't want to do *Singin' in the Rain*. Ava Gardner told me
every time she resisted a role and they forced her to do it, she gave a good
performance. In about fifteen years people will look at *Norma Rae* and *The
Rose* and say, 'We made a terrible mistake at Oscar time.' In *The Rose* Bette
Midler gives a great, lasting performance. Okay, so she's not the easiest person
in the world to work with. She just needs more attention."

With actresses Lorna Luft and Stockard Channing he has tried hard to
put definite talent to interesting use. "I wasn't happy with the way Lorna
worked out in *Grease II*," he says. "It wasn't her fault and she deserves another
chance." He smiles and shakes a finger. "And please remember that I did
not direct that picture." Channing is another story. "I have no comment to
make on Stockard, really. She's very talented and I managed her career for a
while, and now she's working in theater very successfully. She's had a lot of
husbands, all of whom had a lot to say and weren't very helpful. You should
interview her husbands."

Carr is equally noncommittal about a widely circulated story that he
once threatened *Village Voice* columnist Arthur Bell after Bell cast aspersions
on Ann-Margret in print. As a result of the incident, Bell says, his editor
gave him a regular column as a form of protection. "I've never heard that
one before," says Carr. "There are so many versions of that story, it's like
Rashomon. Listen, Arthur was at the New York *La Cage* party on opening
night. There's no problem as far as I'm concerned. Maybe if we discuss him
here in this interview, he can get a television show out of it."

Recently Carr has made what some would call uncharacteristic gestures
toward the gay community, pledging $10,000 to next year's Cable Car
Awards in San Francisco and holding a benefit of *La Cage aux Folles* in
that city this June for the AIDS Foundation. "In New York," says Carr, "we
didn't do anything with benefits on *La Cage*. I remember being upset by
reading something to the effect that here we had this show and I wasn't
doing anything to support the gay community with it. So I've decided to
devote a certain amount of my time to the Los Angeles and San Francisco

engagements. I feel that *La Cage* is a statement, and also that the AIDS crisis is very, very serious. It's such a myth out there that it's only affecting gays. The misinformation is shocking.

"As for the Cable Car Awards, I went because I'd seen someone called Allen White from San Francisco sounding very intelligent on "20/20," and I wanted to go up there and see what the serious gay community was doing for its own people. All anyone ever sees is The Mr. Buns Contest and outrageous people in sequins on the local news, marching in the parades. This is not what the gay community is really about. The sequins belong on-stage. Come and see it in a show. I don't want sequins to be what's discussed on an evening news report about the gay community.

"So I went up to San Francisco, and I was really moved and touched by the work that's going on and the efforts that are being made in terms of medical research. I also found out about a wonderful group for older gay people. It was great. And I decided that there's only so much time in your life to do what you think is important. How often do you have a show like *La Cage aux Folles*, which is such a smash that you can charge extra money for a cause?"

As for Hollywood's traditional attitudes toward gays, Carr sees a change as inevitable. "We cannot go backwards," he says. "There have been a few breakthroughs in what I call popular entertainment. People think *Guess Who's Coming to Dinner* was tame, I know. But I'm sorry, you just didn't *do* that subject before that picture, and that's all there is to it. For gays, the contribution of *A Chorus Line* was enormous. *La Cage aux Folles* makes its contribution. Fourteen-year-olds are going to see *La Cage* because they saw the 'I Am What I Am' number on the Grammy Awards. Today people are a little more tolerant if a son or a daughter comes home and says, 'Guess what...?' Everyone's growing up, I think. It's just a question of time and of people being more tolerant and not questioning so much what people do in bed but what they're doing to prevent 'The Day After' from coming."

In his own public image, Carr is adamantly uninterested. He will not analyze his impact in any way. "As soon as you're in public life, you accept that people will tell stories about you," he says, "People can think whatever they like about me. It doesn't make any difference. I am what *I* am. That's how the song goes, and that's how people live their lives. I have the friends I have. Their pictures are all over the house. One night I can have dinner with Gregory and Veronica Peck and the next night go to a Country/Western bar. Walk around the house and you'll see my life on the shelves."

There are scores of photographs everywhere. Carr with Bruce Jenner. Carr with Mae West. Carr with John Travolta. A smashing shot of Ann-Margret in a red dress. A blowup of Joan Rivers' "*What Becomes a Legend Most?*" advertisement. Then there's the disco in the basement, complete with tiny lights in the floor and copper-colored draperies. The entire room is Egyptian, featuring hieroglyphics and paintings of the Pharaohs on the walls. Pink neon signs proclaim "The Bella Darvi Bar" and "The Edmund Purdom Lounge."

"I decided I would name rooms after people in Egyptian movies," says Carr, a heavy B-movie buff. "I don't consider *Valley of the Kings* a true Egyptian classic. The two classics are *Land of the Pharaohs* and *The Egyptian*. It was so funny. One night Joan Collins was here and I told her that I was planning to name a room after her. She said, "Listen. I am a living, working--and don't you dare to name a room after me as though I were dead!"

Back upstairs, the living room is now crowded with people who have arrived to discuss the *La Cage* billboard on Sunset Blvd. and Carr is required to supervise the giant sequins. His plans for the following week include a two-day vacation at his house in Hawaii, one day working on a new script and an appearance on "The Merv Griffin Show" with the cast of *Where the Boys Are*.

"I'm starting a new project soon for Rock Hudson and Doris Day. We're bringing them back as a team. They'll play the same parts they used to play in those old movies, only they'll be in their fifties." He rubs his hands together in anticipation. "It'll be great. You know, it's nice to have all this new talent around. It's nice to see the kids from *Taps* becoming stars, and Tom Cruise and Kevin Bacon and all those people, but it's good to have our old faves back once in a while too."

Before I go, he says he's hired a woman to work full time trying to sort out the gay community groups in Los Angeles for a benefit of *La Cage aux Folles*, but it hasn't been easy. "There are so many groups, and you have to be so careful. Isn't there a central fund or something which distributes money fairly to all the groups? Something like a gay United Fund? I'm trying to do all of this without having to deal with ego and politics." I wish him lots of luck on *that* project and take my leave.

Nestor Almendros

The Advocate — July 10, 1984

Nestor Almendros is one of the leading cinematographers in the history of world cinema. His work in Europe, notably as director of photography for Eric Rohmer and Francois Truffaut, has supplied the visual magic for such enchanting films as *Claire's Knee, The Wild Child, Chloe in the Afternoon, My Night at Maude's* and *The Last Metro.* His career in America has been equally impressive, adding such hits as *Kramer vs. Kramer* and *Sophie's Choice* to his credits. In 1978, Almendros walked off with an Oscar for his stunning work on Terrence Malick's *Days of Heaven.*

Now, in a radical departure from the glamorous cinematic fiction that has made his name famous around the globe, Almendros has co-directed *Improper Conduct,* an inflammatory feature-length documentary that exposes the repression of Fidel Castro's Cuba, especially as it affects homosexuals. Through a series of beautifully filmed interviews with twenty-eight Cuban exiles (including dancers, artists, transvestites, writers, workers and students), *Improper Conduct* savagely indicts a revolution that Almendros himself once supported, but which, according to those imprisoned has become nothing more than a fascist dictatorship maintaining itself through a regime of fear, torture and imprisonment.

The theme of *Improper Conduct* is expertly reflected in its poster, which shows the lower half of a young man wearing "improper attire," tight white trousers. He is flanked by two soldiers brandishing bayonets. As one of the interview subjects, playwright Rene Ariza (imprisoned five years for "counterrevolutionary propaganda") points out in the film: "To be different, to be strange, to behave improperly, isn't just forbidden, it's totally repressed. It can land you in jail." *Improper Conduct* paints a portrait of a Cuba that is as obsessed with machismo as it is with the persecution of sexual deviants, artistic and political dissidents, Jehovah's Witnesses and members of racial minority groups.

Almendros and his co-director, Orlando Jimenez Leal, are both exiles from Cuba. Jimenez Leal directed *El super*, the acclaimed 1980 film about Cuban exiles   adjusting to their strange and often bittersweet new lives in New York City. The two filmmakers knew each other briefly in Cuba in the early 1960s; they even made a film together called *La tumba francesa*. (*The French Bongo*), an ethnological short about a Haitian sect in Cuba that performs a stylized ritual dance. For both Leal and Almendros, *Improper Conduct* is a very personal movie, a project they had long wanted to undertake.

In the spacious New York loft atop a restored turn-of-the-century actors' hotel that Almendros occupies when in America, the two directors recall their early days in Cuba and talk about the genesis of *Improper Conduct*.

In the 1940s, the young Almendros left Spain to live in Cuba, where his father, a Loyalist, had been exiled following the fascist victory in the Spanish Civil War. From childhood, Almendros was devoted to film, and in 1948 he helped to organize Havana's first film society. After the coup that brought Batista to power as dictator, Almendros was exiled again, this time to Rome, where he studied cinematography. Later he moved to New York, where he taught film. In 1959, when Castro triumphed in Cuba, Almendros decided to go back to Havana. "The revolution attracted me irresistibly," he says, "and I made my first professional films in Castro's Cuba." These short films were directed for ICAIC, a nationalized department of cinema production. Almendros also served as movie critic for the nationalized newspaper, *Bohemia*.

His contentment with the revolution was short-lived. In 1961 he gave a glowing review to a short film by Leal, *P.M.*, a vibrant portrait of Havana by night, which captured a certain spirit of the Cuban people in a *cinéma vérité* style. *P.M.* had no political content, but the revolutionary government banned it on aesthetic grounds and confiscated the prints. For his positive review of the film, Almendros was fired from his post at *Bohemia*.

"They used *P.M.* as an excuse to define the cultural position of the revolution," says Leal. "The film prompted Castro to make his famous speech 'Words for the Intellectuals,' in which he condemned all art which did not have specific pro-revolutionary content. Just the idea that I could even make an independent film inside ICAIC was enough for them. I knew then that it was the beginning of the end for us in Cuba."

Almendros knew it too, and he now professes shame for his early faith in the revolution. "In the beginning I liked working for ICAIC, but as we were obliged to repeat the same triumphalist themes, I began to tire of the demands and the inevitable submissions. I was fired from *Bohemia* not only because I liked Orlando's film but also because I was not kind enough to some of the Soviet films with which we were being inundated at the time. Also, I was too kind to some semi-dissident Polish and Czech films of the period. I saw that this was the end of any possibility of a liberal position within the revolution. Eventually, I decided to leave Cuba because I saw that something worse would happen to me if I stayed there. A third exile seemed my only choice." Soon afterwards, in 1962, Leal left also. "I took the last boat from Havana," he recalls with a rueful smile, adding, "It sounds like the title of a movie."

Leal went to Miami, where for seven months he worked as a newspaper vendor. He managed to make a short film called *In the Park* and to save enough money to go to New York. From there he went to San Juan, where he directed television commercials and began to rebuild his film career. Almendros lived first in New York, where he became involved with the avant-garde film scene, working with the Mekas brothers and Maya Deren, and writing articles for *Film Culture*. Shortly afterwards he flew to Paris, where he met director Eric Rohmer and embarked on his remarkable career in cinematography.

Almendros and Leal barely kept in contact over the years. "We were exiles and very poor," says Almendros. "There was no sympathy in those days for a Cuban exile. If you were exiled from Franco's Spain that sounded much better to people and they could understand it. But not from Cuba." These attitudes are recalled in the opening scenes of *Improper Conduct*, which relate the shock of many intellectuals at the defection of ten ballet dancers from the Alicia Alonso Dance Troupe in 1966, when the company was in Paris.

Only by accident did Rohmer hire Almendros to be the cinematographer on his film *Paris vu par*. "I happened to be on the set one day when Rohmer's cinematographer had an argument with him and walked out," he explains, "and so I offered my services. Of course they were skeptical and said they'd use me only for the day; but when they saw the rushes, they hired me, and that was the beginning of my career. It was like a scene out of *Forty-Second Street*. Then I did *Ma Nuit chez Maude*, *L'Enfant Sauvage* with Truffaut, *Claire's Knee* and the others. But for many years I was literally starving in Paris. I can remember taking the stamps off of letters from friends and scratching off the postmark with a razor so I could use them again."

In 1983, Leal made a film called *L'altra Cuba* (The Other Cuba) for RAI, the Italian television network, and Almendros saw it. "I thought it was absolutely extraordinary," he says. "It was a strictly political film about political people. I got in touch with Orlando and proposed that we do another film with a different focus, about everyday Cubans who were not political people, those who in a normal country would not be sent to prison for their work, people like Heberto Padilla. The film became *Improper Conduct*."

Padilla is a dissident writer whose imprisonment unleashed worldwide protest. In *Improper Conduct* Padilla says: "Homosexuals suffered the most in Cuba because they were so easy to spot. Anyone who displayed extravagant attitudes in the street was arrested and immediately sent to a UMAP." The UMAPs (Military Units to Aid Production) were concentration camps set up in 1965 to "reeducate and rehabilitate" antisocial elements and people who were deemed counterrevolutionary. The UMAP camps were closed in 1969 in response to protest by foreign intellectuals who had visited Cuba, but similar camps immediately took their place. It was at this time, according to interviewees, that Cuba's penal code became the most severe in the communist bloc. Castro's brother Raoul journeyed to other socialist countries, such as Bulgaria, and took their advice on homosexuals. Quoting Sartre, Padilla says: "In Cuba there are no Jews, but there are homosexuals."

Improper Conduct focuses largely on the repression of gays. Stories told by interview subjects relate a system of "informing" on those suspected of homosexuality. "He shook my hand a little too long," someone would say of a neighbor. "We both had friends who were in prison for being homosexual," says Almendros, "and the subject of the repression of gays is certainly the heart of the movie. Everything revolves around it."

When I mention that American leftists, and socialist gays in particular, aren't too crazy about hearing all of this, Almendros first laughs and then becomes indignant. "Well, if they lived in Cuba, they'd hear about it. And while you are speaking, why don't you call things by their right names? It's communism. Don't call it socialism. Socialism works in many places in the world today. The producers of *Improper Conduct* are the Socialist government of France because it's produced by French television which is run by the state."

The filmmakers themselves were shocked by many of the revelations in *Improper Conduct*. "One of the most interesting things," says Leal, "was the curtain of silence around the camps which still exist in Cuba. The idea that Cuba has concentration camps like the camps of Stalin and Hitler was foreign to us because we left so long ago. And those who were imprisoned in them were ashamed to talk about it at first. Also, the liberal intellectuals don't want to hear about [those] things. The awful situation of blacks in Cuba is something else they don't want to face. The two black gays in the film really clarified a lot for us. The government says that the revolution came to free people like the blacks, but if you look at the government, you see only one black face and he's a very nice gentleman who doesn't do anything. Yet blacks are forty percent of the population. Afro hairdos are banned in Cuba because they consider that such hairdos make black people blacker than Cuban revolutionary. You must understand that it is not wise to look extreme in Cuba. Anything different is crushed. The revolutionary position is that the revolution is hurt by anything that is not uniform. There is an obsession with flatness that is frightening."

On the subject of the American left and its reaction to *Improper Conduct*, Almendros is both angry and resigned. "There will be total silence about it, which is one of the techniques they use when a statement is too strong to fight. This was foretold by Georges Semprun, the screenwriter of the film *Z*, when he saw *Improper Conduct* at a screening in Paris. I asked him what he thought the party reaction would be and he replied, 'They will say nothing.' But the reaction in Europe will be more favorable than in America. In Europe the liberals have seen the truth about the Soviet Union, but I think ideological thought comes to America about five years later than in Europe. The trouble with political people in America is that there's a dualism here that doesn't exist in Europe. If you are against the Establishment in America, then all those who are against the Establishment are good. This is nonsense. There can be bad revolutionaries as well as bad conservatives. After all, the enemy of Al Capone can be another gangster, no? Hitler was anti-establishment, and his solution wasn't so good. Things are not so black and white in Europe. Over here, anti-establishment people are really blind."

Addressing herself to this issue, writer Susan Sontag says in the film, "The left in this country will dismiss these injustices because they are basically homophobic. I think that one of the left's weaknesses has always been a difficulty in dealing with questions bearing on the moral and political aspects of sex. First it had to do with the question of women.... The discovery that homosexuals were being persecuted in Cuba, shows, I think, how much the left needs to evolve.... I think we're seeing an evolution in communist culture, towards a military ideal. And this is totally at odds with the basic principles that good leftists thought for years were the communist idea."

Another contradiction that emerges from *Improper Conduct*, a contradiction that had been noted long before the film was made, is that many of the gay Cuban refugees who fled the repression of their homeland did not become champions of gay liberation in a strict political sense once they arrived in this country. "Many gays from Cuba were shocked by their exile," says Almendros, "and when they get here, they are interested primarily in survival. They need to worry about finding a job and eating. When they settle in, some of them will be interested in such activity and some will not, just as with other groups of people."

Almendros says that because he left Cuba so long ago, he has little real understanding of what it would be like for a gay person to come to America today. "I suspect that it takes them a while to learn to live in a free society," he says, "but you should really ask that question of the writer Reinaldo Arenas, who is in the film. He could answer better than I could. Orlando is, of course, not at all aware of the gay world here because he is not gay, and I am not really aware of it because I lead a professional life. I don't like to wave the flag in my personal life. If anyone were to ask me, I would state who I am, but it is simply not my personal style to discuss my sexuality publicly. To have made *Improper Conduct* is my statement. Personally, I think an overemphasis of one's sexuality is another kind of mistake, to define yourself by your sexuality. My life is my work on film, and so I do not wish to discuss it in a personal way."

Almendros is now eager to do a feature film based on the ten ballet dancers who defected from the Alicia Alonso Dance Troupe in 1966. "We have so much fascinating material on them which we had to eliminate from *Improper Conduct* because of time considerations. Ever since those men defected, the government has paid very close attention to who is leaving the country. They make certain that anyone who leaves has family who they have to come home to, so that they will not so easily make the decision to defect. I would like very much to make a film about these people." Almendros obviously takes great pleasure in his work and is quite happy that his message will reach Cuba in spite of censorship. "The people of Cuba will never see *Improper Conduct*," he says, "but the government will certainly pirate a copy and look at it." Some members of the Cultural Office of the Cuban Embassy in Paris have seen the film; in responding to questions by the French newspaper *Liberation*, the Cuban officials replied that they had "no opinion."

"I think one of the great mistakes that the American intelligentsia makes with Cuba and all of Latin America," says Leal, "is that it sees Cuba's problems as separate from the revolution [and therefore solvable], as though these mistakes had nothing to do with the revolution itself. In fact, it's just the opposite. These problems have to do with the basic failure of the ideas of the revolution. As Rene Ariza say in the film, 'It's not peculiar to Castro. There are many Castros. We must restrain the Castro that's in all of us.'"

Paul Verhoeven

The Advocate — September 4, 1984

Paul Verhoeven, Holland's best-known film director (*Soldier of Orange* and *Spetters*), was in New York for a few days to promote his newest film, *The Fourth Man*. We spoke in his suite at the elegant Élysée Hotel, for many years the headquarters of playwright Tennessee Williams and actress Tallulah Bankhead. Despite a tough, tight schedule and a slight case of jet lag, he spoke with great enthusiasm and interest about *The Fourth Man* and the phenomenon of recent European films with gay characters.

"*The Fourth Man* is not considered to be a gay film in Holland," said the director with amusement. "In the Netherlands it is simply an ironic horror film for all audiences. The main character is only by coincidence homosexual. Of course, the situation in Holland with regard to homosexuality is a little bit different than it is in the United States. There was an opinion poll recently in Holland asking the public if it matters to them if someone is homosexual or not, and it turned out that nowadays seventy percent of the population says no we don't care at all and twenty years ago it was twenty-five percent saying they didn't care. So things have changed considerably. The writer of the novel on which *The Fourth Man* is based, Gerard Reve, is one of the most popular writers in Holland, and he has been openly gay since he was twenty-five years old. He has done a lot to change people's attitudes simply by being himself."

Among actors in Europe, there is still a resistance to playing a homosexual role, according to Verhoeven. "Oh, yes, very much so. It is ridiculous, but it still exists. I think actors always have a problem playing characters who are not sympathetic to the audience, because they are afraid that if they play a character like Hitler, for example, the audience will not like them because they don't like the character. But I was very lucky to have two actors who were not at all concerned about this aspect of the film. Even though Thom Hoffman, who played the younger man, is not homosexual at all, he had no problem with those scenes."

Verhoeven thinks that the filmmaking situation in Europe lends itself to making films in which gay characters can appear without comment. "It is very difficult in the United States, where you have a studio system, to reflect life in a realistic way. What I tried especially to do in *The Fourth Man* was to use the homosexuality not as a hot item but just as a matter of fact. There is no statement at all. It's just there, and it's viewed as completely normal within the context of the film. It's easier to expect such a film from a European market because producers in Europe are not bound to investors who want every element of the film to appeal to a wide audience. Also, the risks are not so great in Europe because there is a lot of financial support from the government. It's very risky in the United States because even if an independent filmmaker puts up all of the money himself, the film must be a huge hit or he won't make any more films.

"In Europe the government may put up sixty percent of the money for the film, and they don't really care if the audiences like the film or not, as long as the film is well received by the critics and it brings some prestige to the country in which it was made. So they really promote good films rather than just popular films. The United States is a very powerful country. They don't support their artists because they don't need that kind of prestige. Holland is a small country. We need to be promoted through our art. You never know what's going to happen if the economy gets worse. I believe that when the economy is bad the right wing gets stronger. But for the moment, homosexuality is not a problem at all in Holland."

Kenneth Anger

The Advocate — **November 27, 1984**

Kenneth Anger is more Hollywood than Hollywood. A malevolent yet lovable Jiminy Cricket, Anger is the impish conscience Tinseltown never had and wanted. His notorious book, the underground classic *Hollywood Babylon*, gleefully ripped away the veil of secrecy surrounding the intimate and sometimes bizarre private lives of the film colony's most celebrated legends. A former child star, Anger became Hollywood's bad boy and a legendary figure himself when he made a series of internationally acclaimed films that shocked the public, captivated the highbrow critics and precipitated several landmark court decisions on censorship. The most famous of those films, *Scorpio Rising* and *Fireworks*, have held an endless fascination for audiences throughout the years and exhibit an unrivaled, almost primeval homoerotic sexuality.

The elusive Anger, diabolic and dishy, masculine and fey, frightening but harmless, is at it again. *Hollywood Babylon II* is, if anything, more bitchy and macabre than the original, which the *New York Times* once called "a delicious 306-page box of poisoned bon-bons." Anger elevates gossip to a kind of divine troublemaking and in this new collection of horror stories, he stirs the manure with a pitchfork, tweaking famous noses with undisguised delight. Some of his revelations further document oft-whispered rumors from the past. The book contains the most complete account yet published of Hollywood's "pansy purges," including a frightening episode in which the Ku Klux Klan assaulted gay actor William Haines and his friends after a party in El Porto. Also detailed for the first time is the real reason Clark Gable had director George Cukor fired from directing *Gone with the Wind*. It's rather amazing how paranoid "The King" could be over a few pre-stardom blowjobs.

Most of *Hollywood Babylon II* is simply outrageous fun, more amusing than shocking and more in the spirit of nasty sport than real cruelty. There are some frontal nude shots of Joan Crawford in a chapter called "Witch Joan"; a section on Loretta Young entitled "Attila the Nun"; and a hilarious list of "Odd Couples," including Clara Bow and Bela Lugosi, Edna Mae Oliver and Clark Gable, Marlene Dietrich and Claudette Colbert; plus the best of the lot--the bombshell revelation that Tallulah Bankhead was a chubby-chaser who had an affair with Hattie McDaniel.

Yet for all the startling information contained between the pages, nothing compares with the cover photo of a grotesquely overweight Elizabeth Taylor. The actress is almost unrecognizable, and many people have mistaken the photo for that of Divine. Anger thinks it's just terrific. "That photo was taken in 1979 when she was on her way home after being stoned out of her mind at Studio 54," says the author with a wicked smile.

Anger's Upper East Side New York apartment is practically a shrine to old Hollywood, an immaculate but vividly decorated memory lane containing all sorts of movie memorabilia, old photos and even a small altar to Rudolph Valentino complete with electric candles and red silk roses. The first thing Anger does when I arrive is to open a small drawer and bring out a glossy black-and-white photo. "That picture of Liz Taylor is great," he says, "but let me show you what they *wouldn't* let me print." He hands me the photo and I find myself muttering "holy shit" under my breath. It shows what *appears* to be the profile of Marlon Brando sucking the biggest, hardest dick this side of Santa Monica.

Anger settles into a comfortable chair, laughing at my open-mouthed reaction. He wears a Rangers sweatshirt with the first and last letters missing to spell out his name (a gift from "one of the players — a nice man," Anger explains). How, I wonder would someone come into possession of such a photo, and under what circumstances was it taken? "Oh, you know how sometimes boyfriends will fool around taking pictures of each other," says Anger. "There are a few of those floating around. The dick may or may not belong to Wally Cox. We just don't know. That horrible witch who Brando married — Anna Kashfi — tried to use the picture in court to keep Brando from seeing his children, but the judge wouldn't even admit it as evidence. He just threw it out. It's actually very artistic. I told my publishers that Brando knew I had it, and he's not the type to sue over something like that. He'd just say 'fuck it' because he's above and beyond it all. But they said that some child might open the book and say, 'Mommy, what's that?' so we had to cut it. It annoys me, really, because I had the same problem with Jayne Mansfield's nipple in the first version. I had to fight like hell to keep them from airbrushing it out. It's amazing that nipples and penises are still taboo, isn't it?"

Another quite substantial section of the book nixed by publishers E. P. Dutton concerned the author's passionate hatred for the late Gloria Swanson. Anger's only comment in the published version is a succinct "Ding Dong the Witch Is Dead." The rest of the story was deemed "going too far" by the powers that be at Dutton and ended up on the carpet. When Anger published a letter from Swanson to columnist Walter Winchell in *Babylon I* in which she called Lana Turner a "trollop," Swanson sued Anger for thirty million. Fortunately, he was able to produce a copy of her letter to Winchell. Unfortunately, Anger's publisher, Jann Wenner of *Rolling Stone* fame, deducted twenty thousand dollars from Anger's royalties to cover legal fees.

"It was what they call a nuisance suit," says Anger. "Any rich person can claim you slighted them, and you have to defend yourself. But Swanson was an impossible old witch. She was as mean as they come, and as she got older she got meaner and meaner. She actually turned into Norma Desmond. She was technically a dwarf, you know; she was a human Betty Boop. Her head was too large for her body." The story he proceeds to relate seems harmless and funny, but obviously not to his publishers.

"Once, Gloria and I were on the jury at the Chicago Film Festival, and we were both staying at the Tower Hotel," Anger begins. "One night at Maxim's restaurant in the basement of the hotel, I saw her rush across the room just as a woman was about to put a spoon of sugar into her coffee. Gloria put her hand over the cup and waved her finger in the face of this diamond-covered Chicago matron, shouting, 'Naughty, naughty, naughty!' Can you imagine? So awhile later I went over to Spanish Harlem and bought a small child's coffin painted apple-green. I filled it with about five pounds of white sugar and took it over to her apartment on Fifth Avenue and gave it to the doorman. So she opened it, and apparently she had a huge conniption fit because white sugar to her was like water on the Wicked Witch of the West.

She called the district attorney and tried to have me arrested for attempted murder. She told him, 'I have received a bomb. Someone is trying to poison me!' It took the D.A. quite a while to get it out of her that she was talking about sugar."

Even while calling Swanson an impossible old witch, there's an innate affection in Anger's voice for the old Hollywood and its stars. "My books appeal to people's sense of humor," he says easily. "I really have a tremendous amount of affection for the illusion and fantasy of old Hollywood, and that comes through in my writing. I love how they made Swanson look beautiful even though she was deformed. It's the same with an actor like Alan Ladd. He was so small he was like a little Ken doll, and if photographed properly they made him look like a huge person. I love all that. Someone once asked me why I don't do a *Washington Babylon*. There was the Tidal Basin scandal, George Washington raised cannabis, and Lincoln was rumored to have had three gay bodyguards. There's a lot of stuff like that. But I'm just not sympathetic to people in Washington. I have no affection at all for them. I truly love Hollywood, and that's the difference."

It's no accident that this book deals almost exclusively with the old and not the new Hollywood. He tells me an unprintable story about a current superstar who keeps a huge rock of cocaine on a table in the dining room so that guests can shave off a spoonful at random. "They're just not that interesting," he says, shaking his head. "All the larger-than-life people are gone. I have resisted writing about the new Hollywood stars only partly because they're still alive. The other reason is that they're devoid of the old magic. Hollywood today is doing away with its own magical qualities and burying itself in an avalanche of self-congratulatory awards."

Anger reserves his true fury for the witches and meanies of Hollywood, but he can be quite sympathetic to its victims. In the same way that he wrote about Frances Farmer with sympathy and respect in *Babylon I*, in his sequel he pays affectionate homage to his favorite director, Busby Berkeley. "These are people ruined by Hollywood," he says. "Berkeley was tormented by Jack Warner. What happened to him couldn't have happened anywhere else in the world…only in Hollywood. It was a great, great tragedy that he couldn't go on making movies, especially after coming back years later and making a film like *Million Dollar Mermaid*. His films are awesome works of American art."

It was the old Hollywood and its twisted sense of morality that allowed Anger to explore the hidden, unmentionable homoerotic urges lurking in the corners of the dream factories in his film *Fireworks*, which he made in 1947 when he was only seventeen years old. "I was reading the poetry of Rimbaud when I was twelve," he says. "But there will always be people interested in taboo things. You have to understand that all through history we've had the pendulum effect. The idea of the human race becoming progressively more liberal and tolerant is just a bunch of bullshit. Don't you believe it. There are things going on in South America right now as bad as the Holocaust. Jerry Falwell and his crowd would like to see people put into camps, and we're getting closer and closer to that all the time. There are only a few people interested in exploring hidden sexuality at any given time."

When sexuality was submerged on the screen by censorship, Anger believes, it emerged in interesting covert ways. "All that censorship," he says, "required a high-wire balancing act in order to get some subtlety on the screen. It produced some wonderful allusions, which maybe one-tenth of the audience would get and the rest never saw because they were just there to be entertained." Anger feels the same way about the prospect of movie stars coming out of the closet. Such people, he believes, will always be "out" to the cognoscenti but not necessarily to those who really don't wish to know. "Who are you talking about?" he asks. "Which public are we discussing? Your mother? My mother? Some people will always be more sophisticated than others. You have to understand that for a mass audience, there will always need to be some degree of fantasy in their viewing habits. That's what they want."

When I mention the number of gay people who cooperate in their own oppression, he understands this too. "You're dealing with human nature," he says simply. "You have an incredible spectrum of people out there who are gay. They all don't share similar views. Listen, things don't change that much, even in terms of gossip. When I was a student at Beverly Hills High School, we would hear all these overt rumors about Cardinal Spellman being gay, about how he would even send his private car to the stage door of Broadway houses to pick up his current chorus boy. This is part of American folk history. Yet today in 1984, the New York Times publishing company just suppressed a whole section of a new Spellman biography dealing with his homosexuality. People don't want to know."

Anger feels that most people have dichotomous personalities and are subject to irrationalities in their reactions to things. This is how he explains the antigay and racist attitudes of some Hollywood stars whose "best friends" are gay or black or Jewish. "One of the reasons Katherine Hepburn is so antigay," he says, "is that her brother Tom was gay, and he hanged himself over an unhappy love affair with a boy when he was seventeen. John Wayne was the biggest financial backer of the Ku Klux Klan for years — I mean a *lot* of money — it was his hobby to support the Klan. And privately he would tell people he didn't like working with blacks and Jews."

How does Anger find out stuff like this? "Well, it's what we call 'authentic gossip,'" he says. "Someone working as a stunt man on many of John Wayne's films repeated these stories to several people, and it's just been repeated so many times by so many people." Anger says *Hollywood Babylon* is considered a maverick history of Hollywood, and as such it does the work of recalling the past that Hollywood would prefer to forget. When he publishes photos of Elizabeth Taylor looking like Moby Dick, or Judy Garland looking older than the pyramids, it isn't to say that he thinks they've disappointed us. It's to say that they're magnificent in their own way, in spite of all the ravages of time.

"These people had something called star charisma," he says. "Taylor is the last star, as far as I'm concerned. Garland at her most haggard was still brilliant. To me, it's a great pity that when Liz was fat in 1979 and married to that senator with the huge dick, she didn't immortalize the way she looked by playing the Roman empress Messalina. She'd have looked like a living Beardsley drawing, and it would've been incredible. Now she looks awful with that Miami Beach bleached-out hair. Stars have to be unusual. As far as I'm concerned, nobody will ever line up to see Meryl Streep when she gets old the way we have for Bette Davis."

Anger understands the attraction gay men have had for strong women on the screen, but he thinks it's a lost phenomenon. "Crawford and Davis were the two most obvious examples of stars who were worshipped by gay men, myself included. I remember ducking out of high school to go to the opening day of *Deception*. In a sense I spent my twenties during the best years, the 1950s. Most people say, 'Oh, what a horrible time the 1950s were,' and I always say, 'But we had something you don't have--we had *live* Maria Callas on the stage, and Judy Garland and Marlene Dietrich. We're talking, though about a historical gay man who really doesn't exist anymore. As far as I'm concerned, they can keep their Julio Iglesias."

Anger is very happy with *Hollywood Babylon II* in spite of the cuts, and he would like to begin raising money for another film, one populated totally by Mickey Mouse toys and with a jazz score. "But it's so hard these days to raise enough money," he says. "I made *Fireworks* for two hundred dollar. Now you need at least a hundred thousand to do a decent film. That's why I keep writing. I need the money to pursue the work. I'm an orphan, actually. My father cut me out of his will because I was the gay black sheep. Just like Crawford did to Christina. Can you *imagine* that mean old bitch? But I didn't like my father either, so it doesn't matter. I'm happy. I'm on my own. I write. I make movies. I live in New York. I just wish I could make more films and hope that my work won't be forgotten. I've never had a broken heart because I wasn't a Hollywood filmmaker."

Lily Tomlin

The Advocate — **March 18, 1986**

Lily Tomlin's new show, The Search for Signs of Intelligent Life in the Universe, *is Broadway's hottest ticket, a huge hit that garnered sensational reviews from the critics and has kept packed houses alternately laughing and crying eight times a week. It is more than a one-woman show; it's a theatrical tour de force in which Tomlin, with superb artistry, plays more than a dozen interacting characters, effortlessly switching from one to another for more than two hours until it is impossible to believe that there aren't twelve different people onstage.*

Written by Jane Wagner, Tomlin's partner of fifteen years, the show features few of the characters we have come to identify with Lily Tomlin, yet echoes of her past creations reverberate throughout the evening. The Sixties teenager we met in her last Broadway outing, Appearing Nightly, *has grown up to be a performance artist: a lesbian mother who lost custody of her daughter in a court battle. The daughter is Agnes Angst, a fifteen-year-old pink-haired punk rocker, a Watergate era baby who moans that by the time she was born, Elvis Presley was already fat. Agnes, locked out of the house by her father and his new wife, goes to live with her grandparents, our old friends Lud and Marie, who are upset because Agnes leaves dirty fingerprints on the cheese and wears something that makes the garage door flap up every time she comes home.*

Tomlin is also, by turns, a bored rich woman named Kate who loses the tip of her little finger in a Cuisinart accident, a seminar-hopper named Chrissy who thinks that "if it weren't for false hopes, the economy would collapse," a prostitute who puts a gay man through beauty school to keep him off the streets and, in a long second-act piece that captures the soul of feminism in the 1970s, a new age woman named Lynn who finds that it's difficult to be politically-conscious and upwardly mobile at the same time. Lynn's friends include Marge, a "radical on sabbatical" who writes a column called

"Boycotts of the Month" for a leftist newspaper, and Edie and Pam, a lesbian couple who have a son through artificial insemination with a turkey baster.

The glue of the show is Tomlin's magnificent bag lady Trudy, who acts as consultant to a group of visitors from outer space who are searching for signs of intelligent life in the universe. "It's trickier than you think" says Trudy, commenting: "You'd imagine that by now evolution would have gotten us to the point where we could change ourselves."

In Tomlin's dressing room there's a sign that reads "If You Can Stand Success, You Can Stand Anything." The following interview proved that point over and over again. She handles her life and career inseparably and there's never enough time in a day to do everything she wants to accomplish. Over the course of several days and many interrupted conversations, Tomlin talked about her current success, her relationship with Jane Wagner and her own vision of her work on stage and film.

It is eight o'clock in the morning at the NBC studios in New York, and Tomlin has just finished taping a radio show with Don Imus. In the elevator, Tomlin turns to her publicist Cheryl Dolby and says, "As long as we're in the building, why don't we do the 'Phil Donahue Show'?" Dolby registers a blank look. Tomlin giggles and says with a shrug, "He goes on the air in an hour." Her mischievous grin signals that at first she's only joking but unconventional ideas quickly make themselves at home in Tomlin's head. An investigation reveals that Donahue is doing a show on bag ladies that day and, in fact, he has been trying to reach Tomlin for a week. It is all Lily needs to hear. "Oh, God," she breathes. "Cheryl, run home and get my costume." By nine o'clock she's on the show as a spontaneous guest. Both Phil Donahue and his audience are delighted.

This incident is a good example of the way Lily Tomlin's life in New York has been conducted for the past four months. She's the talk of the town and New York's most sought-after celebrity. Several days a week she attends meetings to plan "Hands Across America," which takes place in May when millions of people will hold hands from New York to Los Angeles to raise money to help the homeless. She is co-chair of the event with Bill Cosby, Pete Rose and Kenny Rogers. If that weren't a full-time job in itself on top of eight performances a week, she also keeps a complete schedule of appointments.

"Let's see," she says on the telephone from her dressing room, "on Saturday I'm going to Brenda Vaccaro's wedding at St. Patrick's Cathedral. On Monday I have Bio-neutronics, which is supposed to give me more energy, and then that afternoon I'm doing a benefit for Ann Richards, who's running for Texas State Treasurer. That night I'm on the 'Larry King Show' on CNN. You can come to that if you want. Or you could come by the dressing room between shows on Tuesday. I don't know if anything exciting will happen, though. My tailor is coming to fit me for some new costumes, and I'm getting a manicure. Oh, I don't know. I hope it won't be dull."

Backstage on Tuesday there are six people from Covenant House, a shelter for kids tossed out of the house to which she gives free tickets every week, three nuns, a priest, Jane Alexander, Helen Hayes, a Seeing Eye dog and fifteen autograph hounds. The shelves in her dressing room are lined with little bag-lady dolls given to her by fans. Displayed prominently is a stunning black-and-white photograph of Tomlin and Jane Wagner. Tomlin's dog Tessie is lying on a pillow in a basket under the dressing table. There are so many flowers that they spill into the hallway and line the staircase.

She deals with everyone personally, intimately and sincerely. Helen Hayes tells her, "For the first time in forty years, I felt envy for another actress today." Tomlin looks dazed. We go across the street for lunch at Charlie's where they've just put Turkey Tomlin on the menu. She gets a big kick out of that.

"So what are we going to do here?" she asks. "Aren't you sick and tired of interviewing me?" I say she's endlessly fascinating, and she strikes a starlet pose that immediately brings six autograph hunters to the table. She orders a tuna salad plate, and we get down to business. Is life in New York anything like she thought it would be?

"Well, I had this fantasy that when I came to Broadway I'd be living a total Gotham lifestyle…that I'd see every play on Broadway, attend every gallery opening in Soho, go to movies in the afternoon, be at every happening in the city…" She pauses and laughs to herself. "As it stands, I have so much to do that mostly I just get up and go to the theater."

I ask if any other stars besides Helen Hayes have groveled at her feet. "Oh, God," she moans, "don't you dare say it like that. I think what she meant was that she felt jealous as an actress that I've created this vehicle, which gives me the opportunity to play so many roles on the stage. But it has been incredible. Of course many celebrities have kissed the hem of my dungarees. Ha! Ha! Now I want you to put in that I laughed there so people won't think I'm arrogant. Truthfully, I almost hate to mention names because I wouldn't want them to think I was using them. But Bette Midler came backstage and Kim Novak was here the other night. Baryshnikov came twice. Actually, I like it when famous people come to the show and then don't come backstage because then maybe they'll write me a note and I can keep it in my celebrity note file."

Tomlin remains an awestruck fan in spite of her own celebrity. Last year she finally got to meet one of her idols, actress Jeanne Moreau. "Oh, I can't begin to describe it," she says, rolling her eyes. "I mean, you can't imagine what it was like. I grew up thinking I *was* Jeanne Moreau. When I lived in New York I'd go to the Charles Street Cinema and watch *Jules and Jim* over and over again. I'd see it maybe a hundred times. So last year I went to the AFI [American Film Institute] dinner for Lillian Gish, and there's this big table of actresses--there's Cicely Tyson, Sally Field, Jessica Lange, me, Sissy Spacek and Eva Marie Saint--and as I take my seat I spot Jeanne Moreau sitting at the end of the table, and I just go berserk. I was raining kisses all over her. I tell you, I did everything but suck the backs of her arms."

The payoff to the story came later when Mary Steenburgen approached Tomlin and said, "You know it was really interesting to see you react that way to Jeanne Moreau...because that's how I feel about you." Suddenly Tomlin is pensive. "Oh, I don't know. Maybe you shouldn't print any of this. I feel like by telling stories like that I'm exploiting people's genuine feelings."

She is extremely sensitive to this sort of thing, a sensitivity that extends to the characters she creates on the stage. Despite her biting satiric mind, she seldom does any character who is hateful or bigoted. I ask if she's ever considered creating caricatures of people like Jerry Falwell. "Well, I don't think so," she says, bewildered. "I wouldn't do them until I could do it in such a way that would illuminate why they're like that so you would feel some connection with them. They're too easy to hate, and they become a symbol of division for us. You don't want to do things just to shock. I'd want to illuminate Jerry Falwell, for instance, so that you didn't feel he was so loathsome that you couldn't have sympathy for him and embrace him. You see, to me, everything should be about healing and unifying. I would hope my show has edge and satire to it but ultimately I want it to heal."

She feels the same way about the gay characters in her show, who are integrated seamlessly into the life of the piece in total interaction with the heterosexual characters. "Of course they are," she shrugs. "It's not a matter of creating characters to make some sort of statement. I might do absolutely anything if it had some real artistry or social perspective to it, if it had humanity and tension and depth, all the things you want your work to have. Once you decide that you're going to do a piece on the women's movement in the 1970s you just have to have lesbian characters in there if only because it's part of the truth of the time. I don't know about anyone else's experience but representing my experience of that time, you have to select a range of women. Now you could also select a dozen different kinds of women who are lesbian. Edie is a black lesbian…that's the image I have of her for myself even though I don't want to make such a specific point of it. I just see physical types when I work, and I want to recreate their voices and their demeanor."

It never occurs to her that people might conceivably be turned off to such characters simply because of their sexuality.

"Oh, I don't even think about things in those terms. I know intellectually that such people exist, but I want to believe in the inevitability of people's positive response. I like to expect the best from each creature. My audiences are so mixed anyway. I always say that there are at least five hundred people out there who under ordinary circumstances wouldn't be caught dead in the same room together."

The next evening Tomlin arrives at CNN studios to do a live call-in show with host Larry King. She insists on doing her own hair and makeup, and when she is seated on the set she's not satisfied until the lights are readjusted to her specifications.

"Was I too hard on them?" she asks later. "It's just that I know myself very well, and I want everything to be perfect." It is this sense of perfection that has characterized Tomlin's attitude towards her work from the early days of her career and that has made it more difficult than usual for her to work collaboratively on films. We talk about her film career, and I ask if it's difficult for her to surrender her usual control over her material to a collaborative effort.

"Well, I'm so used to deciding what my characters are going to do and say that I do have some problems with movies, but I'm getting more used to it." She had some rude awakenings after her initial film experience with Robert Altman in making *Nashville*, which brought her an Oscar nomination. "*Nashville* was a special case," she says, "because we were encouraged to improvise, I had relatively little screen time and Altman was very free-wheeling. Since then I have tried to bring as much creativity to my roles as possible. But it can be confusing because as I understand a part, I try to make the best selections I can to bring the role to fruition, and whenever people don't agree with my choices I get confused."

One thing she has never been confused about is the politics of a situation. A good example of this is the original script for her last film, *All of Me*, with Steve Martin.

"When the script first came to me there were all sorts of unconscious things in it…things against women and stuff like that. You see, it's the consciousness that influences me most about material, and very often people just have blind spots. In the initial draft of the film, whenever someone crossed Edwinna she'd slap them because she was so arrogant. Now, I allowed a certain amount of that because the character was emotionally immature. But then later, the slapping carried over into the sex scenes and that wasn't okay, see? But they changed it to my satisfaction. The image of a man in bed with a woman and him slapping her was just gone, and as far as I was concerned, that was a real bottom line for me in accepting the role. But if you're going to print any of this you have to say how open they were to discussing these things and to making the changes I wanted. They weren't so invested in any of it to the degree that they weren't willing to change it. See, if I cast my lot in something and agree to participate in it, then I really can't blame anyone else for how it turns out. I did it. There I am. The only responsibility I feel is to try to put out something I can believe in, something which doesn't hurt me when I look at it. I never want to feel that I've compromised something affirming. As long as I sense a loving and lighthearted intention in something, then I'm comfortable to be a part of it."

She has become less defiant in recent years than she used to be. "I've learned to be more forgiving," she says. "There would be a time in my life when certain things were just not allowable and I'd be more rigid in my reactions. Now I've learned how to effect change without being so confrontational. She laughs when she thinks about how she behaved on the set of Robert Benton's *The Late Show*, in which she starred with Art Carney. "Oh, it was just funny. I didn't think I was being lit properly. I have very black hair, and we were shooting in small spaces and they were bouncing a lot of light off the ceilings. So I wanted more fill light because it affects everything. It affects your character and your performance…everything. And of course if you're a woman, they just think you're being vain. And all these guys on the crew would pat my hand and patronize me and say things like, 'Oh, you're a pretty girl. I'd marry you.' Ha! So I started carrying a mirror on the set, and I would refuse to shoot the scene until they changed the lighting. Well, they didn't like that a lot. They'd go by me on the set and spit on the floor and I'd say, 'Do you think your opinion means very much to me?' and they'd tell all these racial and sexual jokes, and I'd say, 'I don't want those stories told in my presence.' I was a real cutie pie. They loved me. Then one day the crew held up a big sign that said, 'Pretty Is As Pretty Does.' Ha! Ha!"

She has said that two roles she would love to have played were the Jane Alexander part in *Testament* and the Cher role in *Silkwood*. "But if you're going to name those films," she says, "you have to say how brilliant I think those women were in those roles." Why hasn't she attempted a dramatic role since *Nashville*? "Well, I don't know that people will ever think of me that way or give me that much opportunity, especially after failing as I did in *Moment By Moment*. People are eager and willing to have me in comedies or eccentric parts, but I think it's a stretch for them to see me in some kind of conventional leading lady part. I don't say I buy that but those are the facts."

How did the failure of *Moment By Moment* affect her relationship with Jane Wagner, who directed the film and with whom she has worked for fifteen years?

"Well, ask me some questions. I'll talk about it. As difficult and painful as it was, as any big failure is for anybody, I still don't see it in those terms at all. It was only a movie. There was a lot of criticism and personal pain…it happened and we had to live through it, that's all. It happens to people all the time. What can you do about it?"

She thinks for a minute. "What really happened is that we lost control of *The Incredible Shrinking Woman* because of *Moment By Moment*. We were in preproduction on *Shrinking Woman*, and because of the failure of *Moment* they cut back the budget, and we lost John Landis as director. I'm sure Universal didn't want Landis to get his hands on a special effects movie where he could spend millions of dollars and certainly not with me at that point. The film could've been much better, but things were just taken out of our hands. It could have been richer and more satiric and more adult and yet still appeal to kids because of all the special effects. As it ended up, it has no ideas. The ideas were taken out of it because they just thought it had to be simple-minded. And in the meanwhile I had turned down *Nine To Five*. I wasn't too sure about the style of comedy they would be doing, and I felt that since I was the one so identified with comedy, more so than Jane Fonda or Dolly Parton, all the comedy would fall on me. So I said no. Jane Wagner was the one who really convinced me to change my mind.

I came home one day, and they had to have a final answer by six o'clock, and I just wasn't doing it. Jane said to me, 'You're going to regret this for the rest of your life. After Jane Fonda has pursued you and courted you and struggled to make this film for you and Dolly, you're just going to throw it back in her face. You're going to regret working with those two women so much…you better get on the phone and tell them you changed your mind.' Ha! Nobody's smarter than Jane! She's got such great instincts."

"So *Nine To Five* was a blockbuster and a tremendous personal success for me, and then we did the Las Vegas special for television, which got great reviews and we won an Emmy for it…so when you think about it all in perspective, it really wasn't so grim. Of course we'd try to protect each other. I'd tear negative things out of magazines about *Moment* and throw them away so Jane wouldn't see them, and of course she was doing the same thing. Ha! So now with this show she's finally getting the attention she deserves. She's been doing interviews since the show opened, and of course nobody is smarter or more ironic. It's particularly gratifying that Jane should be getting all this recognition now because she never got any of the real credit associated with my work. I mean, if I could do half the things attributed to me...well then I should be the President. Ha! Ha! Ha! Oh, wait! The best was Joan Rivers. She came backstage one night with Edgar, and they were sobbing and she looked at me and Jane, and she said, "I don't care what you two have been through in the past. You were meant to meet, you were meant to be together and you were meant to create this play."

Two days later Tomlin is on the phone saying that Colin Higgins, who directed her in *Nine To Five*, has produced a videotape about the Louise Hay seminars for people with AIDS, and she would like me to see it. "It's just so positive," she says, "and several of the people with AIDS in this videotape are really surviving through the way they view their illness."

Tomlin has done several benefits to fight AIDS, including one at The Metropolitan Opera House last fall. I ask if she's seen Paul Mazursky's new film *Down and Out in Beverly Hills*. (I was offended by a scene in which Richard Dreyfus is giving mouth to mouth resuscitation to Nick Nolte, and Better Midler yells, "Don't! You'll get AIDS!" I say that in addition to being medically inaccurate, the scene is gratuitously nasty, casting people with AIDS as lepers. I'm particularly upset that Midler would even agree to speak such irresponsible dialogue.)

"Well, I did see it," she says, "and I did have a problem with it just because it was so jarring. Whenever anything is out of consciousness it's always jarring if you're sensitive to it. If Midler had any problem with it and she rationalized it, then she probably rationalized it by telling herself that she was satirizing that character she played. Yet, I've never been able to rationalize that it's fine to say anything just because the character saying it has no consciousness. You have to think about the impact it's going to have out there in the world. Also, when you make a movie you have to realize you have very little control over who's doing the editing and how something is going to ultimately be presented. It could have been all right. If there was some kind of illumination around it or if her consciousness was suddenly raised so that the audience learns something through her that might be a justification for doing it, but if that's not what follows then it's just done because AIDS is in the news and it's a pop reference."

Did she perceive any fallout in Hollywood from the press coverage of gays when it was revealed that Rock Hudson had AIDS? "Well, Rock was the one who revealed that an image an actor is able to project...it's like that

old monologue I did when I said, 'You don't have to be one to play one...'
It's good in all respects actually because there was an awakening around that
and a raising of consciousness but then there's the aftermath of that, which is
that a lot of fear surfaced. First of all, we're going to see that Linda Evans will
not get AIDS. That's what was really going on around the Hudson stories
because of their love scenes together in 'Dynasty,' right? So that will blow
over. But the media has always fed the most negative input to the culture.
They could take a different approach and come from a healing perspective
instead of being divisive."

Suddenly Jane Wagner picks up the extension phone. "Hi, you guys. Lily,
did you mention the videotape that Colin Higgins did? It's the most upbeat,
encouraging thing. It's just wonderful."

Lily tells Jane that we were discussing the AIDS panic in Hollywood,
and Jane says, "I think at the moment it's doing a lot of damage. It's giving
people with deep-seated prejudices someplace to put all that. My hope is
that because of AIDS, maybe we'll go through a bad period, but in the end
I really think scientifically and medically this will be a breakthrough for our
understanding the immune system. And in the end I think people will be
more understanding."

Lily interrupts, saying, "Yes, but in the end it's really media created. If it
wasn't given such a negative focus, we might all learn something."

"You know what freaks me out most of all?" says Jane. "Reagan
announced during his State of the Union address that he's having the Surgeon
General investigate the AIDS crisis. As if they weren't just the most backward
people imaginable who will certainly discover the most reactionary aspects
possible. That frightened me instead of making me more secure. The more
the government is involved, the more frightened I become."

Lily says that the car is waiting. "We're going over to an auction of Ruth
Gordon's clothes. I'll have a messenger come over to you with that videotape
tomorrow."

The next night, leaving the theater, Tomlin is besieged by people who
want to touch her, talk to her, get her autograph and ask her a few questions.
In a limousine on the way home, she talks about that kind of attraction
people have for someone who's so visible in the culture.

"Whenever you do something like I'm doing it always happens that people imbue you with a knowledge that you really don't possess. Often I am seen as more than I am. When young kids come to me--by young I mean fifteen or twenty years old--they romanticize me and think of me as something much larger and more knowing than I actually am. I usually take them by the shoulders and say 'I don't know any more than you do--I just practice more!'

"It's like when you go to the dentist and you get nitrous oxide. While you're under you think you've figured out the meaning of life. I was so sure of this that I was determined next time to remember it all, and I took a little notepad and a pencil with me and tried to stay conscious long enough to write down my thoughts. Then when I left the doctor's office I looked at the piece of paper, and it said "Galoshes." The sound of Lily Tomlin's laughter echoes through the canyons of Manhattan as the limousine speeds away from the lights of Broadway.

Pedro Almodovar

The Advocate — May 12, 1987

Spanish filmmaker Pedro Almodovar was introduced to American audiences last year with his unconventional and rudely funny film *What Have I Done to Deserve This?*, which featured a down-trodden, glue-sniffing housewife who sells her son to a dentist and kills her husband with a soup bone. Almodovar, whose films are wildly popular in Spain, made his mark as a leading light in the post-Franco liberationist movement, which celebrated old-fashioned values like sex, drugs and rock 'n' roll. Although *What Have I Done to Deserve This?* served as his breakthrough project, he has made six features since 1980 and a string of Super 8 films with titles like *The Fall of Sodom* and *Fuck Me, Fuck Me, Tim.*

Almodovar's new film *Law of Desire* was a huge hit at this year's Berlin film festival and is currently causing a stir in this country after shocking audiences at festivals around the globe. Almodovar has a facility for making mainstream audiences care about the most unconventional of characters, while at the same time challenging the audience's perceptions of the rules by which we live.

Law of Desire opens with a stunning, sexually explicit sequence showing a handsome young man being directed in an erotic film by the leading character, a movie director named Pablo Quintero. With Quintero as his focal point, Almodovar unfolds a story of romantic and sexual obsession set against the backdrop of the new Madrid — a place of casual, fun-loving, open sexuality and freedom.

The plot of *Law of Desire* is almost indescribable. Part fantasy, part murder mystery and part erotic comedy, the film (anachronistically) celebrates unfettered hedonism while strangely reinforcing traditional emotions with which a mass audience can identify. Pablo Quintero lives inside fetish and fantasy. He is in love with a handsome young man named Juan, who does not share his feelings and goes away to live at the seashore. Pablo writes passionate letters — the kind he would like to receive — and sends them to Juan, who signs them and returns them. Pablo's typewriter, which he uses to write his screenplays, is the repository of the life he would like to lead but from which he is deliberately, coolly removed. Direct sexuality seems to mean nothing to him; only the promise of desire is alluring.

Pablo's sister, an actress named Tina Quintero (superbly played by Carmen Maura), used to be his brother. She is a transsexual who had a long affair with their father, fleeing with him to Morocco for a sex-change operation. Pablo and Tina share a complex love/hate relationship, and are dependent upon each other for validation and support. Pablo can have many men but enjoys them only through his creative fantasies. Tina has no men in her life but her passion is immediate, raw and more real.

While Juan is away at the seashore, Pablo becomes involved with Antonio, an opportunistic hustler who — although it is her first homosexual encounter — falls in love with the director and becomes obsessed with possessing his entire life. Eventually Antonio murders Juan out of love for Pablo and takes Tina hostage, bargaining with the police for one hour of passion with Pablo before he kills himself. Though it may be difficult to believe in light of such descriptions, the film is a comic tour de force that takes everything and nothing seriously.

For Almodovar, the spirit of the film itself — rather than its unconventional characters — provides the autobiographical touch, which is evident in all of his work. "My part in the film," Almodovar says "is the strong, wild, primitive romanticism of the story. Everyone in the cast and crew was wiped out at the end of shooting. We felt as thought we had just made *The African Queen*. The characters I create are very alive, and consequently they have intense, unusual problem. In Spain, such characters are not so outrageous. Audiences cry for Tina Quintero when she confesses her loneliness and her dissatisfaction with her life, when she reaches out to her brother to be a witness to her past and her life. Audiences are not being shocked that she is a transsexual. To them, she is like a neighbor."

This most important scene in the film is one in which Tina tells her brother that in spite of her unhappiness and confusion, she would make the same choices again if she had her life to do over. "This is crucial," says Almodovar. "This is what life is about--to be completely unrepentant — otherwise what did you life mean? What was it all about? Tina would go crazy if she thought her life meant nothing in the end."

The same is true of Almodovar's use of homosexual passion in a completely casual manner. *Law of Desire* is one of those films in which the issue is not the sexuality of the characters but rather the irreverently funny and tragic love story in which they act out their passion. "This is the first film for me," Almodovar says, "in which the relationships happen to be primarily gay, and it was very important for me to do."

The opening scene was the hardest for him. "It is very difficult for men, straight or gay, to overcome our education. It was painful, almost embarrassing, for me to shoot a scene where a man says 'Fuck me, fuck me' out loud. That scene is almost like a horror movie for some people, in the degree of discomfort it causes audiences. Originally, all I wanted was one naked body in front of the camera and the voice of the director telling him what to do, but it was just too intense. I couldn't bear it, and in the end I added cutaway shots to the director and his assistant just to relive some of the tension."

The sexually explicit sequences in the film are shot with the actors completely naked and there is no mention or even consideration of either the AIDS crisis or the idea of safe sex. When it screened recently in the New Directors New Films series at New York's Museum of Modern Art, the film was immediately criticized by some gays as shocking for "promoting homosexuality in this day and age." Almodovar says he understands their concern, in light of the impact of AIDS in the United States, but points out that there is no widespread concern about AIDS in Spain at the moment. It was only this year that newspapers began printing stories about the issue, and gays are not yet as paranoid about health issues as their American counterparts.

"What can I say about this problem?" sighs Almodovar. "One must continue to explore romanticism and sexuality on the screen. There is this kind of awful conservative morality that has developed since AIDS, which is frightening and dangerous, like when the Pope--who is really crazy--tells people that AIDS is a judgment of God. I think we have to be very radical

right now on these issues. It seems to me that all the freedoms we have
won can disappear very quickly. This young new generation has absolutely
no experience in protest. It isn't in style anymore to protest. I feel I have a
personal duty to be very radical right now in defending individuality above
all. I have made a film about a man who is so obsessed with possessing the
soul of someone he loves that he is willing to lose his life in exchange for one
hour alone with that man. This isn't a tragedy. It would have been a tragedy
if he couldn't have had that one hour."

The world in which Almodovar operates is the attractive but possible
tenuous Madrid of today, which enjoys hedonistic pleasure after years of
military rule. Almodovar used to have nightmares about the military. He
says that since the new freedoms in Spain, he doesn't have those nightmares
anymore; however, he acknowledges that just as there are many Spains, there
are many Madrids.

"The film is very much like Madrid, as it is these days--amusing, funny,
casual, liberated. We are now probably the most liberal country in Europe.
But Spain is very paradoxical and very divided. There's a very liberated part of
the country and a very Victorian part. When you live where I do, in Madrid,
you can easily forget that I'm only talking about my world in Madrid, which
of course does exist--but it isn't all of Madrid." He pauses, shrugs and smiles.
"But it is *my* Madrid."

Whoopi Goldberg

The Advocate — November 22, 1988

The last time I met Whoopi Goldberg was at the Chateau Marmont in Los Angeles. She had just finished filming *The Color Purple* with Steven Spielberg, and her one-woman show was selling out in New York at Broadway's Lyceum Theater. We talked then about her rapidly changing career, the paucity of roles for black actors (don't call her a comic, or she'll kill you), and the public response to the recent death of Rock Hudson.

It was a long, intense conversation. I had just been diagnosed with AIDS and was living in San Francisco. She was already doing a series of benefits to raise money for social services. Within three months she would be nominated for an Academy Award for Best Actress, and I would move back to New York to form a group called ACT UP with playwright Larry Kramer and a group of angry Manhattanites.

Now, three years later, Goldberg has just completed her seventh film, *Clara's Heart*, for director Robert Mulligan as well as a hilarious HBO special called "Why Am I Straight?," which rips apart the Reagan administration for its failure to meet the challenge of the AIDS crisis. When I walk into her suite at the Ritz Carlton in New York, the first thing she says is, "Boy, am I glad you're still here." I give her an ACT UP shirt that says, "The Government Has Blood on Its Hands," and she puts it on exclaiming, "Great! I'm supposed to meet Dukakis next week, and this is the shirt."

It isn't easy to grab time with Goldberg these days. She's come a long way from being the local Bay Area performance artist who played at San Francisco's Valencia Rose and the 544 Natoma performance gallery, doing her Moms Mabley show for audiences of old and new friends. She is stunned to learn, in the course of conversation, that Peter Hartman, the owner of 544

Natoma who gave her an early start, died of AIDS in July of this year. She hadn't heard the news because she's been on the road, promoting her movie, her cable special and the record album of the show, which has just been released by MCA. I apologize for bringing sad news.

"No." She shakes her head sadly. "This is how I find things out. I just wish it would end." During the course of a very short hour, she discusses movies, racism, Hollywood hypocrisy, AIDS and homophobia with the intensity that has come to characterize her life and work.

What was the genesis of Clara's Heart?

It's a film that the producer, Martin Elfand, has been wanting me to do for three years, but I wasn't ready until now. In a way, it's fate, because our original director, David Anspach, had a parting of the ways with the studio, and that's how we ended up with Robert Mulligan, who has always been a favorite of mine. Also, three years ago we wouldn't have had this kid, Neil Patrick Harris, who is astonishing. So, in the end, I think it all worked out the way it was supposed to.

You're happy with this film, but that hasn't always been the case. Some people think the films you've chosen have been mistakes. How do you see the choices you've made on-screen?

You know, in terms of the choices I've made on the screen, I have to say that it's real easy to do what you want to do. What's not easy--what's a problem--is getting what you choose on the screen. I look at some of the films I've done, and I say, "Wait a minute. That's not what I read. I don't recall this movie." *Fatal Beauty* was nowhere near the script I first saw. The script I agreed to do was a nasty, dirty film about drugs. What they edited together was this glossy eight-by-ten of some planet where people are killed--but never by drugs.

It's frustrating, because you know it's all marketing people. They look at the film and say, "Well, she has one or two funny lines here. Let's cut it up and make it a comedy." And you try to be diplomatic about it. You don't run up to them afterward and scream, "You assholes! What have you done?" But it's terribly depressing. You always do films you want to do, but they're not necessarily the films you eventually see on the screen.

There are only four black people in America who work well on the screen Richard Pryor, Eddie Murphy, Bill Cosby and you--and they're all comics. Will this ever change, or is it a losing battle?

It will change. The fact is that there are four of us, and two of us are the top moneymakers in the business. Look at Oprah Winfrey, Michael Jackson, myself, Eddie — that's more color in Hollywood and New York than has been seen in the entire history of the movies. In four or five years, I've made seven films and developed a body of work. While critics have not liked the material I've done, never have they ever had anything bad to say about my acting ability, which is why I still have a career. Cicely Tyson wishes she could have seven films behind her right now, and she's been around for one hundred and ninety years. It's a slow process.

What I personally find interesting is that that with all the gay men who are in Hollywood -- and who *run* Hollywood -- they can't seem to present gay people on the screen. It's like the early Jews of Hollywood who were everywhere — Mayer, Goldwyn, Warner -- all Jews. And did they make movies about Jews? I think not. And now there are all these gay Hollywood producers, and they won't even consider me for the leading role in Larry Kramer's *The Normal Heart*, which I would love to do. They can't stretch their minds that far.

See, I think the whole point is to get the information out there, and I don't care how we do it. The whole AIDS issue has become politicized in the wrong way. We don't even see it as a public health issue anymore, thanks to a well-timed media blitz by people like Jerry Falwell. I think the government created this disease, and it got out of hand. But they are never gonna cop to that. Not in our lifetime. But you just can't justify it to me any other way, because gay folks have been on this earth since air. And the President should know better, with the amount of gay friends he and his wife have had over the years.

It's fear. That's why Hollywood producers who are gay don't produce AIDS benefits. They're afraid someone will think they're queer.

That's what it's really about. Last year, after I went on the March on Washington, people said to me, "What are you doing? They're gonna think you're gay." People think that already, because I hang out with a lot of women.

There hasn't been a studio head I've worked for who hasn't come out and asked me if I'm a lesbian.

What do you say?

I say, "Normally, this would be none of your business. However, I will answer you." And say, "It's possible. I'm not practicing at the moment, but I will not say it will never happen or hasn't happened in my past."

But what's the point? The point is, when you have people who are so caught up in image, it's a crying shame. Friends of theirs are dying every minute, and I'm just so tired of it all.

Why do you think the black and Hispanic communities have not responded to AIDS the way the white gay male community did?

First of all, there has always been a separate black gay culture from the middle class. See, I grew up around tons of gay folks. There were always what we called "the big girls." And part of the problem is that the black gay community never felt that they were a part of this crisis. They felt this was specifically white gay men, not realizing how many [black gays] were out there in the bathhouses and hanging on the streets.

You know what kills me? You think about AIDS hurting the image of the black community, and then you look at the Tawana Brawley [rape] case. Reverend Sharpton? You can't get much lower than that, I'm sorry. And reverends who have all this shit worked out in their minds have, in fact, set us back a hundred and fifty steps.

I know how painful it is for performers to talk about other performers in a negative way, especially when they're friends, but do you have a take on why Eddie Murphy is so insensitive on these issues?

First of all, he's very young. He's what? Like, twenty-three? Young men are often overly concerned about manhood, and in there lies quite a bit of humor. I believe, in my heart, that Eddie is very concerned and doesn't really see the problem. It's not much different from Richard Pryor early on; he really pissed off the gay community. These guys don't want to be thought of as "sensitive." Young people espouse things they don't fully understand. I'm sure Eddie Murphy doesn't perceive that he's promoting violence against gay people.

I have the same problem with my own young person, and sometimes I want to take her face apart tooth by tooth. She said she didn't want to be around someone who has AIDS. I said to her, "Now, how can you possibly say that? You've been around nine hundred people who have it. If there was a problem, you'd be dead a hundred times by now." And she said, "Yeah, you're right." A lot of it is ignorance and bravado.

As far as Eddie Murphy is concerned, what we need to do is sit down with him one-on-one instead of having the community up in arms against him, because that promotes defensive behavior. If you could interview him, you could say, "Do you know what your work is encouraging?" It's tough for him to see the truth because he's also surrounded completely by a lot of macho guys.

The black community has a different take on being gay. When you talk about "big girls" and "booty busters," it's not offensive to kids in my neighborhood. I don't really think [Murphy] knows what's offensive. You gotta talk to him. And if I can help to set that up, I'd like to do it.

So what's next for you? Is there another movie?

Not right now, because I'm doing "Star Trek." I've been telling them for a year that I want to do the show, and finally they said, "Are you serious?" And I said, "Yes, like cancer." And so I'm doing a regular, recurring role. I've always loved the show. I play a humanoid who runs their bar, and people just talk to me.

It's easy to see why people talk to Whoopi Goldberg. She's on top of the issues, and she's not full of shit. As she walks through the lobby of the hotel on her way to her limousine, people turn to stare. Her shirt reads, "The Government Has Blood on Its Hands."

Ian McKellan

Village Voice — **June 22, 1988**

Clause 28, the most odious antigay legislation in Britain since the Victorian era, became law last March. The statute, which forbids "local authorities" from promoting homosexuality, has been interpreted to apply to everything from school curricula to library shelves, from publicly funded plays, films and television shows to the licensing of gay bars. It isn't yet clear how British courts will apply Clause 28. But as a law seeking to regulate the representation of sexuality, it has set the stage for unprecedented protest, culminating in the largest gay rights march in British history. Writers, artists and performers have spoken out--and in some cases, come out. Ian McKellan, one of Britain's most renowned Shakespearean actors, told his public he was gay during a prestigious theatrical awards ceremony. And McKellan donated the entire proceeds of his recent American tour to the London Lighthouse, and AIDS hospice.

What made you decide to come out?

I was in San Francisco last fall doing *Acting Shakespeare*, my one-man show, and some friends dragged me through long trauma sessions arguing that there wasn't a single celebrated actor, conceivably in the world, who'd come out. And they felt it would be a potent symbol for other people if it happened. Also, I had become tired of avoiding questions about marriage in interviews. So I came back to England ready to come out, and the ideal opportunity came with Clause 28 — it didn't seem I could make a public statement against it unless I was absolutely honest as to why I took it so personally. So the truth popped out, and in popping out, the millstone was released, and I realized that being in the closet had been a terrible burden.

Why hadn't you come out sooner?

I thought that to declare myself gay might be a limitation on the audience's response to me. It was always that, rather than the fear that if I were open, I wouldn't get work. I mean an actor's job deals with sex to a great extent. The first thing an audience looks at when an actor enters is his face, then his crotch. The last thing you check before going on is that your flies are done up, or undone, depending on what you're playing. It's very unlikely that I would be offered a straight romantic part in a movie now.

What parts have you been offered since coming out?

One offer was to play Noel Coward, which I wouldn't do. The other was John Profumo, the cabinet minister who allegedly was sleeping with a prostitute who also was sleeping with a member of the KGB. I took the part thinking it would be a wonderful message for my next role to be that of a notorious heterosexual.

How important is it for gays to see themselves represented on stage?

It doesn't happen often enough. There is a company called Gay Sweatshop, which has toured Britain for twelve years and has a good reputation, but gay plays are unlikely to find a place on the West End. Even classical plays with homosexual themes, like Ben Johnson's *Edward II*, are neglected. Nobody in that play, incidentally, ever worries about the central character's homosexuality. What they object to is that his boyfriend is a foreigner, not that he has a boyfriend.

Your one-man show is about Shakespeare....

You can't understand a play like *As You Like It* unless you realize that it's not just about straight love but about bisexuality and lesbianism. Shakespeare knew that because he knew people so well, and it's all on display. People often ask, was Shakespeare gay? No, he was beyond being gay. He wasn't even bisexual. He was everything with equal passion.

I understand John Gielgud finally made a statement about Michael.

In an interview, he talked about the man he has lived with for a very long time, though he didn't actually say they were lovers. And I think he was prepared to write a letter to the prime minister against Clause 28, which, in the end, we didn't send. He is privately, extremely supportive.

Why did you choose to come out at the Olivier Awards [a British version of the Tonys]?

Because it was broadcast live. They couldn't stop me.

What was the reaction in the press to your announcement?

Once you say publicly that you're gay, Rupert Murdoch has nothing to write about. If you're not a hypocrite, there's no story for them. Leading a double life is something like acting, but it's the worst kind of acting. And coming out has put my job and my way of living into perspective. Until a year ago, the only thing I felt expert in was theater. Now I realize I have another expertise--and source of pride: my sexuality. The world probably needs that a great deal more than it needs my acting.

Given how the two relate and overlap, I think I shall see acting from an entirely different standpoint now. To be going through my fifties with that pride is a great relief. It's a great joy.

That's a perfect way to finish.

Bye bye, darling.

A Lavender Lens

With a culture so polarized around the notion of being a winner or a loser--with thumbs held up or either plunged down--the job of a fair-minded reviewer has never been more difficult. Add to this the public's long-standing disdain of critics in general and the task seems near impossible. It was the playwright Edward Albee who said, "The difference between critics and audiences is that one is a group of humans and one is not."

Well! Vito Russo was very much all-human, thank you: a man of his times with a critical eye given to nuance and kind words as much as bad raps when they were deserved. His is a rare feat of opinionated balance, but he did it—and with panache.

As the following reviews demonstrate, Vito was always generous with his opinion. He never stinted in telling you the truth about something he had seen—good, bad, or ugly. But his gift as a critic was to go the extra distance. If a piece of work was poor, he'd say how come and then maybe explain ways it could be made better. When he really liked a movie, such as Robert Altman's Nashville *or the Walt Whitman docudrama* Song of Myself, *he'd not only ring bells for it, but honestly says why so.*

He had no use for gratuitous judgment; not the facile pull-quotes craftily tailored for Sunday morning papers, or the self-aggrandizing put-downs prized by so many of his peers. Vito was unquestionably a lover of the movies. But unlike some lovers we may have known, who reveal less with closer viewing than first promised, Vito remained a gentleman throughout. His analytical, precise, and caring reviews are proof of that.

Gay Liberation from Germany with Reluctance

Gay Activist — April 1972

Europe's first gay liberation film will arrive here this week after a struggle to reach our shores which has lasted three months. The film, *It Is Not the Homosexual Who Is Perverse But the Situation In Which He Lives*, is the work of a young gay German filmmaker, Rosa von Praunheim, who describes his film as made by "homosexuals, for homosexuals." Von Praunheim, a member of the Hamburg Co-op, has also made an eighteen minute film entitled *Sisters of the Revolution*, a women's lib film.

It Is Not the Homosexual... is the story of Daniel, a young gay man, beginning to come out and meet various people in gay life, only to be put off by the seemingly self-imposed loneliness and frivolity of it all. The film takes the very strong viewpoint that "all gay things are not good" and that the gay life of the old, pre-movement times must vanish and be replaced by a new order, created by and for gay people. It is a plea, also, for gay/straight separatism, undoubtedly a very controversial issue. In the film, Daniel meets a group of people at a gay bar who are into alternate lifestyles, and they set up a communal living arrangement which strives toward creating a culture based totally on gay experiences rather than mimicry of straight lifestyles.

The strong political viewpoint of the film, coupled with its total dedication to a homosexual culture, has caused it to become the center of a storm of political controversy in Germany. It was banned from German television one hour before air-time and is now inciting debate and chaos outside of theaters where it is playing to overflow audiences at every screening. One American recently returned from Germany reports that the lines were so heavy for one screening that people were fighting in the streets to get into the theater.

The film almost had to be canceled due to lack of funds on the part of the filmmaker and also because the government decided not to title certain films from the Co-op. It was very strange, however, that most of the other films which were not chosen for titles were silent films or ones with music only. Rosa's film, although very heavy with dialogue, was the only one with so much to be translated not chosen. He then decided that rather than have American audiences misinterpret the film because of the language barrier, he would not have it shown here at all.

He was then prevailed upon, however, both by the Museum of Modern Art and by the Gay Activists Alliance Arts Committee, to come anyway with the film. In the interim, von Praunheim made an English translation on tape and is bringing both tape and film to New York. The film will be run at the Firehouse in English, with the help of a special Seaman magnetic projector, especially equipped for synchronizing tape with film.

At this point one wonders if all the hassles have been worth the final outcome. Will von Praunheim's film have a message for American homosexuals? Will it stir the same political controversy here that it is causing in Germany? Will it bring us to an alliance with our brothers and sisters in Europe, or will our ideologies prove to be too far apart for us to come to terms with now? All of this remains to be seen. Certainly, there are issues here that deserve discussion among our community. Certainly there are basic ideas which do not change, such as our hatred of repression, and our wish to effect a long and meaningful change.

Von Praunheim has said that homosexuals and liberals hate the film, as a rule, because it seeks to destroy a lifestyle they have become used to over years of repression. He treats the film almost as a comic strip. No depth of character in acting, no trying for feeling and flashy performances; just a group of homosexuals trying to change things in their own way.

Well, we'll see, won't we...?

Panic in Needle Park

After Dark — July 1971

Watching *The Panic in Needle Park* is like being at the scene of an accident — you can't bear to look, but you can't look away. Jerry Schatzberg, whose last film was the ill-fated *Puzzle of a Downfall Child,* has given us a powerful and frighteningly realistic look at some of the people we pass on the street every day--the heroin addicts of New York's Needle Park. Located in the West Seventies, Needle Park is the burial ground for America's lost children, the last stop on the roller coaster ride to a living death.

The Panic in Needle Park, screen written by Joan Didion and her husband John Gregory Dunne, and adapted from the novel by James Mills, is the defeating and heartbreaking story of Helen, all-American girl from the Midwest, and Bobby, New York-born street dweller and drug addict, and their world of hustlers, johns and cheap hotel rooms. When they meet, he is on heroin and the panic (shortage of drugs) is just beginning. As their relationship grows so does his habit and soon, out of sheer (and completely believable) love for him, she takes her first shot. The next day when he looks into her eyes and discovers what she has done, he simply holds her and murmurs, "Now, when did that happen?" From that moment on, they don't have a chance. They know it and we know it, but we hope for them right to the final shot, cut off abruptly, telling us that this is their life and will be until they die.

Kitty Winn as Helen and Al Pacino as Bobby, in their first film roles, reduce you to a state of helpless compassion as they become slowly but irrevocably aware of their fate. Winn makes such amazingly subtle transitions that halfway through the film you suddenly see her again for the first time--a hard, determined hooker, unable any longer to help herself or Bobby as she betrays him to the police. Pacino *is* Bobby; playing stickball with the neighborhood children, fighting an overdose in a hotel bathroom, or sitting in a seedy luncheonette, proudly greeting friends as if he were holding court, he carries with him the air of one defeated by his very birth into a society bent on his downfall.

Adam Holender's camera has recorded the places and the people of the West Side in such a sure, exacting and natural manner that we see again and again the things we have shut out of our minds and vision for fear of becoming too familiar with their impact. Now that Holender has shown them to us, we shall never be immune again.

This is a film of horror and of pity and of love. The kind of love that really happens, not the kind we usually get. It will knock you down without ever picking you up again, but it will force you to see and to remember that not all lovers are tragically beautiful; some are just tragic and they live on the same streets you do.

Nashville

The Advocate — July 16, 1975

Robert Altman's new film, *Nashville*, is of such importance that it will not only be the popular and critical success of 1975 but will also be discussed for years to come in terms of its relevance within the context of film history, being compared to *Citizen Kane* and *The Blue Angel*. It is a film which uses the Middle American mind and sensibility as embodied in the city of Nashville, home of country music, to explore both the music and the mentality with which it has become synonymous.

The story concerns five days in the lives of twenty-four people, all of whom have come together in Nashville for one reason or another during the presidential campaign of Replacement Party candidate Hal Philip Walker. Walker advocates, among other things, taxing the churches, removing lawyers from Congress, and changing our national anthem to a song everyone can remember. His campaign manager is staging a political rally for him, and the other twenty-three characters are framed by his efforts to get the "stars" of the Nashville music industry to sing at the televised benefit.

It is a brilliant tapestry, giving us not only a glimpse of the America that is Nashville but a hard look at how the music of the city relates to that America and its equation of cleanliness, godliness and short hair. The stunning and original way in which Altman weaves the lives of these people together is the freshest and most vividly exciting piece of theatrical filmmaking ever seen on the screen. Even the music itself is a character which sweeps along, giving a thrilling and vibrant background to a group of carefully delineated characters who never for a moment become clichés. Their music defines them and their place in both Nashville and the larger society.

There are stunning bits of work which, as the film unfolds, reveal layer upon layer of new dimensions to discover. Lily Tomlin makes what is probably the most important dramatic debut of the decade as a black gospel group's only white singer, whose husband is the Nashville music industry's lawyer. In one sequence during which she sits in a nightclub watching Keith Carradine sing "I'm Easy," a song which he wrote for the film, her transitions as the camera moves in on her face are an acting textbook.

She is joined by one of the strongest lists of actors to appear on the same screen in memory. Most of them wrote their own music and lyrics for the film and perform brilliantly. Karen Black as a sort of Tammy Wynette character named Connie White does things in her backstage scenes which I've only seen one other performer carry off, and, oddly enough, that was Lily Tomlin in a sketch about a country singer for one of her television specials. She is a terrific success. Henry Gibson as Haven Hamilton, the benevolent dictator of the Nashville music scene, is so good he's almost frightening, and Barbara Harris as Albuquerque, like the great actress she's always been, practically steals the film in the final hair-raising scene.

I could go on forever. *Nashville* is filled with beautiful, foreboding and dizzying revelations. It puts us on the edge of a precipice, always one step from the brink. Its underlying theme of the inherent violence in Americana is intricately woven into the being of its characters, cutting innocently from one image to the next with a bittersweet and melancholy directness.

One of the most unsympathetic characters, Opal, a reporter from the BBC played by Geraldine Chaplin, almost accidentally defines this undercurrent in a lucid moment when she says that all people who own guns are the real assassins, since they inspire the innocent ones to pull the trigger. We then see a very innocent young man on the phone talking to his mother and warning someone to stay away from his fiddle case. It almost takes two viewings to appreciate the images and their import.

The spectacle of Ronee Blakley as the pure and popular Barbara Jean, whose inability to cope with her success and subsequent breakdown, is haunting. Karen Black telling some young fans at the edge of the stage that they should "study real hard because anybody can grow up to be President" is chilling when the scene cuts once again to the intense young man with the fiddle case.

Such emotional cues are abundant: Barbara Baxley's raucous and beautifully realized Pearl, who worked "for the Kennedy boys because they was different"; Allen Garfield's stubborn refusing to let his wife Barbara Jean be involved in a political statement, somehow coming out as a portent; Haven Hamilton glad handing a black singer in the wings and muttering "lucky he's alive." It's all counterpointed with music which runs from "If makin' love is margarine, then you're the high-priced spread" to "You may say that I'm not free, but it don't worry me" and conspires to hold you in awe.

The music, then, is the real language of Altman's vision. His daring and inventiveness have paid off at last; he has produced an American classic. I could make some quite horrid parallels about the generation for whom *Woodstock* was the major musical message, now relating to *Nashville*, and what that might mean in terms of using music as politics, but I'm sure you'd rather not think about that.

Rocky

I Am Magazine — 1976

It's been a long time since we've had a film like *Rocky*. Some movies are like big hearted slobs who turn up just when you need to borrow a twenty; *Rocky* arrived in time to give us a break from anti-heroes, earthquakes, non-heroes, and giant gorillas. With simple faith and belief in the basic goodness of the human spirit notably absent from the screen in recent years, we are desperate for a film which tells us that everything can still come up roses.

In the 1940s we watched Mr. Smith go off to Washington courtesy of Frank Capra's corn and gladly believed that good could triumph, especially with Jimmy Stewart in the Senate. But it's been twenty years since a Bronx butcher named Marty found the miracle of true: love with a shy schoolteacher at a Saturday night dance hall. Since then, it hasn't been too easy to believe in fairy tales.

When, in *Nashville*, a country singer reminded young fans to "study real hard because anyone can grow up to be the president," we snickered because the dream was a transparent sham. Then a peanut farmer became president of the United States and Sylvester "Sly" Stallone came along with *Rocky* to remind us that some people still get a shot at the title. It's movie magic all the way.

Stallone, a New York actor frustrated by the limitations of bit parts, turned his creative energies towards writing a screenplay which would showcase his talents and articulate his vision. "I wanted the human spirit to triumph for once," he told the press. Irwin Winkler and Robert Chartoff agreed to produce it, and John Avildsen (*Joe* and *Save the Tiger*) was hired to direct. The film was shot on a shoestring budget in twenty-eight days. When *Rocky* opened it became a crowd-pleasing hit and catapulted Stallone from obscurity to stardom, and recognition as a sensitive, talented screenwriter. The long shot Stallone took on *Rocky* is essential to the success of the film. His simple belief is what we respond to in *Rocky*, a belief which emerges through his finely drawn characters as well as the dreams they represent.

Rocky Balboa is almost too good to be true. A gentle giant with large soft eyes, he's the unspoiled common man who moves through the squalor of his Philadelphia slum neighborhood with the simple trust of a child. Everybody loves Rocky, who's just the opposite of Johnny Boy in Martin Scorsese's *Mean Streets*. There's no guile, no greed in Rocky, he's just a pug who works out at the local gym and dreams of beating the rap someday. He wins an amateur bout occasionally but he's past any real greatness and he knows it.

To keep himself in spending money he runs strong-arm errands for a neighborhood loan shark named Gazzo but the harsh reality of small-time gangsters never touches Rocky Balboa or the film. Rocky is too decent to break a few fingers when a client doesn't pay up and Gazzo really likes the kid so there are no ugly repercussions. This isn't *Fat City*. It's a dream city, a Barnum & Bailey world with a paper moon, pure Hollywood of the 1930s making a comeback to give us an old-fashioned hero.

John Avildsen's leering accent on the seamier side of the American dream seems more subdued here, partially because Stallone has written simple characters who articulate simple dreams and simpler frustrations. Rocky's best friend Paulie is played with moving directness by Burt Young. Paulie is a mass of inarticulate failure, jealousy and frustrations, the embodiment of what Rocky is trying to escape. Stallone's screenplay shows us Paulie's pain as well as his rage, making us like him almost in spite of ourselves.

Paulie's sister Adrian, beautifully acted by Talia Shire, is Rocky's painfully shy girlfriend who blossoms under his touch as only a movie heroine can do when love comes just in time. Shire not only makes us believe that beauty if removing her glasses and combing her hair but that she can both love Rocky and rescue him from Palookaville.

When heavyweight champion Apollo Creed, a broad caricature of Muhammed Ali, challenges the local "Italian Stallion" to a Bicentennial match as a tribute to the land of equal opportunity and a few cheap laughs, Rocky doesn't even seen the hook. He smiles at the chance of a lifetime and starts training like crazy for his last chance. The belief Stallone infuses in his portrayal of Rocky works the necessary miracles, and in a few weeks, ignorant of the condescension of the promoters and the press, Rocky is in shape, having transformed himself from a cheap joke into a contender who just might go the distance.

Again we're wary when Rocky's friend Gazzo offers him a couple of hundred to tide him over until the match. We say to ourselves, "Oh, there he goes. This guy'll own him in a minute." But it doesn't happen. Not in *Rocky*. Gazzo is really just helping him out. Everybody loves Rocky.

We believe in Rocky because it's obvious to us that Stallone believes it and he's placed the same faith in us as an audience that he places in Rocky as a dream. Like Marty the butcher from the Bronx, Rocky Balboa doesn't want to be president; he just wants a piece of the action before his time is up. We want Rocky to be a hero. It's also fitting, somehow, that the Bicentennial should have given us Rocky, a man who triumphs even over the crassness of that event by being, and living, the spirit of the American dream. He follows his personal dream and, miraculously, wins the title. Not the one he fights for in the film but the one that tells him he's a somebody, a person of worth and value. As Ernest Borgnine said to his newfound plain Jane in *Marty*, "Dogs like us, we ain't such dogs as we think." If Rocky can go ten rounds, there's hope for all of us.

Welcome to L. A.

The Advocate — 1976

Welcome to L.A. has a lot of sunshine but absolutely no warmth. Alan Rudolph has written a directed an ice-cold vision of a group of depressed and depressing people barely coping with life in the city where the sun seems always just about ready to set in a blaze of tacky reddish-gold. Rudolph's point of view is what used to be called decadent six years ago, and he has altered it slightly by adopting Robert Altman's style of plot construction and going for a broad generalization of what Altman did in depth in *Nashville*. Rudolph worked with Altman on *Nashville* and wrote the screenplay for *Buffalo Bill and the Indians*.

Welcome to L.A. was written around Richard Baskin's dirge-like *City of the One Night Stands*, and he performs it relentlessly during the film, in counterpoint to the actions of the characters that are busy missing each other emotionally and physically. As Rudolph acknowledges, it's a film of behavior rather than plot, and if you don't mind pointlessness, watching these super-talented people behave for us is at the moment one of the best shows around.

In *Nashville* there was a burning sense of consequence to the proceedings. The characters performed in direct relation to the political and social isolation they felt, soothing each other as people when necessary and maintaining a sense of humor about themselves, however lopsided. The people in *Welcome to L.A.* are totally humorless, and the alienation they feel isn't at all pathetic because we care as much as they do — which is to say not at all.

In spite of the dismal outlook of the film, I found that I like it because Rudolph *does* manage to capture something. I can best define it as a sensibility having to do with the city of Los Angeles, which he shows us without ever actually showing us the city itself. We see Los Angeles in the way Sally

Kellerman (a magnificent performance) is photographed through the rear view mirror while driving her car, like a splashy Hollywood billboard, her lips and hair much too oversized for real life. The characters constantly look into mirrors, are reflected by mirrors and glass and at least one each, look directly into the camera on purpose at the request of the director. Since people in Los Angeles are more often than not posing for the rest of us in one way or another, this seems about right. The only insight available is that everyone in the film wishes to be seen as they see themselves, and everyone else is refusing to do so. Keith Carradine as Carroll Barber, a composer, re-creates his *Nashville* role with a beard (a very unattractive beard) and prays that his pauses will speak volumes. They do not.

I like very much Rudolph's energy and style. I like watching *Welcome to L.A.* because it was superbly lit and photographed and beautifully performed by a cast of interesting, dynamic people, but as a friend said after a recent screening, "People are sleeping with each other but not caring about each other and this is something *new* he's telling us?" With all that talent, Rudolph should try for something better than *Airport '69*.

A Gentle and Truthful Vision of Walt Whitman

The Advocate — March 10, 1976

On Tuesday evening, March 9, CBS will present a one hour special entitled *Song of Myself*, highlighting the life of American poet laureate Walt Whitman from his early twenties to the period just before his death at age seventy-three. The program is part of a series called "The American Parade" featuring central themes in American history, and deals, for the first time, with the homosexuality of the poet whose songs of male love were considered controversial at one time.

Shot in beautifully muted golds and browns, the show opens with Whitman sitting for a famous photograph, holding a paper butterfly and musing about his life to Tom, the photographer to whom he says, "I only met one artist in all my life, Tom, one real artist...that's you. All the others couldn't resist the temptation to prettify things...to make 'em better than they really are...don't prettify me...I never prettified anything in my life."

The large part of Whitman's life was dominated by the adverse public reaction to his *Leaves of Grass* which he published at his own expense in 1855. A disappointment to his family and friends for being a dreamer, not making money at writing "things people read," Whitman was an indomitable spirit who was "never ashamed or embarrassed of anything in his life," and in his own words, "never will be."

The show covers his battles with his father, his nursing soldiers through the Civil War and his meeting with his lover, Peter Doyle, a streetcar conductor who shared ten years of his life. The entire hour is a series of images, enhanced by Whitman's poetry which is woven in and out of the soundtrack over scenes of Whitman and Doyle walking through the woods, arms around each other, "When he whom I love travels with me or sits a long while holding me by the hand…" Or Whitman telling Doyle that he feels a comradeship with Lincoln saying, "I'm told that he's read *Leaves of Grass*. He knows who I am…we nod. Our chin whiskers bobbing at each other — A President, a poet…a special kind of comradeship…" And Peter Doyle smiling gently at him, saying. "Wait…maybe he's just friendly to everybody."

It's a short hour, too short to really explore with any kind of depth or analysis the greatest poet in our history, but it succeeds in being a gentle and truthful vision of a man misunderstood by his times. His battles with "Boston bluebloods" who wanted him to "change his poems" are only alluded to and his relationship with his family is reduced to their reaction to his homosexuality and the sexuality of his work, but we get a sketch here etched in strength and it all comes from the words of Whitman himself used extensively throughout.

The opening narration indicates that Whitman "broke convention in what he wrote and how he lived" and refers us to the first Amendment to the Constitution which "allows any man the freedom to go against the grain…to find his own place in The American Parade" as if that were true. Whitman's works were changed to make them heterosexual in nature and only now is the truth being spoken after decades of American lies. CBS is to be congratulated for being a part of this revelation in the year of our Bicentennial but it is not enough, obviously. It's a lovely, moving hour of poetic images and worth watching, but only as a promise of things to come.

Rip Torn, who portrays Whitman, gives an impressive and delightful performance. His eyes burn with knowledge and simplicity and truth and his transitions are effortless and convincing. When interviewed here recently and asked about Whitman's homosexuality, Torn replied, "Dealing with it was unavoidable but I did a lot of research and I think he was probably a bisexual." Torn uses as proof of this Whitman's *Hymn to a Woman's Body*, saying "There's sufficient evidence in his work that he was not without heterosexual drives." This obsession people have to make all gay people acceptably bisexual apparently knows no bounds.

When asked about people's reaction to Torn playing a strong homosexual role, Torn replied that "one character intimated that I was homosexual — me with wife and three kids. I let it pass." What was the alternative, I wonder, to letting it pass?

Television is the most powerful medium of our times because it comes into gay homes and straight ones and teaches us about each other. The discovery of our heroes is only one way it can teach us the truth. Whitman's homosexuality was an intrinsic part of his nature, like Rip Torn's heterosexuality. When I walk down the street and some people mistakenly think I'm heterosexual, I do not let it pass. We have to start celebrating who we are. Don't miss *Song of Myself.*

Puttin' Down The Ritz

The Advocate — September 22, 1976

The Ritz, Terence McNally's wacky Broadway farce about a Cleveland garbage man eluding his mafia brother-in-law at a gay bathhouse, has lost a lot of steam in transition from stage to screen. The one-joke situation — trapping a straight man in gay surroundings, compounded by the usual mistaken identities and sexualities — is explored only in the broadest possible terms by both McNally, who adapted his own screenplay, and Richard Lester, who directed the film. Relying on mock horror and exaggerated consternation, Lester has paced the action at such a feverish intensity that there's no time to get to know the characters. They just keep whizzing by like Looney Tunes.

On Broadway, *The Ritz* worked better, largely as a result of director Robert Driva's sense of timing and the incandescence of Jack Weston as Proclo, the rotund refugee, and Rita Moreno as Googie Gomez, the supremely untalented Puerto Rican chanteuse in The Ritz's nightclub, "the Pits." In a sense, the play functioned as a piece of provincial theater, emerging directly from a strong New York sensibility. It is a limited sensibility though, stemming from the Bette-Midler-at-the-baths days when straight and gay people met briefly in such surroundings, producing some very funny moments.

The story goes that McNally saw Moreno do her Puerto Rican singer routine at a party one night, singing "Everything's Coming Up Roses" and decided to write a play for the character. Onstage, the performances — combined with an obvious sense of good will inherent in the play — made *The Ritz* an inoffensive piece of fluff for both gay and straight audiences. Nobody was laughing *at* anyone: it was simply the situation that produced the laughter.

Onscreen, however, Lester doesn't seem to get the jokes. He directs the film as if the existence of gay people in such surroundings were the joke. Unfortunately, his pacing has only two speeds: a hundred miles an hour and stop. After each laugh the film grinds to a halt so that the audience can "get it," something which was unnecessary for Broadway. It looks as if Lester keeps waiting for the general public to catch up. If pregnant pauses were elbows we'd all have black and blue ribs.

Also, Lester has no clue as to why this particular situation is funny. McNally, being Catholic, knew how to weave a tapestry of humor built on cross references to the church, the Italian family and the gay subculture. Scenes like the one in which Kaye Ballard, as Procclo's wife, feigns a coronary upon discovering her husband in a fur coat, then starts to scream about Father Bonelli in confession, were cut because Lester didn't appreciate the humor in them. One of the highlights of the play, a talent show in the nightclub, has been shortened to almost nothing in the film, robbing us of what little color existed. The cuts took away any glimpse we might have had of real characters caught up in a farce of their own making. They're cartoons instead of people in a cartoon situation.

Still, there are some very funny things in *The Ritz*, if you can distance yourself from the stereotypes. F. Murray Abraham as Chris, Weston's self-appointed guide to "fairyland," is funny and displays a sense of consciousness in his humor which is lacking everywhere else. All the other gay characters in the film, aside from being singularly unattractive, are "types." There's a man in leather and chaps; a chubby chaser who brings a suitcase full of food to his room as "bait"; even a raincoat or two. I thought *that* one went out with black sedans parked in front of playgrounds.

While maintaining a sense of humor about ourselves and a sense of the human comedy, sometimes created out of such situations (and they *do* happen) we must, nevertheless, examine the impact of such exposure on our image. At least in a film like *Ode to Billy Joe* we get a sense of who we are and the historical perspective of American attitudes towards gay feelings. A sense of shared experience prevents us from feeling cheated by the truth we see on the screen. In *The Ritz*, however, we do feel cheated because a film like this cheapens the strides we have made in gay visibility by using it to limit rather than expand our presence in society. It's almost like getting a good laugh out of us before we finally surface.

Of course, we've come a long way from the Tallyhatchie Bridge, and *The Ritz* has all the earmarks of being one of the transitional period films that mark of not understanding and communication, at least a certain amount of faith that the public is ready to deal with us. Or are they? At a swank opening night party for *The Ritz* at The Four Seasons, I asked Rita Moreno if she didn't think the film would reinforce Middle America's stereotypes.

"Don't give me stereotypes! We're a *farce*, darling. It's not the job of farce to educate Middle America. We are not a documentary." Two days later at a fashion show on Fire Island, she reacted to my *faggot* t-shirt with "I hate that word. It's like *spic*."

Jack Weston, who may finally get the offers he deserves after his performance in *The Ritz*, was less sure what the effect of the film would be on attitudes towards gay people. "It could go either way. Either they'll just think of all the gays being like that or they'll be more open to the subject. I *hope* it doesn't reinforce any stereotypes because I really feel bad that at the end of the film my character has broken through with some positive sense towards Chris when he says 'If you're in Cleveland, my wife makes a terrific lasagna.' It shows people as people and I think when shown in Dubuque it will be a watershed film with respect to gays."

Kay Ballard had her own complaints about the film. "My objection is that there are no really handsome gay men in the film. All the gay guys I know are beauties. They all look like Tyrone Power. Why didn't they use great looking guys? Besides, Lester didn't know what he was doing. He cut so many things; a lot of it makes no sense anymore."

Obviously, everyone has a version of "who we are" in the public mind. *The Ritz* should be seen by gay people if only to point up the seriousness of our present dilemma onscreen. McNally is the one who should have sought refuge. Lester has put cement shoes on his play and dropped it into the river. Maybe Billy Joe McAllister is better off.

Sundry Nights at the Movies

The Advocate — November 3, 1976

Norman Is That You? finally slipped into general distribution and it might be the first pro-gay fag joke. I know that's like being slightly pregnant but producerdirector George Schlatter manages to combine generally good intentions with a production only a hack could love. Filmed mostly on videotape, the film looks like it was shot in a Castro showroom; mostly Fidel with a little Bernadette thrown in.

The short-lived Broadway comedy went on to become a dinner theater hit and it's easy to see why. Playing both ends from the middle, it makes no statement whatever except that which each viewer imposes upon it. Redd Foxx discovers that his wife (Pearl Bailey) has run off to Mexico with his brother and that his son is a "tinkerbelle." Only Michael Warren doesn't play it like a "tinkerbelle." That would alienate some people. His white lover does it instead, recreating the Michael Greer role from *The Gay Deceivers*. Get it? One plays the husband and one plays the wife — just like us, George. Throw in a little consciousness, a few statistics and the homophobes can identify with Foxx's Neanderthal reactions while we bask in the information that Stephen Foster is brought out of the closet. He's only been dead for one hundred and twelve years.

Some of it is funny, especially Wayland Flowers and Madame, who steal the picture. Flowers has always had the facility for showing us how to laugh at ourselves and he is simply used well here. I also liked the opening and closing songs, "An Old Fashioned Man" and "One Out Of Every Six." I would even like to believe that some of this nonsense will change one heart about gay people, but I can't sell myself that dream. The cheapness of the film makes it all so inconsequential.

People have a tendency to refer to Martin Ritt's new film *The Front* as "the new Woody Allen film" which it is not. A funny, thoughtful and sometimes fascinating dramatization of the effects of blacklisting in television during the McCarthy era, it employs Allen as a schlepping opportunist who "fronts" for blacklisted writers, selling their scripts under his name and collecting a percentage for the service.

Many of the people connected with *The Front,* including director Ritt, writer Walter Bernstein and actors Zero Mostel and Herschel Bernardi, were actually blacklisted in the 1950s. This information is given rather solemnly in the closing credits, lending an almost documentary quality to the work. In fact, it saves the essential seriousness of the film from a badly contrived ending. Allen's character, Howard Prince, is a bookie and part-time cashier suddenly turned celebrity by his use of other people's words. He is slimy and unscrupulous in the familiarly nebbish way we have come to see in his own films.

But there is more to *The Front* than he allows his character to see. He never betrays a real understanding of the terror created by the blacklist. More alarming, he doesn't pick up any consciousness about the entire witch hunt along the way; it's as if he were dumb and blind. We sit in the audience infuriated by the revelations on the screen, and the person to whom they are being revealed is unaware of them. His sole motivations are greed and a case of lust for television script editor Andrea Marcovicci, who has fallen in love with the writer she thinks he is. He treats her like a dame from one of his own comedies for about two hours in a five minute scene at the end and is radicalized by her politics. No way. We don't believe this sudden transformation. It's as if he were saying, "You mean you'll keep loving me if I hate blacklisters? Where do I sign up?" It almost ruins the film.

But not quite. There is much to recommend *The Front.* It's an honest exploration of a shameful period in American history and succeeds beautifully in exposing the waste and madness that destroyed careers and made a fearful weapon of patriotism. Most of all it makes clear how present a danger this type of thinking is and how it could happen again tomorrow. The other performances in the film are quite good, especially Zero Mostel as a blacklisted comic and Herschel Bernardi as a spineless television executive. Remak Ramsay paints a chilling portrait of a network "advisor" who checks people out for the Committee on Un-American Activities. "I don't take sides," he says; "I just advise on patriotism." Marcovicci gives a warm, human and intelligent portrayal of a woman whose conscience cannot allow her to sit by and watch the horror.

Some measure of how close we are to the subject matter is evidenced by the refusal today of NBC and CBS to let director Martin Ritt use their facilities for the filming of *The Front*. People are still scared and it could easily happen again.

John Schlesinger's *Marathon Man*, adapted for the screen by William Goldman from his own novel, is a highly complicated thriller involving an exiled Nazi war criminal (Laurence Olivier), a Columbia University graduate student (Dustin Hoffman) and various spies, counter-spies and thugs who switch sides every five minutes. In a plot difficult to follow, let alone retell, Hoffman is pursued by Olivier and his henchmen for information they think was whispered to him by his dying brother (Roy Scheider). Olivier is after a ransom in diamonds sitting in a safe deposit box in a midtown Manhattan bank, but isn't sure it's safe to pick them up. Hoffman hasn't the slightest idea what anyone is talking about. He thought his brother was working for an oil company. The plot thins.

The film reduces the complex relationships in the novel to a kind of shorthand in order to retain as much of the action as possible. Schlessinger is obviously desperate for a commercial hit and has gone after the car chase crowd with a vengeance. At times the film resembles *Mad m*agazine's Spy vs. Spy comic strip, with bombs bursting in air like clockwork.

Hoffman's relationship with his professor at Columbia and his passion for clearing his father of McCarthy charges become slight references, reducing his character to a scared rabbit, running from shotgun blasts. Schlessinger still has an eye for people and a sense of locale but gets no chance to explore them. The gay relationship between Roy Scheider and William Devane, fairly up-front in the novel, is thrown away here—not, I'm sure, for any political reason, but because there is so much information it simply gets lost in the shuffle. When Hoffman asks Devane who they're working for, he is told that when the FBI and the CIA won't touch a job it's given to The Division. Oh! The Division! Sure. Of course. Right. If Schlessinger doesn't get back to making real movies about real people soon, we will have lost a great talent.

Burnt Offerings, directed by Dan Curtis, is an old-fashioned, scary movie about an isolate country house that regenerates itself every summer by taking the life from its temporary inhabitants. Karen Black and Oliver Reed are a city couple who find this mansion for only nine-hundred dollars for the entire summer. That should have been their first clue to run like hell, but in horror movies the people are always stupid enough to stick around until they get polished off. The film is full of lovely and menacing touches. The clocks have a mind of their own, doors slam shut unaided and the swimming pool does strange things to people who splash around in it.

Bette Davis gives a surprisingly rich performance as an elderly aunt growing more elderly by the minute; and Eileen Heckart, in a brief appearance at the outset, lends a slightly batty air to the proceedings with help from a dotty Burgess Meredith. There are a lot of holes in the film, the biggest being the total innocence of the characters. After Reed tries to drown his son in the pool, Black suggests that it's all over and they should all come to bed and forget it. The next day, Davis is crocheting by the pool and comments, "My, it looks marvelous — why don't you jump in?" Our giggles are a little uneasy, though, because being scared is such great fun.

Black pouts too much and a subplot about her sexual problems with her husband is mishandled and slows the film down considerably, but *Burnt Offerings* is a great Saturday night chiller.

A Matter of Time

The Advocate — **November 17, 1976**

Vincente Minnelli's *A Matter of Time* is an exercise in memory for everyone concerned, including the audience. It isn't a good film, but it's a film that is very difficult to dislike. There are too many subtle forces on the screen that work to prevent us from dismissing the picture as being based on an outdated dream. It's easy to see why Minnelli would be fascinated by this story based on Maurice Druon's *A Film of Memory*. It embodies the kind of romance he was so good at creating when such films actually worked. We even believed them for a minute.

Alas, filmmaking isn't what it used to be and the music isn't so grand in this tale of a chamber maid getting the Vickie Lester treatment from an aged Contessa (Ingrid Bergman) who has "lived." There are a few musical interludes — more an evocation than a solid attempt — and even the dubbing is bad, giving the proceedings a slightly discordant air.

The Minnelli sensibility, however, is also at work, constantly reminding us that this film has been made by someone who knows the real thing even after the bubbles have gone. He cared about this picture. In fleeting moments, there is a bit of memory for everyone here. A homage to Judy Garland is certainly implied in Liza's *Star is Born* verve, and a few minutes at the piano backed by a group of tired musicians has a delicacy in spite of an arrangement of Gershwin's "Do It Again" that would horrify her mother. Bergman, a remembered character remembering the past, floats across a room at sunset and thousands of birds fill the Rome sky. It *is* a film of memory and we do want so very much to believe it again for just a minute.

There's an audacity at work here as well that drove Liza Minnelli to express herself though this film. We see how gawky and awkward she seems and we are grateful she doesn't have green fingernails. After all, she can't take John Kander and Fred Ebb with her everywhere she goes, and perhaps this is what she looks like when she isn't playing Sally Bowles. It leads us to discover something about both the father and the daughter, and although they don't have the proper means to express themselves, somehow one is glad they try.

Small Change

The Advocate — November 17, 1976

Francois Truffaut's love for children and his preoccupation with childhood is on display again in his latest film, *Small Change,* which opened this year's New York Film Festival. We have seen Truffaut deal with childhood before, notably in *The 400 Blows* and in a more analytic way in *The Wild Child.* In *Small Change* he presents us with a string of childhood moments framed by a school term in the medium sized town of Thieirs. The film introduces a dozen or so young people aged two months to fourteen years, and we stay with them in their big and small moments--examining their boring Sunday afternoons, their first attempts at clumsy romance, their petty larceny — until school lets out for vacation.

The film has some great moments. Twin brothers try hocking their schoolbooks at a local bookshop and are asked for a note from their parents. Stumped, one them tries angelically, "Even orphans?" It doesn't work. The young daughter of a police captain tries to take her ratty, stained animal purse to dinner with her parents on a Sunday afternoon. When they tell her she must leave it at home, she decides not to go and they leave without her. As soon as they're gone, she takes her father's bullhorn and announces to the courtyard that she's hungry and that her parents have locked her in the apartment and gone to dinner.

She receives a basket of food on a rope rigged by sympathetic neighbors outraged at the cruelty of the parents. A very young baby follows a cat out of a window and falls what looks like four stories only to bounce once on the grass and giggle, "Gregory go *boom.*" His mother promptly faints.

It isn't just a string of vignettes, though. Truffaut, by using a script and child actors instead of recording the spontaneous actions of children means to define a certain type of child in us all. He has also chosen to make the film deliberately "cute," dealing only dispassionately with the abuse of a child by his mother and not at all with the kind of abuse children often heap upon one another. Seeing two of the teachers who interact with their students on a daily basis in and out of school, we get bits and pieces of a nonpolitical message of love for children and proper treatment of them when they're young.

But mostly, it's just a series of charming charades played by cunning, uninhibited little actors. By piecing together only the nice things children do, Truffaut has created a loaded composite of what he would like the idea of "child" to mean. As long as we're getting to pick out our versions, though, I must say I rather like the way W.C. Fields saw it.

Network

The Advocate — **December 15, 1976**

Sidney Lumet's *Network* is an outrageous motion picture, just like it says in the ads. In fact, the film illuminates the method of that ad's appeal. Centering on the people who create our images, the film is really a series of ideas that carry the dehumanization of the individual to its quite sane and logical conclusion. It doesn't take any prophetic vision to see the corrupt values responsible for what we see on our television sets. If there's a market for it, they'll do it. Just turn on a network news show any night of the week and see for yourself.

You are likely to find anchorman Howard Beale (Peter Finch) on the UBS six o'clock news announcing that he's been fired because of poor ratings. He says he intends to shoot himself on the air next Tuesday. He is yanked off and fired. The next morning, enter Faye Dunaway, powerhouse vice-president of programming with a newspaper in her hand. The story made the front page. The ratings are up. Are we going to throw this opportunity away? The next night Howard Beale is back on the air to inform the public that, "We'll tell you any shit you wanna hear." The people love it. Dunaway says he articulates the rage of the common man. The ratings soar. In the words of one executive, "It'll wipe that fucking Disney right off the air."

Dunaway is weary of scripts for situation comedies that all call for (pick one) "a crusty but benign" police captain, doctor, district attorney. She sees a career in turning the network news into a smash with a thirty-five percent of the share. Her campaign to take over the news department precipitates an affair with UBS News President William Holden. This affair continues even after she has calmly seen him fired. She is total television. She fills out the rest of the news with Sybil the Soothsayer, who "tells tomorrow's news today," and a flashy gossip columnist, all on a garish revolving set.

She also creates a show called "The Mao Tse-Tung Hour," which opens with real footage of an act of terror supplied by members of The Ecumenical Liberation Army in return for a piece of the show. She's thinking of doing a homosexual soap opera — "The Dykes." What do you think? Huh?

Meanwhile, Beale, preaching in front of stained glass, has gotten people all over American to open their windows and shout, "I'm mad as hell and I'm not gonna take it anymore." The ratings go over the top. When Beale announces that the network has been bought out by Arab money, however, he hits a nerve. In a strange, almost religious scene, he is told by corporate magnate Ned Beatty that he has "meddled with the forces of nature." There is no America. No democracy. The individual is finished. He is to begin preaching "corporate cosmology" if he wishes to remain a prophet.

Paddy Chayevsky's script delves a lot deeper than an examination of the "thrill -a-minute" mentality of television. When his characters talk to each other about human relations they sound like robots in unfamiliar territory.

Dunaway: *I reached for the phone a hundred times to call you but I was sure you hated me for taking your news show away.*

Holden: *I did, I guess, but I just can't get you out of my mind.*

Yet when they're behaving like robots, they sound perfectly natural. For example, Dunaway nonchalantly threatens to fire about six people for not having read a report.

Dunaway's role was originally written for a man and the simple decision to use a woman in the part becomes an interesting occasion. Her intensity, drive and ambition will be seen by some audiences as "masculine." The fact that she recreates a male-oriented metaphor for women. In one scene she and Holden   are headed on foot for a motel room; she is delivering a rapid-fire monologue on the ratings in New York, the percentages in Los Angeles, and syndication problems even as they begin to have sex. She climaxes, sitting on him, still intensely spouting ratings and makes you believe it. Sex and power rarely become one for women on the screen. A closed deal is like a good fuck.

In *Long Day's Journey Into Night*, Katherine Hepburn slaps Dean Stockwell and embraces him in the same continuing gesture. Lumet evokes the same sensibility here with separate levels of emotion in operation at once. Dunaway and Holden play it perfectly. Good performances also come from Finch, who manages to bring dignity to a character scared in a jungle, and from Beatty, who makes the corporate creep an ominous presence.

There's a tendency to see *Network* as a sort of far-out vision of our depersonalization. Yet a local New York news show recently announced the addition of a fortune teller to its staff. Can a man really be killed on the air for getting low ratings? Or are Lumet and Chayevsky also waiting to see if we will buy a "perfectly outrageous motion picture"? Would they tell us any shit we wanna hear? I wonder what kind of ratings *Network* will get.

La Cage Aux Folles II

New York Native — **February 23, 1981**

My favorite moments in *La Cage Aux Folles II* came during the opening credit sequence, which featured some of the funnier scenes from the original film. I didn't think *La Cage Aux Folles* was a good film but I laughed a lot and had a thoroughly enjoyable time. I did not, in spite of the long lines at the 68th Street Playhouse, talk myself into believing that the film would make democracy safe for homosexuals simply because we were all laughing together. And besides, we weren't laughing together. The straight people in my particular audience were laughing *at* while the gays were laughing *with*, and at completely different times.

For me, the original film provided some classic gay/straight comic confrontations and two wonderful performances by Michel Serrault as the excessive but hilarious Albin (professionally, transvestite star Zaza Napoli at La Cage Aux Folles nightclub on the French Riviera) and Ugo Tognazzi as his exasperated, long suffering lover Renato.

The tag line in the ad campaign for *La Cage Aux Folles II* is "...the relationship continues." But it is a promise unfulfilled. Whatever sketchy, undeveloped relationship existed in the original film between Renato and Albin is hopelessly lost in part II, replaced by the crudest cartoon posturing imaginable. In *La Cage Aux Folles* there were a few faint glimmers that these two shared something together and that gave the comedy a little bite. The impending marriage of Renato's son prompted the tension of trying to keep the bride's father, a conservative politician, from discovering that the "mother" of his new son-in-law is actually the notorious drag queen Albin.

Although the pace of the farce is deadly in the first film and lethal in the second, the original contained a few sustained bits that actually worked, such as Renato trying to teach Albin how to walk like John Wayne and Albin failing miserably to butter a piece of toast. There's also a lovely moment at the end when the moralistic father of the bride shouts, "*Who* is the mother of this boy?" Renato nods at Albin who rips off his wig, holds out his hand and says "Enchante, monsieur." A small victory, but our own.

La Cage Aux Folles II is conceived entirely from the Milton Berle School of Drag humor. The joke is seeing a man dressed like a woman and the movie is boring because of it. Unlike its predecessor, this one is not in any sense gay. It is rather a film about gays for straights — *Zaza Napoli Meets The Pink Panther*. Due to circumstances much too stupid to repeat here, Albin gets involved in an espionage caper to do with microfilm and consequently must jump out of a cake looking like Ethel Merman. If that sounds funny, it wasn't.

Michel Serrault still cuts quite a figure as Albin to say the least but the genuine laughs are so far apart they're like favors to us, rewards for sitting through the rest. And all those laughs are visual gags. There's no tension, no situational humor, no gleeful expectation of what might happen next. Serrault gets to butch it up as a macho carpenter in one scene and I loved it for a minute but every combination of that joke is attempted for the next hour and it gets tedious. First we have a gay man dressed as a woman trying to pass for a man, then a group of straight men try to pass for gay, then a gay man dresses up as straight but all they're really doing is running around changing clothes.

A potentially funny sequence with Albin as an Italian peasant woman working in the fields ("I don't like being a woman in this country") is virtually thrown away. Albin's talents as Zaza inside the club were wisely kept from us in the first film. The scene in which Zaza does Marlene Deitrich in blackface could have been terrific but it's as flat and uninspired as a crepe. There's no pace at all. The film just flits around looking for something to show us.

In addition, there's a lot of vicious fag-baiting in this one which goes beyond pointing out who the bigots are by putting "queer" and "fag" into the mouths of obvious fools. The epithets hurled at Renato and Albin throughout *La Cage Aux Folles II* are gratuitous and cruel. When, towards the end, Albin says to Renato, "Well, you can't say we haven't been happy together," it gets a laugh because nobody is supposed to take this relationship seriously.

Part III is in the works for next year, and I hear they're thinking of calling it *La Cage Aux Folles Meets Abbot and Costello*.

The Tragic Dullard

New York Native — **March 23, 1981**

Bob Rafelson's *The Postman Always Rings Twice* is a beautiful film about something ugly, a morality tale about gross immorality, and a deeply felt statement about two people who seem to have very little feeling. It asks us to consider that beauty can enter the lives of the ignorant and the dull, that morality exists independently of the basest intentions, and that one can feel something tragic has happened to people who are not even capable of articulating their own dilemma. The contradictions in *Postman* are reminiscent of those in Arthur Penn's *Bonnie and Clyde* and Noel Black's *Pretty Poison* but the sexuality only hinted at in those films is central to Rafelson's *Postman*, and its frank, natural exploration provides a stunning — if strange — love story.

James Cain's melodramatic novel of sexual obsession and murder certainly presents Frank and Cora as ordinary people. Frank is a drifter in the California of the 1930s Depression who takes a job at a roadside café, where he meets Cora, the proprietor's wife. Driven by an overwhelming sexual passion which blots out any considerations of justice or decency, they plot to murder Cora's husband and succeed despite one abortive attempt and their own outright stupidity. They are exonerated of the murder through a legal technicality, and here's where Rafelson's version of the story--starring Jack Nicholson as Frank and Jessica Lange as Cora — departs from Cain as well as from the Lana Turner/ John Garfield film directed by Tay Garnett in 1946.

In both the Cain novel and previous film versions of it, including a seldom seen French interpretation and a recently screened Italian translation by Luchino Visconti called *Obsessione*, the story is one of passion, crime and conventional retribution. The Cain novel is framed in flashback, opening and closing with Frank's confession to a priest while on trial for the murder of Cora. In the 1946 film, Garfield and Turner never quite trust each other. After their acquittal in the murder of the husband, their suspicion of each other destroys them. In the climactic car crash scene, Cora looks at Frank as if wondering at the last instant if he is in the process of murdering her. Any real love shared by the two is denied the audience so that we can think of them as complete snakes, unsalvageable as decent people.

Rafelson's film uses sexual obsession as a doorway to true love, a daring thing to ask people to accept. Frank and Cora, mindlessly sexual at first, live speeded-up lives for us. We seem them in a childish sort of sexual thrall. They're spiteful and petty throughout, but we see a woman begin to accept love and maturity and a drifter begin to accept middle age, the prospect of children suddenly changing both of them into different kinds of dullards. Only their illusions about themselves are pretty, but we see that they believe in them. In the end, Frank and Cora are married. On their way home from an afternoon picnic, they laugh happily with the sun slanting down into the west. Suddenly an oncoming car causes Frank to swerve and Cora is thrown from the car, killed instantly.

Frank is probably tried for the murder of Cora here, too, but Rafelson doesn't consider it the irony of the tragedy. The tragedy here is that Frank loses the love he has found in Cora, and the film ends with him weeping by the roadside over her dead body. It has never occurred to him that they both broke the rules and might be punished someday by losing each other. The fact that these people can be tender and loving in spite of the fact that they've committed a horribly brutal crime is what's fascinating here, like Bonnie of *Bonnie and Clyde*, just before the police blow her brains out. It makes us wish they'd never killed anybody so they could be free to explore this gentle love they've found together.

The film is satisfying in a number of ways. The husband, played by John Colicos, is a boastful, proud, chauvinistic Mediterranean man who can't conceive of his wife ever cheating on him. In the 1946 film, Cecil Kelloway played a sort of senile leprechaun who was blissfully unaware of his surroundings. Here it's the fatal flaw of the husband that he considers his wife his property. When he has a surprise for her, it's a satin dressing gown he has bought for himself, a measure of his cocky sureness of her devotion to him.

Add the fact that it wasn't so easy for a woman to leave a man in the 1930s, and murder doesn't seem out of the question.

The sexuality of the film is the purest expression of sexual passion I've seen on the screen since Oshima's *In the Realm of the Senses*. It may be the first expertly made American film in which sexual heat is presented as a natural state. The scene that will be talked about most is an early one in which Nicholson and Lange has sex on a kitchen table soon after her husband makes his first excursion into town. But the extraordinary scene of sexual desire for me came when, toward the end, they have finished off the husband by pushing the car over a cliff. Suddenly, Lange leans back on the rocks and lazily opens her legs. Nicholson is at first shocked, but it is clear that the heat of the violent murder has made them both horny and they fuck slowly but intensely on the side of the hill.

Nicholson turns in a low-keyed performance--a distinct relief after his eye-popping in *The Shining*--but it is Lange who is the revelation. It's a knockout performance from a woman who was all but written off as an empty-headed model from that *King Kong* remake a few years back. She's intensely sexual, lazy, stupid, electric and completely compelling. She makes Cora into a woman with a sexual and emotional force of her own, not just a glamorous trigger for tragedy.

Rafelson said in an interview that his characters are "alienated losers... rather than ordinary people." But I think that alienated losers are ordinary people. Most people on earth are alienated losers who will never achieve their little dreams. The revelation here is in Rafelson's illumination of the fact that such drudges can fully experience depths and heights of passion and despair usually reserved for "special" characters, the heroes of the cinematic world. *The Postman Always Rings Twice* doesn't turn Frank and Cora into any kind of recognizable heroes, but the way their brief passion is lit up for us is heroic.

Drugs and Dopes in Atlantic City

New York Native — **April 6, 1981**

Louis Malle's *Atlantic City* comes under "serious, touching, yet rough look at American dreams," which European directors are so good at because of their alleged cultural distance from us. But I don't think there's ever much distance.

I think we're all fascinated with America's tawdry success story, as though everyone was a foreigner, and America was a place we all watched on television. *Atlantic City* is a lot of fun, both an idealization and a cruel indictment of a place predicated on dreams yet inhabited by those to whom reality has been less than kind.

Lou (Burt Lancaster) used to run numbers along the boardwalk, but in a city on the verge of a new era in casino gambling, he's a useless shadow. Nobody needs an aging gangster-groupie with no real underworld power when nuns are lined up at the slot machines and Howard Johnson's is running blackjack tables. Lou lives in a condemned apartment building, about to be torn down to make way for yet another spectacular casino. He takes care of Grace (Kate Reid), the widow of his old boss. She came to Atlantic City in the 1940s to enter a Betty Grable look-alike contest, lost, married a gangster, and made the resort her home. Now she sits in a rococo bedroom looking like Baby Jane Hudson, screams at Lou and plays with her poodle.

When Lou isn't rubbing Grace's feet or walking her poodle, he's peeping through his blinds at Sally (Susan Sarandon), who lives across the court in the same building. He stares at her while she rubs lemon juice on her breasts and arms. She works at the oyster bar of a casino and is interested in becoming the first woman blackjack dealer in Monte Carlo. Her husband (Robert Joy) is a hateful little dope-selling punk who knocked up her sister and is in the process of ruining her life by stealing her money and dealing drugs with people completely out of his league.

Of course, these unlikely characters all get to meet and fall in love. Except Sarandon's husband, of course. No sooner does he enlist the aid of Lou in selling some heroin than he gets rubbed out by the mob, leaving Lou with something like ten thousand dollars worth of the stuff stashed in a sugar canister. Lou pays for his funeral and begins to court Susan Sarandon. Malle really pulls all the stops on everything here. Lou and Sally have their first real meeting at the hospital. She's racing down the hallway screaming, "I don't *want* the fucking body!" to a mortician, and in the background, Robert Goulet is dedicating the new Frank Sinatra wing of the hospital with the help of three showgirls in scarlet while confused patients shuffle about in stupors. The movie is filled with these kinds of satiric or eccentric moments, which almost force you to mutter: "Jesus, Americans are so tacky."

Lancaster is wonderful, and because of his and some of the other performances in the film, it is certainly worth your time. He has some really lovely moments and plays the kind of a guy who's been a nebbish all his life and for once gets to be the star, running the show. He keeps up a running stream of boasts and memories about the good old days, and eventually you realize he's son of a crackpot. Walking along the boardwalk, Sarandon's husband tells Lou he's never seen the Atlantic Ocean before. "Oh," says Lou, "you should have seen the Atlantic Ocean in the Forties. The Atlantic Ocean was great in the Forties." Reid is overdone but doesn't really overdo it as Grace. "I always wanted shoes with clear plastic heels," she tells Lou, "with goldfish swimming inside them because you 'd have to walk so delicately." Nice crackpots.

Hollis McLaren, who played the schizophrenic friend of Craig Russell in *Outrageous!,* here plays an equally spaced-out, pregnant hippie named Chrissie, Sarandon's sister. She gets it together with Grace, who hates her at first but succumbs after a foot rub and a lecture on Krishna. McLaren doesn't mind that her husband deals heroin. "Dope is for everybody," she tells her sister dreamily. And that's the way the movie feels about the American dream.

Lou and Sally have a "touching" little intergenerational affair. He proves himself by killing two dope-dealing thugs for her. Chrissie goes home to have her baby, the plane ticket paid for by good old Grace. Lou and Grace sell the last ounce of the stashed heroin together at the end and sail down the boardwalk with a fresh thousand–dollar bill. Sarandon heads for the nearest airport with the rest of the money in a stolen car, hoping to get to Monte Carlo to fulfill her dream. And the punk husband winds up dead, which is fine by everyone because he was such a bastard. America the beautiful!

What Does This Woman Smell Like?

New York Native — June 1, 1981

Meet the Fishpaws. Francine Fishpaw is a tragic, totally victimized American housewife whose husband, Elmer, runs the local porn theater, currently showing *My Burning Bush*. Being a good Catholic housewife, Francine is horrified by this and further humiliated by the picket lines outside their suburban home. "They spit on me at the shopping mall!" she wails to her fiendish husband. Francine's daughter, Lulu, is the high school tramp and her son, Dexter, is the Baltimore Foot Stomper, a criminally insane punk. Her only real friend is Cuddles, her former maid, who inherited a fortune and now spends her time shopping for debutante clothes. *Polyester* is the story of Francine Fishpaw's descent into misery, despair and alcoholism. "I look at my future," she sobs to Cuddles over a bottle of Scotch, "and all I see is a long highway filled with toll booths and no exits."

In many ways, *Polyester* is business-as-usual for director John Waters and the rest of the Baltimore Barrymores who gave us *Pink Flamingos, Female Trouble* and *Eat Your Makeup*. Waters hasn't let the prestige and power of 35 mm film and decent color cinematography — not to mention the presence of Tab Hunter — affect his profoundly disturbed and essentially filthy sensibility. Even with an "R" rating, *Polyester* once again recreates the world according to Waters in the same fundamentally distasteful ways we have come to expect from him.

At the center of the film is its greatest asset, Divine's performance as Francine Fishpaw. In a major departure from his previous work, Divine plays the long-suffering Francine absolutely straight. There isn't a hint of malice in the woman, none of the villainess of yore and not a trace of self-consciousness. Most surprising of all, there's no revenge exacted at the end. Francine Fishpaw is the American dishrag, the completely subjugated woman, and she's played to a fare-thee-well by Divine in the most inventive, tightly controlled performance in the film.

It's colorful and funny, but for me it's no *Female Trouble*, a true Waters epic. Edith Massey shleps around as Cuddles, the destitute man's Eve Arden. Ken King is terrific as Dexter, the angel-dusted psychopath, and Mink Stole does the sexy secretary who runs off with Francine's husband. But there is a major disappointment in the use of Tab Hunter as Todd Tomorrow, the hunk who promises to take Francine away from it all, only to betray her in the end. It's hard to tell whether he's used badly by Waters or whether he's just dull. In any case, like Elizabeth Taylor in *The Little Foxes*, he *looks* sensational. For some of us, that's enough.

There's a gimmick involved called Odorama. Scratch-and-sniff cards are provided with smells numbered from one to ten. On cue from the screen, one is supposed to scratch the right number and take a whiff of the action. The smells range from a rose to a fart (number two, for those of you who would rather pass) and at a certain point after the pizza smell, everything begins to run together. A much more effective piece of wizardry is the set decoration by Vincent Peranio, who turns Divine's suburban home into a velvet-flocked wallpaper and Mediterranean furniture circus. The opening sequence, in which the camera tracks through the house and discovers Divine sitting in the bedroom in a bra and girdle, is the best in the film.

I liked *Polyester*, but there were things I missed. At one point, Lulu calls Francine a "fat galoot." In any other Waters film, she'd have said, "Screw you, you fat fucking slob." The raunch of the language in Waters films was never and is not now incidental or disposable. It goes with the way the characters live, and its absence changes their frame of reference drastically. It's as though a group of black-and-white cartoons were dropped into a color film. One notices. But it's still trash. And for that we can be grateful.

Taxis and Tearooms

New York Native — **October 5, 1981**

Taxi Zum Klo (Taxi to the Toilet) is a new film from Germany that was shown last week at the New York Film Festival. A low budget premiere outing by writer, director, and actor Frank Ripploh, it is possibly the first film to raise sexual and emotional issues of contemporary male gay life in a funny, shocking and entertaining story about a guy who can't say no. It's going to cause him a lot of trouble.

Ripploh is a compulsive cruiser, the kind of guy you get to know real quick because you've seen his act at every subway toilet and backroom fuck bar in town, in this case Berlin. Frank is a schoolteacher who prowls around sex places every chance he gets and tries, in vain, to keep his job and his lover Bernd, a sweet thing who dreams of cooking dinners at a house in the country and petting little sheep on his days off. Frank's drag name is Peggy but she's no housewife. He is totally free sexually and very impatient with tradition, monogamy, fidelity or responsibility. Not to mention Bernd.

Taxi Zum Klo is a landmark film of stunning quality, considering its $50,000 budget, but, more than that, it does something few films, straight or gay, have ever done. It champions promiscuity as joyful, enriching and valid, putting the compressed pleasures of the moment on a par with a lifetime of relating. It does so implicitly. Frank is a likeable, funny fellow who is admired by his students. He meets Bernd at a late-night cinema, and they become lovers. What follows is a sort of classic melodrama which never becomes melodramatic. Frank corrects his students' papers while sitting on the john fondling a cock through a glory hole. Bernd is furious because his roast is ruined.

Behind the love story between Frank and Bernd, one lurching towards real life and screen disaster, is a commitment on the part of the filmmaker Ripploh to deal realistically with the modern gay male libido. The film derives its title from a sequence in which Ripploh, confined to a hospital bed with hepatitis, takes a taxi in his nightclothes to his favorite toilet to cruise for awhile and then speeds back to the hospital. Though the man obviously fancies himself something of a sexual catch, he is in fact rather ordinary, even sloppy and repulsive at times. It's his sense of irony about himself and his humor in the smallest of scenes which make him a pleasure to watch.

The conflict between Frank's lifestyle and his definition of relationship comes to a head at the annual drag ball, to which Frank goes as a fairy princess and Bernd as a sailor. Frank puts the make on a stable boy, he and Bernd argue, and by the time the dust settles it is early morning. Frank doesn't have time to go home to change and reports to school still in drag. He impulsively asks his students to act out some of the things they've always wanted to do but wouldn't dare, and the film ends on an anarchistic but confused note. Frank loses his job and Bernd as well.

Taxi Zum Klo is terrifically satisfying as a film and as politics. It is explicitly, sometimes disturbingly sexual and never sacrifices its point of view to balance or convention. Ripploh presents a case for a kind of gay relating which falls in between the two normally accepted options, promiscuity or monogamy. It doesn't "work" for Frank and Bernd because they don't find that middle ground. One wants to settle down and the other wants excitement, sexual danger and the challenge of the unconventional. The film points to a solution, but Ripploh "loses" in spite of his freedom.

The point of Ripploh's anthem to "being" should be to legitimize his experience for others. He realizes and acts out a grown-up truth which gay men are only beginning to learn. One can be whole and happy even in the midst of a lifestyle which seems based on transition and insecurity. But there's a romance about *Taxi Zum Klo* which belies Ripploh's lessons. Bernd is seen all hazy and Hallmark-wistful petting a sheep in a field. Alone, Frank is left to watch his eye makeup run in the mirror and ponder his unconventional triumph of style and sex. Come, now. These are traditional images of loss and defeat.

But *Taxi Zum Klo* has a lot going for it and must be seen. Ripploh's triumph is personal and professional. *Village Voice* critic Stuart Byron has correctly identified *Taxi* as "the first masterpiece about the mainstream of male gay life as it has developed since Stonewall." Yet you may wish to quibble with Ripploh's revolutionary outlook. It is my firm belief that most gay men, like most straights, abhor promiscuous behavior and that what they really want is a gay *Gone With the Wind* on screen, a traditional love story which will make them feel included in this charade we call society. So be it, though without my participation, please. Yet even they will not be able to ignore the fun and the sheer audacity of *Taxi Zum Klo*. A school in Berlin lost a good teacher, but we've gained a great moviemaker with a refreshingly cracked vision.

Mommie Dreariest

New York Native — **October 5, 1981**

Frank Perry's *Mommie Dearest* will do for battered children what *Lipstick* did for rape victims. Nothing. It looks like one of Joan Crawford's films of the mid- Fifties. In fact, it looks like *Queen Bee*, in which Betsy Palmer hangs herself in a closet because Joan's such a bitch. The design of the film is somewhere between Sam Fuller and Ross Hunter, an unlikeable, mean-spirited, yet impeccably glossy Technicolor extravaganza in which style overcomes content and obscures any possibility of meaning. An instant revival house classic, it should open immediately at the Regency and forget any first-run pretensions. *Mommie Dearest* belongs on a double bill with *Whatever Happened to Baby Jane?* Right now.

If you read and liked Christina Crawford's literary retribution against her adoptive mother you won't be sorry that it isn't a better film. Like the best-selling book, it is contemporary schlock horror that will be a tremendous crowd pleaser despite its considerable deficiencies. The people who love this movie are the crowds who ran to the Joan Crawford auction a few years back and snapped up all those old shoulder pads with a vengeance.

The opening sequence is stunning and the best in the film. Brilliantly edited, it promises a film experience that never materializes, documenting the early morning regimen of a working superstar with economy and precision. The rest of the picture is a heavy-handed construction of the unsubstantiated case against Crawford. Although the movie spans over thirty years in the life of the star, there are so many holes in the continuity that the viewer is never sure what year it is or which husband is in residence. The story omits mention of Crawford's two other children and concentrates on the trials of

Christina, giving much shorter shrift to little Christopher strapped to the bed.

Perhaps as an echo of the book's construct or the film's ad campaign, the picture is designed to give "the illusion of perfection." Crawford's house is probably the finest single achievement of the film, a lavish color coordinated palace reflecting the star's Harriet Craig complex. The trouble is that in thirty years there isn't an indication that an ashtray has been moved across a table. Surely Joan would have redecorated between 1939 and 1955. She gets old but the set decorator never changes the bedspread. The whole film is shiny-new. There isn't a gritty or realistic thing in it, not even the dirt in the garden during the world-famous rosebush chopping scene. ("Christina! Get the axe!") The newsreel cameras that arrive to photograph Christina's birthday party are as spotless and new as the clothes on the journalists who use them. Everything is seen through the eyes of a cinematographer on one of Crawford's old movies, and if that's supposed to be the point, it's a small one.

Faye Dunaway's electrifying portrait of Joan Crawford makes *Mommie Dearest* a much more important experience than it has a right to be. She works so hard so long that she creates a gallery of memorable moments with staying power. But that's the kind of movie it is. You'll hear everyone telling the Pepsi board meeting scene over and over again. People will gleefully recount the night of the wire coat hanger and powdered cleanser rampage. But the blanks are never filled properly. You never understand why Crawford went on binges. There's The Promiscuity Scene, fuck-me pumps held grandly aloft. There's the She Used to Drink Sometimes scene. There's even a When She Won the Oscar   scene. But there's no attempt at insight into the relationship between Crawford's personal temperament and her fierce career ambitions. We're supposed to buy that she beat the kids because they make noise while she's trying to get some sleep.

Diana Scarwid, whom I loved in *Inside Moves*, is just weird as Christina. She acts the part of a petulant ten-year-old even when she's supposed to be twenty-five. Female impersonators will get a lot of mileage out of her Southern accented "Why did you adopt me?" scene. Much better by far is the young Mara Hobel as baby Christina, who, after her mother has dragged her out of bed, beaten her with a coat hanger and slammed the hell out of her with powdered cleanser, sits amid the wreckage and whispers quietly in her mother's grown-up voice, "Jesus Christ!" My sentiments exactly when the lights came up. I didn't like it; I wish I hadn't gone to see it, and you shouldn't go either.

The Women

New York Native — October 19, 1981

George Cukor's *Rich and Famous* is a pleasant surprise. The gossip surrounding the shooting of the film in New York last year had Cukor senile and nodding out in the middle of scenes. I pictured something like Vincente Minnelli's tragic swan song *A Matter of Time* or Billy Wilder's successful but still disappointing *Fedora*, the work of directors well past their peak who refused to lie down. But *Rich and Famous*, while not one of Cukor's classic sophisticated comedies of the golden years, is a beautifully made, old-fashioned movie with a beginning, middle, and an end. It's got energy, charm and a literate screenplay. It's also extremely stylish, recalling the glamour of films from a different age.

Rich and Famous is a remake of Vincent Sherman's 1943 Bette Davis/Miriam Hopkins shoot-out *Old Acquaintance*, a likeable chestnut which is not challenged by this new version. Jacqueline Bisset and Candice Bergen play the Davis/Hopkins roles respectively, as a writer of serious art and a pulp fiction peddler who attain wealth and success but end up alone in the end. Much of the spark of the original film was generated by the chemistry between Davis and Hopkins, who hated each other cordially and tore up the screen. But *Rich and Famous* better illuminates the nature of the friendship between the two women, and though Bisset and Bergen have their moments, it doesn't rest on fireworks between two powerhouse performers.

The film opens at Smith College in 1959, Bergen leaving school before graduation to marry and settle in Malibu, saying goodbye to Bisset at the railroad station. Ten years later, Bisset is an unmarried feminist writer who agonizes over her work. She is lecturing at UCLA, and Bergen is a prissy Southern housewife who has written a trashy expose of her Malibu beach colony neighbors. Bisset plays the far more interesting character of the two, a Scotch-drinking, fairly promiscuous, vital and intelligent woman with complex ideas and feelings about everything. But Bergen's portrait of the shallow, petulant overnight success is really her best screen performance, and she tackles it so lustily, it becomes the highlight of the picture.

Like the original, *Rich and Famous* is a traditional movie with lots of glamour, fabulous clothes and witty dialogue. It covers a lot of ground and uses an economy rare in current films, taking us from 1959 to 1981 without resorting to montages and other tricks. The story runs true to the John Van Druten play from which it is taken but updates some of the sexual and emotional issues that were taboo in the 1940s. When *Old Acquaintance* began shooting, the Breen Office ordered certain cuts because the Bette Davis character was "obviously having an affair with a younger man" and script contained "gross illicit sex, alcoholism and numerous affairs."

All of this is explicit in *Rich and Famous*, and it is sometimes rather shocking even by the standards of today's films. Bisset has sex with a man in the toilet of an airplane while landing at Kennedy airport and picks up a stunning hustler on Fifth Avenue, but both scenes are filmed with the old George Cukor charm. One feels that the edited Claire Bloom scenes from *The Chapman Report* might have looked like this.

Rich and Famous is a modern, entertaining soap opera. It is not a mess, something which cannot be said of most popular films these days. It also has a sense of humor about itself — as in the Malibu party scene, when Bergen says, "Half of Hollywood is here," and the camera pans the terrace to pick out Christopher Isherwood, Don Bachardy, Ray Bradbury, Gavin Lambert, Nina Foch, Roger Vadim and Paul Morrissey, a strange collection at best. Bergen refers to a Rock Hudson–type actor as having become "*far* too familiar with drugs, some of which he puts up his nose!" Bisset, on the other hand, must manage lines like "I was very young. Paris was very old. He was intense. I was shy." She doesn't have the style Davis had saying, "It's late and I'm tired of youth and love and self-sacrifice," but she does have some of the assurance of that actress and even some of her mannerisms, especially when angry.

In some senses, *Rich and Famous* is a "gay film" the way some pictures used to be called "women's films." The relationships between men and women in this picture are intelligent, and people relate and move in a sophisticated way.

I don't know why that should be unusual but I guess it has something to do with the reaction to the *Raiders of the Lost Ark* syndrome of grunts and groans on the screen lately. Cukor has made an old-fashioned film and for that we are grateful. I saw it twice just to see Bergen's reaction to a young reporter at the Algonquin Hotel. It is worth your time.

Pentimento

New York Native — **August 15, 1983**

It's clever of Woody Allen to have released his priceless new film *Zelig* during the annual summer hack wave so as to shine all the brighter against such nitwit hits as *Flashdance, Staying Alive* and the latest *Porky's* pig-out. *Zelig* is an artistic and technical jewel of a film which would shine in any season. Set alongside *Jaws 3-D* it's a positive miracle. I'm sure the summer release is a calculated move on the part of Allen and company. *Zelig* needs a "masterpiece" buildup if it's to survive the inevitable backlash when it begins playing the hinterlands. Like its title character, the film lacks emotional identification. It's a sort of *Star Wars* for intellectuals, a virtuoso display of impertinence and movie magic.

The strange case of one Leonard Zelig, played by Allen, is told in old newsreel footage and photo montage so convincingly faked that for the first fifteen minutes we are still waiting for the film to begin. The docu-fraud is so complete that it is matchless in our film-going experience. It produces a rare sense of wonder such as people must have felt in the early part of this century when D.W. Griffith used the camera in a new way for the first time.

Leonard Zelig is a man so terrified of asserting himself that he takes on the physical characteristics of those he's with when threatened. In the style of Movietone News we learn that Zelig's condition made him as famous in the 1920s as Lindbergh. In his diary, F. Scott Fitzgerald remembers Zelig at a party on Long Island, noting that he seemed a waspish Republican with the guests and a working class Democrat when talking to the servants. We see Zelig in old photos with Eugene O'Neill, Jack Dempsey and President Hoover. He is visible in old sports footage, warming up behind Babe Ruth in a Yankee uniform. Impeccably aged film shows Zelig as an Asian, a Native American, a Black jazz musician, an elderly Greek. Standing next to a fat man, he grows huge. Zelig comes to the attention of the psychiatric establishment.

Allen observes that in America, one can become a very famous doctor or a very famous patient. Zelig becomes a national curiosity and the pet project of a gentle psychoanalyst, played enchantingly by Mia Farrow. Zelig captures the imagination of the public and becomes a byword of the jazz age. The tabloid newspapers dub him "Chameleon Man." Fanny Brice sings him a song atop the Ziegfeld roof. Al Jolson slips his name into a lyric. Helen Kane (The "Boop-Oop-A-Doo" girl) records a hit called "Chameleon Days." The Lizard Dance sweeps the nation and Zelig is given a ticker tape parade down lower Broadway. In France, Zelig is termed a symbol "of absolutely everything."

Zelig is eventually cured of his unwanted affliction with the (secretly filmed) help of Mia Farrow, whom he marries. But not before the tide of public opinions turns on him. After being exploited by his sister and her oily husband like a sideshow freak, chorus girls and creditors come out of the woodwork far and wide to slap him with polygamy suits and old subpoenas. Finally, Zelig disappears only to turn up later at a Nuremberg rally, behind and just slightly to the left of Hitler during a speech. He spots Farrow in the crowd and waves shyly. It's a great sequence, Zelig blending impishly into what threatens Allen most.

We, of course, never come to "understand" Zelig. A newsreel has no heart and our distance from Zelig's personal feelings about his predicament reflects Allen's own confusion about the nature of fame, the human urge to fit in, and his purpose on this planet. Zelig became like the people around him because he didn't want to stick out, be wrong. He wanted people to like and accept him so he became them. At parties he didn't want to admit he hadn't read *Moby Dick*. *Zelig* is an extension of Allen's lifelong fear of being hated for being famous. Zelig is actually a fairly ordinary schmuck whose father, on his deathbed, said that life is one long miserable journey, urging him to "save string." That he should become famous is out of proportion with his sensibility.

Leonard Zelig is, in fact, one of the more painful Allen alter egos. Think of it. What if one was so afraid of standing apart that one developed the physical ability to blend in. And then became famous for that ability, standing apart even more. Allen is famous for not wanting to be famous lest the crowd turn on him. Happily for all concerned, especially those of us sitting out there in dark, he continues to voice his confusion in ways that produce screen art. *Zelig* isn't as romantically charming or as genuinely real as *Annie Hall* and it's not even as wildly funny as *Love and Death*. But it's a flawless counterfeit, a perfect marriage of form and content. It's the kind of thing made by a man who'd like to be at his own funeral. A famous man who wants to be left alone.

Doña Herlinda's Sweet Subversions

The Advocate — June 10, 1986

Jaime Humberto Hermosillo's new film, *Doña Herlinda and Her Son*, is a deliciously funny, offbeat comedy about mother love and the sweet subversion of social convention. Doña Herlinda is an upper-middle-class Guadalajara widow who has a beautiful house and a son who's a doctor. For some mothers this would be enough, but not for Doña Herlinda — her handsome but decidedly dreary son Rodolfo has an equally handsome musician boyfriend named Ramon.

Far from discouraging this relationship, the sphinx-like Doña Herlinda encourages it, innocently suggesting that Ramon move into her house. ("Rodolfo has *such* a big bed.") Yet while Ramon and Rodolfo make love quite audibly in the next room, Doña Herlinda sits in bed serenely leafing through magazines filled with pictures of wedding gowns. Mama has plans of her own. You can almost hear the wheels turning.

Doña Herlinda is omnipresent. In the opening sequence of the film she interrupts her son and his lover having sex--not once, but twice, by both beeper and telephone. This sets the tone for her omnipotent control of the proceedings throughout the film. With crackpot simplicity and a fatuous smile, Doña Herlinda keeps her son's lover distracted with movies, ice cream sodas and shopping sprees so that mama's big boy will be free to court a young lady named Olga, who will provide respectability and—eventually--grandchildren.

The plot works. Rodolfo married Olga, and Ramon serves as best man. Wife and lover discover that they have more in common than just sharing the same man and become friends. When Olga goes into labor with her first child, Ramon is busy fucking Rodolfo in the bedroom. Ramon becomes the child's godfather. Mama provides the final touch by building a luxurious new house where they will all live happily ever after--mother, son, wife, baby and lover. Doña Herlinda's final beatific smile is triumphant.

Hermosillo handles this revolutionary (for Mexico) subject matter with the same lightheaded simplicity he gives Doña Herlinda herself. None of the actors has ever worked in a film before, and they give the impression that this unlikely story is taking place in upper-middle-class homes all over Mexico. Doña Herlinda is the kind of woman who, in real life, would be described as a vicious, controlling bitch. Yet here she's lovable and charming, the perfect doting mother who sees only what she wants to see and lets everyone have their way--as long as she gets hers as well.

The least attractive character in this captivating tale is Rodolfo, the apple of everyone's eye. A handsome, hairy mama's boy, he is fawned over, fussed about and protected from any harsh realities. If his mother isn't in the kitchen cooking for him, it's his lover or his wife. Rodolfo expresses no preference except to be served by life in the most convenient possible manner. This is cultural. A central issue in the film is the fact that Rodolfo is a traditional Mexican male who expects both his lover and his wife to remain feminine. The twist, of course, is that mama runs the show and Rodolfo ends up in the feminine role, both sexually and socially. His wife has plans of her own; to leave the baby with mama and spend a year getting involved in politics. Rodolfo could end up as much a smiling idiot as his mother, but with no similar satisfaction.

There are enough laughs in *Doña Herlinda and Her Son* to make up for the occasional awkwardness of the neophyte actors. Guadalupe Del Toro's performance is enchanting and alone worth the price of admission. Hermosillo has fashioned the kind of comedy that wins over even the most conservative audiences while giving the rest of us plenty to enjoy on a level that the general public won't even visit.

Russo on Film

Although Vito was a frequent freelance contributor to The Advocate over many years —as he was to numerous other publications — he was given a regular column in the prestigious and widely read gay newsmagazine near the end of his life. These following articles are his views and news on the queer cinema of the late-1980s. His column, "Russo on Film," appeared once a month in the biweekly Advocate until his death from AIDS in 1990.

Spellbound in Darkness

Ken Russell's *Salome*: Gutter and Spit
in the Eye of Sanity

May 10, 1988

In Ken Russell's new film, *Salome's Last Dance,* the director has an unbilled cameo role as a photographer in a male bordello. He looks like Santa Claus in a Coca-Cola commercial and is photographing for posterity a production of Oscar Wilde's *Salome,* which is being presented for the author. It is Guy Fawkes Day, 1892, and on this evening Wilde will be arrested for his crimes against nature. "If your acting is as indecent as your photographic studies," Wilde tells Russell before the curtain rises, "we're in for an outrageous evening."

So begins another Russell odyssey into erotic camp and outlandish costume. You never know what you're going to get with Russell. His cinematic obsessions have cured my insomnia more than once. Yet I keep coming back because, like the musicals of Stephen Sondheim, Russell's films demand to be seen even when they don't work.

Salome's Last Dance works beautifully. Because Russell is secure about his own voice in this outing, the film is intentionally hilarious. It is also mercifully brief, a mere ninety minutes. That's no small favor to someone like myself, who thinks absolutely everything these days is much too long. The film itself hardly exists; it's just an elaborate excuse for what is probably the definitive production of Wilde's *Salome.* A grand old time is had by all.

We know exactly what kind of territory we're entering as soon as Wilde is informed that the exotic aroma he detects in the Victorian drawing room of this male whorehouse is "a blend of green carnations and the pubic hair of virgins." As a metaphor for the deterioration of the public and private Oscar Wilde, the action framing the main event is pretty straightforward. The production of *Salome*, however, is fairly dazzling. There are three drag queens right off the boat from Fire Island, gossiping about Jesus' miracles, and three midgets dressed as rabbis, who argue about everything. There's also Glenda Jackson playing Herodias as a deranged Auntie Marne. When Herod offers to give Salome the veil from the sanctuary if she will dance for him, the entire cast yells, "Oy vey!"

Apart from the astonishingly good performance of Imogene Millais Scott, who plays Salome, Russell's film offers the kind of delirious abnormality that is fast becoming endangered. With the death of Divine and the advent of films like James Bridges' dreadful *Bright Lights, Big City*, I'd say we need all the glitter we can get. So much the better if it happens to spit in the eye of sanity.

A full-page ad in the March 18 issue of Daily Variety read, "MYTH: 'If I play a gay role, I'll never work in this town again.'" Under the heading "FACT," the ad then listed ninety-six famous actors and actresses who have played gay characters. The ad was placed by producer Jerry B. Wheeler, who has made no secret of the difficulty he's been having casting the role of the coach in his proposed screen version of Patricia Nell Warren's *The Front Runner*. Wheeler has a deal with Hemdale Releasing Corporation, and Marshall W. Mason is set to direct.

I assume that the problem is probably that Hemdale wants a star in the role of the coach to ensure box office. I may be way out of line here, but I think that's a mistake. Sure, it would be nice to have a Harrison Ford or a Jeff Bridges playing a gay part in a major motion picture, but I thought we'd learned this lesson with *Making Love*. I'll say it again for what I hope is the last time: Major motion pictures targeted at a mass audience have to reach the lowest common denominator out there, and in doing so they must necessarily sacrifice all the things that make a movie exciting.

The Front Runner would make a great and potentially profitable independent film. It is my opinion that Hemdale and Wheeler should courageously forget about trying to turn *The Front Runner* into a Hollywood film and make a really magnificent independent with unknowns. If *The Front Runner* is a good film, people will flock to see it without a star. If it's a compromised, mass-audience feature, even Tom Selleck as the coach won't save it. That's why *Parting Glances* is infinitely more satisfying than *Making Love*. Movies should not be produced with the goal of making homosexuality "popular." I'd rather see a good movie than a star vehicle. Guts, please.

Vanities of the Nitwits

Low Laughs and High Stakes in the Movies This May

June 7, 1988

There is nothing in Harvey Keith's documentary *Mondo New York* that hasn't been seen or done before. This pathetic little tour of downtown Manhattan is a desperate plea for attention by a group of people referred to in the production notes as "anti-stars." Actually, they're anti-talents.

At the kickoff, some greasy moron who claims to worship Richard Speck bites the heads off two live white mice and sets off some fireworks on his chest. Then you visit a cockfight, a Chinese slave auction (asleep yet?), an S-M club, and a voodoo ceremony at which a chicken is decapitated.

The performance artists who appear in the film include John Sex, singing "Hustle with My Muscle"; Dean Johnson, singing "Fuck You"; and Karen Finley, who covers herself in raw eggs and sequins to deliver a monologue on greed.

This is all old news to anyone who was alive and awake twenty-five years ago. If these people really cared about the lack of values in this society, they wouldn't be torturing animals for entertainment. One sequence, shot in Washington Square Park, features two very talented and funny comics named Charlie Barnett and Rick Aviles. They are in the wrong film. *Mondo New York* makes you want to take a shower and vote for George Bush. It's the best argument I can imagine for the gentrification of the Lower East Side.

The new comedy *Casual Sex?,* directed by Genevieve Roberts, is just an old teen beach movie with updated language. Two girlfriends check into a health spa in California to meet boys, and both end up happily married. The alleged twist here is that they are both afraid to sleep around because they're scared of getting AIDS. When one of them discovers, in her doctor's office, that she has tested negative for the virus, she falls to her knees and starts babbling that from now on she'll be a good girl.

There's something really slimy about squeezing adolescent laughs out of the AIDS crisis, especially in this nitwit context. We are constantly told by the media that the heterosexual risk of AIDS is roughly equivalent to the risk of getting hit on the head by a falling piano. Yet virtually all the public AIDS education is targeted directly at this allegedly low-risk group, and now movies meant as light entertainment use fear of the epidemic as an excuse for teenage comedy. AIDS panic among heterosexuals exists now for the same reasons people go to cheap horror movies. They like being scared without actually being in any danger. It stinks.

Meanwhile, the battle continues to get a serious movie about AIDS produced. Barbra Streisand has failed to go into production with a screen version of Larry Kramer's *The Normal Heart* after two years of fitful negotiations with the playwright. He finally asked her if she would release the property, and the latest word is that David Picker, former president of Columbia Pictures and Kramer's old boss at United Artists, will produce *The Normal Heart* with an all-star cast. The script is finished, and money is no problem, but an all-star cast demands a star director, and at the moment that's the hitch. John Schlesinger said yes and then said no. James Bridges just said no, as did Norman Jewison. And the quest continues. In the mean time, Kramer has written a political farce about Nancy Reagan called *Just Say No*, and Charles Busch is reading the script with his eye on the lead.

An interview with Lily Tomlin published in the latest *American Film* magazine reveals that there are some gratuitous antigay situations in her new film with Bette Midler, *Big Business*, which Tomlin and her partner, Jane Wagner, were unable to change during shooting. According to Tomlin, director Jim Abrahams thinks that the idea of a man being attracted to another man is a joke in itself. Tomlin and Wagner tried to place the humor in the context of the situation, but Abrahams was having none of it, and once again homosexuality is the punch line and homosexuals are the punching bags.

Tomlin has been increasingly outspoken about what an unpleasant experience making *Big Business* was for her. Midler, on the other hand, apparently has no powers of analysis and never seems to notice such things.

She didn't notice a tasteless reference to AIDS in *Down and Out in Beverly Hills* and her comments about working at the Continental Baths in a recent *Vanity Fair* interview revealed a woefully limited consciousness about the politics of the AIDS crisis and gay sexuality in general. Some people are just willfully stupid about anything that doesn't pertain directly to their own careers.

Lost treasures from the troves of gay film history are constantly coming to light, but seldom do we find a sympathetic gay hero emerging from the days when sissies were good for nothing but a quick laugh. The 1938 Australian film *Dad and Dave Come to Town*, one of a popular Ma and Pa Kettle-type series directed by Ken G. Hall, provides us with such a character.

Mr. Entwistle, played by Alec Kellaway (Cecil's brother), is an effeminate floorwalker in a dress shop who foils a plot by a rival shop to put the store out of business and becomes the hero of the film. Kellaway's portrait of an outrageous queen into taking control of his business joins the ranks of the best of Franklin Pangborn and Eric Blore.

The Torch Is Lit

Fierstein Play Before Lens with Stellar Cast

October 5, 1988

Harvey Fierstein's Tony Award-winning drama *Torch Song Trilogy* has finally started filming in New York under the direction of Paul Bogart. The dazzling cast, headed by Fierstein in the leading role of Arnold, includes Anne Bancroft as his mother; Matthew Broderick as his lover, Alan; Ken Page as Murray, the wisecracking friend; and Charles Pierce as one of Arnold's sister drag queens.

Fierstein, in a recent telephone conversation, found it difficult to contain his exuberance. "Even I can't believe it," he says. "It's so gay! It's like a hundred times gayer than the play. Finally, something that can be called a real gay movie. I just keep thinking, Jesus Christ! A movie where the straight people are the strange ones."

Originally, New Line Productions, the company that put up the money, was nervous about a movie with back-room sex scenes in the age of AIDS. "They got over it," says Fierstein. "Let's face it; the action takes place in the 1970s, and besides, this is our history. I'm not covering up who we are. Also, anybody who would bitch about AIDS when they see this movie would be the first one to scream 'whitewash' if we left it out."

The scene they are shooting on the day of our telephone talk is the one in which Matthew Broderick is murdered in New York's Tomkins Park by teenage fag bashers. "Just think of the effect," says Fierstein. "Matthew is a teen idol now, and to have the audience love him in the first part of the film and then watch him get bashed to death by teenagers for being a faggot will be devastating. Matthew usually gets three and a half million a film, and he did this film for virtually no money because he believes so much in it."

Torch Song Trilogy will wrap on July 15 for a December release. Fierstein says he wants the proceeds from the opening-night benefit to go to people with AIDS, the Antigay Violence Project and The Institute for the Protection of Lesbian and Gay Youth. The outspoken, fiercely committed writer-performer has been exceptionally busy. He just completed filming "Tidy Endings," the third act of his latest play, *Safe Sex*, for HBO. The story of the confrontation between the wife and the lover of a man who has died of AIDS was directed by Gavin Miller (*Dreamchild*) and stars Stockard Channing opposite Fierstein. It airs next August.

Phil Zwickler's acclaimed documentary about the stormy battle for the New York gay rights bill, *Rights and Reactions*, will be aired on KCET, in Los Angeles, this month. A hit at the Berlin Film Festival, the film opened in Boston in May and had its New York theatrical premiere at the Film Forum on June 15. The producers of the film version of Hubert Selby Jr.'s novel *Last Exit to Brooklyn* are looking for someone to play the lead role of Georgette, described as "an eighteen –to-twenty-year-old boy who is witty, flamboyant, energetic and passionately romantic." Send photos and resumes to Deborah Aquila and Jeffrey Passero at Deborah Aquila Casting in New York City.

Losing it at the Movies

**Escapist Fare Dominates San Francisco
Gay Film Festival**

August 2, 1988

San Francisco's twelfth annual International Lesbian and Gay Film Festival began on a political note this year when Mayor Art Agnos exhorted a capacity opening-night crowd at the Castro Theater to raise their voices against a rising tide of antigay sentiment. Referring to the "Silence = Death" buttons worn by some people, Agnos told the audience that "silence is always an ally of the powerful over the vulnerable."

Few of the films at this year's festival matched the political passion of the mayor's opening-night speech, but an increasingly apolitical generation of San Francisco gays did not seem to notice, being either silent themselves or dead from the neck up. This is now a city divided between battle-scarred older gay men who are weary of the struggle and a younger generation who think they are immortal and have no reason to fight. Both groups packed the Castro Theater nightly for ten days--a record twenty-thousand people--searching not for meaning but for escape.

Escape was in plentiful supply at what is still the best, most exciting and most comprehensive festival of its kind in the world. The opening-night offering was Pedro Almodovar's 1983 feature *Dark Habits*, a pleasant enough one-joke comedy about a convent filled with outrageous, irreverent nuns (Sister Manure and Sister Sewer Rat among them), who harbor a tacky bolero singer on the lam from the police. *Dark Habits* serves to fill in an early career gap for those of us devoted to this rising young Spanish director, and we await even more eagerly his latest film, *Women on the Verge of a*

Nervous Breakdown, which Orion Pictures has just picked up for worldwide distribution.

The fun continued, unabated, with the festival's tribute to the late Divine, an evening of film clips from *Pink Flamingos, Polyester, Female Trouble* and *Hairspray*, among others. The show opened with the famous dog-doo-eating scene from *Pink Flamingos* and closed with the scene of Divine being raped by a giant lobster in *Multiple Maniacs*. Or maybe it was *Mondo Trasho*. But it was definitely a giant lobster.

Director John Waters was on hand to accept this year's Frameline Award for his superstar, and, of course, the audience was nearly as colorful as the action on-screen. Asked *by San Francisco Chronicle* writer Edward Guthmann to relate some of his fondest memories of Divine, Waters replied, "The time we went shoplifting and Divine walked out with a chain saw in one hand and a TV set in another and didn't get caught."

Derek Jarmans' new film, *The Last of England*, a non-narrative collage about Britain today, pleased a minority of hard-core fans but outraged most of the audience with its experimental structure and assaultive editing techniques. This was not a crowd prepared to do its own thinking in response to disconnected imagery. More to their taste was Stefan Henszelman's 1986 Danish film *Friends Forever*, about a handsome sixteen-year-old boy named Kristian, who has a crisis when he discovers that his equally handsome best friend, Patrick, is gay and is having an affair with the captain of a soccer team.

Handsome is the operative word here. On a warm and sunny Saturday afternoon, more than one-thousand gay men jammed the Castro Theater to see a twelve-minute French short called *Bel Ragazzo*, simply because of a widely publicized still photograph of its star in a tom T-shirt. That *Bel Ragazzo* is a nice film is beside the point. This audience's response was to an armpit and an exposed tit. Maybe next year Frameline should start showing cartoons.

For the grown-ups, there were British shorts, a group of well-made, colorful and informative pieces that were decidedly political in nature. It would be a little odd if they weren't, considering what's going on in England (with Section 28) at the moment.

Richard Kwietniowski's *Alfalfa* has been deservedly praised on two continents. Described as a fag's thesaurus for those in the know, the film raises more issues about gay sensibility through mainstream language in nine minutes than most features do in two hours.

Charlotte Metcalf's *Vivat Regina* explores the possibility that the London production of *La Cage aux Folles* was prematurely closed because of panic over AIDS. Although the film relies more heavily on camp attraction than is perhaps necessary ("I'm still big!" says one character. "It's David Merrick who got smaller!"), it gives a good sense of the political climate wrought by AIDS in Britain today.

A handsome, expensively mounted soap opera from Australia also packed the theater, thanks largely to the presence of its pretty star, Mark Lee, of *Gallipoli* fame. Michael Thornhill's *The Everlasting Secret Family* is perhaps the silliest gay film ever made, an overwrought combination of *Dynasty* and *The Picture of Dorian Gray*. This story of a group of powerful businessmen and politicians who recruit young men into their secret homosexual society has been attacked by some as dangerous and homophobic. Perhaps, but it's a moot point because hardly anyone will ever get the chance to see it. Hemdale, its American distributor, has already dumped it directly onto the home video market without a theatrical release. This is an illustration of one of the chief functions of a gay film festival. The San Francisco audience was among the few groups of people who will ever see this film on a large screen.

Another, more important, purpose of a gay film festival was also achieved this year in the discovery of a talented young independent filmmaker from Los Angeles named Gregg Araki, whose *Three Bewildered People in the Night* was a festival highlight. Writer-producer-director Araki spent only five thousand dollars on this gritty black-and-white feature and, shooting at night with minimal lighting, has painted a vivid portrait of the adolescent alienation that has come to symbolize his home city. Araki is so talented; one wishes he had more to say. The uncharitable might remark that one wishes he had something to say. The ambivalence of his three characters, one of whom is a gay performance artist, quickly becomes annoying.

The film is about three young and allegedly creative people who don't know what to create and aren't sure what they want to do with their lives. Film should explore these feelings and somehow make sense of them, illuminating something in the characters that helps us understand our own ambivalence. These three characters, especially the gay one, just whine. They piss and moan about their lives when it's clear they don't have lives to moan about.

Black coffee and cigarettes are not the meaning of life. It was difficult, during this festival screening, to ignore the irony: an audience containing many people with AIDS, people who are hanging on to their precious lives by their fingernails, watching a movie about privileged, self-indulgent adolescents who want to commit suicide because they're bored. Still, one wishes Araki well. It would be nice to see what he can do with a lot of money and a different subject.

The festival, as in past years, also revived several old films for examination by a new generation. It was a great pleasure to see the rare 1957 version of *Maedchen in Uniform*, starring Lili Palmer and Romy Schneider, in a beautiful 35-millimeter print in glorious color. Unfortunately, a screening of the 1936 classic *Dracula's Daughter* was marred by audience members' mindless knee-jerk booing of sexist remarks, which prevented more sophisticated audience members from hearing all the dialogue. Apparently it's big news to some people that fifty years ago, movies were often sexist. Some audiences don't know the difference between fascism and feminism.

The historical coup of the festival was a screening of a beautifully restored print of Mauritz Stiller's 1916 film *Wings*, perhaps the first gay film ever made. Although the film is little more than a beautiful curiosity, the screening, accompanied by live organ music, was a special event. Gay historian Alan Berube introduced the film by pointing out that *Wings* was made before his parents were born. He said it provided him with a window into gay life of another era.

The festival hosted many guest filmmakers, among them the aforementioned Araki, who wins the festival hairdo award; Greta Schiller and Andrea Weiss, who premiered their new film, *Tiny and Ruby Hell Divin' Women*; and Monica Treut, whose latest feature, *The Virgin Machine*, closed the proceedings.

But the entire two-week festival was dominated by the physical and spiritual presence of the preeminent experimental artists James Broughton and Barbara Hammer, who were at every screening. Hammer screened her new video, *No No Nookie TV,* exploring the feminist controversy around sexuality with electronic language, and Broughton was honored on the occasion of his seventy-fifth birthday with screenings of his films. The work of both filmmakers has recently been made available on video.

Finally, this year's festival spotlighted a group of videos that included an all-day symposium on AIDS at the Roxie Theater. This is the kind of programming that should be encouraged. It seems that video makers are much more political and willing to be more dangerous in their attitudes than filmmakers are. Although there are economic reasons for this, video seems to lend itself to a more radical exploration of gay life than film is attempting at this moment in history.

By way of a small observation, it is alarming how basic and unimaginative the majority of AIDS videos are, compared with those on other subjects. Ten years into this epidemic, videos aimed at education are still in their "AIDS 101" phase, describing what T-cells are and self-consciously calling for condom use by teenagers. If this is all that's out there, we're in a lot of trouble.

Now, on to Los Angeles for that city's gay and lesbian film festival, beginning July 8. A highlight will be the screening of lengthy, completely restored clips from Andy Warhol's greatest early films, including *Blow Job*, *My Hustler*, *Lonesome Cowboys* and *Kiss*.

Cocktails and Fish

Swimming against the Mainstream

August 30, 1988

Movies are so aggressively heterosexual this summer that even those of us who hate both winter and Christmas are praying for December so we can wallow in *Torch Song Trilogy*. Tom Cruise's latest film, *Cocktail*, arrived amid the August doldrums and has all the requirements of a blockbuster hit. A sex comedy written specifically for the nitwit population, it's about rich white people, has crab jokes and features an MTV score guaranteed to overwhelm the feeble acting and direction.

Cruise plays an Irish version of John Travolta's character in *Saturday Night Fever*, an ambitious boy from Queens who comes home from the Army determined to make a fortune in the business world. The trouble is that cutie pie isn't very bright, you see. But he does have a dazzling little smile. After a few stabs at reading a book, he decides that the wonderful world of bartending in singles clubs will provide him with a ticket to the top. Assisted by a seasoned sleaze bucket (Bryan Brown), he learns to toss bottles in the air and spot rich women on the make. This makes him attractive to the type of woman to whom such behavior is attractive, and he's on his way.

Cocktail is a duplicitous film that spends two hours making promiscuous sex, drinking, smoking, false values and macho sexism look attractive and then turns around in the last ten minutes to say that fidelity and loyalty are really where it's at. Tom Cruise has been running around the country giving thousands of interviews in which he describes *Cocktail* as though it were some sort of low-budget independent art film instead of the manipulative trash is really is. Two weeks ago he told a reporter, "I don't think it's my job to educate people on safe sex. Do I have to wear a condom in my scenes on the screen? This is an R-rated film. This is the 1980s. There is AIDS. There is alcoholism. People should be able to figure it out for themselves."

If the New York preview audience was any indication, they've already figured it out. People are hip to the marketing strategy in New York. It was so obvious that this was an advertisement for dangerous behavior that the ultimate cop-out to morality at the film's end was all but laughed off the screen. When the lights came up, Cruise's co-star, Elizabeth Shue, turned to me and asked, "Why was the audience so cynical? They all laughed at the happy ending. They didn't do that in Los Angeles!"

I rest my case.

As long as we're on the subject of stinkers, I might as well offer the dissenting opinion on a film virtually everybody seems to think is hilarious. I thought Charles Chriton's *A Fish Called Wanda* was the dreariest waste of valuable time since Lee Radziwill remade *Laura*. I'm treading on thin ice here, because people who are fans of what I call Monty Python-type humor are as rabidly loyal to it as Judy Garland freaks were to the lady herself.

A Fish Called Wanda starts out promisingly enough. It's about a bunch of deliriously crackpot jewel thieves who spend their time trying to stab each other in the back at every turn. This is a time-honored device, and it's worked in countless films--but not this time. First you have to buy the premise that everybody in London wants to fuck Jamie Lee Curtis. Okay, this isn't real life; it's farce. But then you have to go with endless dreary and, quite frankly, cruel jokes revolving around stutterers, gays and animal torture.

I think black humor is just swell. But in order to make it work, the audience has to like the characters and then relish all the horrible little things they perpetrate from a position of conspiracy. It's impossible to get with any of these people. John Cleese represents repressed British sexuality let loose. How's that for a hot new idea? Kevin Kline plays the kind of sexist moron real people cross the street to avoid in bad neighborhoods. When Kline pretends to be gay to pry information from another crook, it's so Neanderthal in concept that you just want to leave the theater. If you want to save seven dollars, you won't go in the first place.

Start voting with your wallet. They'll keep making these dogs if you're willing to ay for them. If you're set on a late-summer mainstream movie, go see Tom Hanks in *Big*. Or even *Who Framed Roger Rabbit*. If you've already seen them, go again. Hanks gives a perfectly lovely performance in *Big*, and the scene where he and his boss tap out "Heart and Soul" and "Chopsticks" on a giant piano at F.A.O. Schwarz is absolutely enchanting. *Roger Rabbit* deserves to be seen twice, if only because it's impossible to catch all the tricks the first time around. These films are sentimental and manipulative, but they're honest about it, and they aren't insulting or dangerous to your psychic well-being.

The Temptation of Acceptable Lies

Why No Protest of the Whitewashing of Gay Lives?

September 27, 1988

Five years ago, when Martin Scorsese originally announced his intention to film *The Last Temptation of Christ*, fundamentalists all over the United States objected in principle because they'd heard that Jesus would be portrayed as a homosexual. This was, of course, untrue. But in the end, it didn't matter. The focus of the protests eventually centered on Jesus' heterosexual temptations.

The degree of controversy generated by alleging that Jesus Christ might have had human emotions started me thinking about the quality of the films we're used to seeing in this country and how little substance or truth we're exposed to on a regular basis.

Every day of the week, films open in which women are mutilated by chain saws, beheaded with butcher knives and dismembered by monsters and mass murderers. Every day of the week, films open in which alcoholism and promiscuous sexuality are treated lightly. Every day of the week, another film opens in which the most disgusting forms of violence are celebrated for hooting bands of mindless teenagers.

These films fill the theaters of our country, and yet demonstrators do not fill the streets to protest such anesthetizing, dehumanizing experiences. Instead, they rush to cry out over the defamation of a historical figure many of us believe to be a fictional character in a very dull book.

My point is not that censorship is ever justified ever justified, no matter what the target. Protest is not censorship. Yet there are some forms of protest that have the same effect as censorship. It's interesting to note which kinds of images are protested and which are not.

Even more interesting to note are which protests are picked up by the press and which are not. Increasingly, legitimate protest is seen as that which promotes traditional values and does battle with the forces of humanism and change. Protests against traditional values are given no media coverage and rarely have any effect.

Gay groups around the country have been protesting against Kellogg's homophobic Nut'n'Honey commercials for almost a year with no press and no results. Yet Jean-Luc Godard's *Hail Mary* was canceled from the Bravo cable channel last month because of forty-one letters of protest from religious groups. A secular nation is being turned into a religious dictatorship before our eyes.

I make note of this for a reason: Fifty years ago, the Motion Picture Production Code decreed that "any inference of sexual perversion" on the screen was "strictly prohibited." In plain language, this meant that one could not make reference in motion pictures to the existence of homosexuals.

Censoring the fact of our existence effectively made us invisible. We lived in a world where, for all practical purposes, everyone was heterosexual. Queen Christina of Sweden, Alexander the Great, Hans Christian Andersen, Cole Porter, Lt. Charles Gordon, and, yes; even Bonnie and Clyde were fastidiously--if fraudulently—made heterosexual for a mass audience. If audiences will not accept the truth, give them an acceptable lie.

There is no longer a production code, but there is still censorship. Steven Spielberg whitewashed the lesbianism in Alice Walker's *The Color Purple*; there was no effective protest. Bernardo Bertolucci completely negated the homosexuality of the emperor of China in *The Last Emperor*; nobody cared, and nobody spoke out.

Paramount insisted on cutting the homosexual encounter from the film version of James Kirkwood's *Some Kind of Hero*, and there was no outcry. Richard Attenborough sliced most of the gay monologue out of the film version of *A Chorus Line*, and there were no objections.

This is all to say that we have come full circle and it might as well be 1933. Most lesbians and gay men in this country are a bunch of fat, lazy slobs who are willing to allow their humanity, visibility and dignity to be systematically wiped out by a culture dedicated to false values and heterosexual supremacy. We have no spokespeople, no leaders and no defenders. We are looking forward to a world in which Jesus is God and there are no homosexuals. And nobody cares.

Pedro Almodovar's latest film, *Women on the Verge of a Nervous Breakdown* has been announced as the opening-night feature of this year's New York Film Festival. Although the inspiration for the film is Jean Cocteau's famous theater piece, *The Human Voice*, only a remnant of the situation remains: a woman alone with a telephone. The rest is pure comic invention, including a cast of the most unconventional characters found on the screen in many a year.

Harvey Fierstein's *Tidy Endings* has had its nationwide premiere on the HBO cable channel. This post-funeral confrontation between the ex-wife and the lover of a man who has died of AIDS stars Fierstein and Stockard Channing. Originally, this play was the third act of Fierstein's *Safe Sex*, which had a brief run on Broadway last year.

It is a bitter and powerful piece, all the more effective for its brevity. It isn't often that material so sophisticated is let loose on the general public. Fierstein is writing here about issues that are familiar to anyone in the gay community. Many critics have found the invective directed at the wife by the lover a little harsh - even brutal. There's a homophobic edge to such criticism. The straight world isn't used to a gay character flogging a member of the comfortable majority with the ugly truth. Let's hope they're forced to get used to it.

Writer-director Colin Higgins, who gave us *Harold and Maude*, died of AIDS last month in Hollywood. Those of us who identified with Ruth Gordon's free-spirited philosophy about life and death in that cult film will always hold the memory of Higgins dear in our hearts.

Different From the Others

Experimental Gay Films Challenge Viewers

September 25, 1988

The second annual Lesbian and Gay Experimental Film Festival drew thousands of alternative cinema fans to New York's East Village last month, constituting a triumph for organizers Sarah Schulman and Jim Hubbard. The overflowing houses were also a victory for the art form, proving that there is a substantial audience out there willing to support film experiences that require imagination, dedication, intelligence, and, occasionally, the patience of Job.

Experimental films have always had limited appeal. For most audiences, movies are nothing more than entertainment. Experimental films do sometimes entertain, in the broadest sense, but they also challenge the viewer to do some independent thinking; to participate in the experience. In the world of experimental cinema, the audience often works very hard. You can't just sit there and let it wash over you; you have to decide what you think you're seeing, and then it's up to you to figure out what it means to you as well as whether that's what the filmmaker intended you to "get."

For most people, that's no picnic. They want to see a narrative story with identifiable types of characters and be brought to a neat conclusion at the end. They also want to be told what to think when it's all over.

Most of the sixty-two films in the festival were non-narrative efforts, visual poems that sought to create a series of individual impressions on the viewer, while a few were experiments in narrative, meant to challenge our perception of conventional storytelling. A good example of both styles used effectively was Josef Steiff's *Catching Fire*. This twenty-three-minute film repeats images of the family, friends and lover of a man hospitalized with AIDS, going through the rituals of caretaking and mourning. The film achieves a haunting eloquence by juxtaposing this with shots of a safe and comfortable home threatened by a forest fire.

A different approach is taken in Jerry Tartaglia's six-minute film *A.I.D.S.CR.E.A.M*, which addresses in fragmented images and repetitious phrases ("Four out of five doctors recommend no sex for gay men") the de-sexualization of gay culture and the danger of AIDS-phobia. What was clear in all of the films screened was that while lesbian films are becoming more erotic-- witness, among others, Lisa Guay's *The Quest*, about vaginal fisting--gay male content is fastidiously moving away from sex even when sex and/or AIDS is the subject. The censorship of imagery in the newer films typifies the rise of the asexual gay-boy culture currently flourishing in New York and San Francisco. In this new world, gay boys are designed to be cute and alluring and slightly "toyish," but they don't fuck around, and their frame of reference is strictly pop culture.

This attitude is, I think, exemplified in Jeff MacMahon's *Cross Body Ride*, which functions as a dance piece featuring two handsome men rolling around on a beach in Venezuela and in a rumpled bed. Films like this one come down to a question of how does it look, because looking is what we do at the movies, and in this case, we are looking at traditional GQ magazine-type imagery utilized in a manner that can only he described as coyly openly gay.

In contrast, the films revived from days gone by bad an almost terrifying sense of sexual urgency. Especially exciting was the late Curt McDowell's *Confessions*, made in 1971, at once honest, compelling and shocking in its nakedness. In both the McDowell film and in Michael Wallin's classic *The Place Between Our Bodies*, made in 1975, the explicit sexuality between men is offset by a sweet innocence. What we're missing in the 1980s is the sexuality as well as the sweetness.

I do have my personal prejudices here. I'm a great fan of narrative commercial film, and I don't particularly like my favorite traditional images subverted unless it's done so brilliantly that I'm sufficiently dazzled to forgive the transgression. I realize that those are fighting words to an experimental artist, but what the hell; anyone who doesn't like it can twirl on it. I am thinking particularly of a film by Roger Jacoby called *Aged in Wood*.

Now, as anyone worth knowing will tell you, *Aged in Wood* is the name of the play in which Margo Channing starred in the film *All About Eve*. Jacoby's short film, described accurately in the program notes as composed of "mostly grain and very little image," offers on the soundtrack the comments of a group of people watching *All About Eve*. There's a lot of dialogue from the film itself (which we should all know by heart) and scattered commentary. The only decipherable phrase came during the moment when Birdie, played by Thelma Ritter, gives Bette Davis "that look" on her way out of the bedroom. We hear what is, I hope, a queen's voice saying, "Watch this look between Thelma and Bette--this is pure knowledge." Now, that's funny. But it makes you (a) want to see *All About Eve* and (b) wish that Jacoby would make a film with a drag queen dressed as Thelma Ritter, being interviewed by a gay talk show host. In focus.

But what's the use of talking? There's just no denying that a lot of this stuff makes you want to run out and see *Singin' in the Rain*. Yet it's eminently worth your time. It's rewarding to stretch a little and take a shot at learning a new way to look at images. And occasionally, it's more than rewarding; it's exciting. A festival like this one is like a vast attic filled with a lot of boring stuff and some real treasures, and you have to be willing to sift through the rubble. There's a lot of talent out there, and if you're patient, you can take home some valuable images.

Among the other films that demand to be seen were Abigail Child's dazzling *Mayhem*; Jim Hubbard's evocative *Cruising*, with silent footage from the demonstrations against the Friedkin film (you find yourself "cruising" the crowd); and Karl Soehnlein's *My Space*, with its simple *I Remember Mama* narration. These are talented artists with something to say. I would say they deserve our attention at least as much as television movies on Liberace, complete with twenty-five of his most popular songs.

A quick update on the commercial homophobia front: Paul Mazursky has done it again. I was hoping that his tasteless lapse into AIDS-phobia in *Down and Out in Beverly Hills* was a momentary aberration. Now in *Moon over Parador*, we not only have references to "fags in the state department" but, for good measure, "*maricon*," in case our Spanish-speaking viewers feel left out. This is not the Paul Mazursky who made the superb *Next Stop, Greenwich Village*. It makes you wonder why one of his countless gay friends doesn't slap him silly.

Stepping Out From the Gay Film Ghetto

Screen Gems from the New York Film Festival

November 21, 1988

The works of no fewer than five gay filmmakers were shown this year at the New York Film Festival at Lincoln Center. What is so particularly satisfying about that fact is that they were not ghettoized or labeled as gay movies but were presented as superb films that happened to be made by gay directors. Few of them were explicitly gay in content, but each had an undeniable, distinct gay sensibility.

The opening-night film, a resounding popular success, was the latest effort of Spain's Pedro Almodovar, *Women on the Verge of a Nervous Breakdown*. In this film, his funniest and most accessible to date, the superb Carmen Maura gives a tour de force performance as a woman who learns from her telephone answering machine that her lover has taken a powder. In a series of farcical events worthy of Feydeau, she throws the telephone through a window, sets fire to her bed and mixes a gazpacho with a few hundred sleeping pills. She's so terribly busy being pissed off, however, that she forgets to drink it, and the madcap plot rolls on and on in waves of hilarity.

What's gay about *Women on the Verge* is the way it looks. Almodovar is a fan of certain American films of the 19'50s that only a discerning queen could appreciate. In style, decor and sensibility, *Women on the Verge* resembles *Funny Face*, *Written on the Wind* and the films of Frank Tashliln. Everything is beautiful. Everything is perfect. People suffer in penthouses with gorgeous views. Maura even wears earrings made from espresso coffeepots that hang to her shoulders.

Other offerings by openly gay artists included Derek Jarman's intense and evocative *The Last of England*, which encapsulates in a series of rapid images the terrifying collapse of England under the Thatcher government. *Honor and Obey*, a short film by avant-garde filmmaker Warren Sonbert, is a tightly edited panorama of silent images from around the world, opening with two gay men having an argument on a New York City street. Nobody would know that they happen to be gay men, but since I'm acquainted with them, that's the case.

Perhaps the most exciting film in the entire festival was made by England's Terence Davies, whose short film *Trilogy* was shown several years ago in San Francisco. His first feature, *Distant Voices, Still Lives*, is quite simply a masterpiece. An elliptical, non-narrative homage to Davies' family in London during and after World War II, it is a film of overwhelming power and beauty. Davies labored for six years to create this perfect piece of work, which functions as a film in precisely the way our memory works. Using flashes of popular music to typify his family life, he evokes both the light and darkness in the way we all remember the past. The film won top honors at Cannes and has now been nominated for best picture at the European Film Awards, to be handed out in November in Berlin.

Davies created *Distant Voices, Still Lives* as a tribute to the women in his family: his mother and his sisters. "Like a lot of gay men," he says, "I prefer the company of women. I'm enthralled by their conversation and all the minutiae of their lives. I was brought up by my sisters, and I can remember the smallest things, like the scent of Evening in Paris perfume."

To bring back the past, Davies made use of a new bleaching process, draining the film of all primary color except the bright-red lipstick of the early 1950s, creating a texture in the place of color that stops just short of sentimentality. Each sequence bleeds to a searing white as the drama of ordinary lives is given melancholy immediacy by the camera of a master. Among the dazzling, unforgettable images are the faces of a London cinema audience weeping as they watch *Love Is a Many-Splendored Thing* while the rain pours down on umbrella tops outside the theater in homage to *Singin' in the Rain*, one of the landmark films of Davies's childhood. Sequences in which his mother sings "I Get the Blues When It Rains" and his family joins together and sings, "They Tried to Tell Us We're Too Young," are simple and overpowering.

Marcel Ophuls's *Hotel Terminus* was a moving experience on more than one level. A four-hour twenty-five-minute documentary on the life and times of Nazi war criminal Klaus Barbie, the film illuminates one simple truth for all its complexity. After all the documentation of Nazi horrors compiled by the man who gave us *The Sorrow and the Pity*, the experience comes down to one anecdote that is applicable to us today:

A Jewish woman in Lyons tells of being marched away with her family. A next-door neighbor called Mme. Bontout, she recalls, opened her door and tugged at the child's sweater, trying to save her by pulling her into the apartment. The neighbor failed. A soldier struck her and shoved her back into her flat. But the child, now a grown woman, never forgot.

Hotel Terminus bears a dedication that reads, "This film is dedicated to Mme.Bontout. A good neighbor." In this age when "good" people stand by and do nothing, it is wise to remember that perhaps what we need are simply a few good neighbors.

Hollywood Hardball

Can the Industry Afford to Give Up Its Gay Stereotypes?

December 20, 1988

In 1967, screenwriter Abby Mann told *The New York Times* that he set the action of his murder mystery *The Detective* in the homosexual underground of New York's Greenwich Village because, "I wanted to show that in our society, it's easier to be accepted as a murderer than as a homosexual." Mann's observation is borne out in spirit, if not in fact, by the attitudes of the industry and the general public toward movie stars who play homosexual roles on the screen. You've heard the classic actor's complaint a hundred times. It's always phrased in roughly the same terms: "If I play Medea, no one will think I'm really a child murderer, but if I play a homosexual, everyone wants to know if I'm really gay."

Significantly, the analogies used are always odious ones, comparing homosexuality to child molestation, murder and other universally detested activities. The people who use such comparisons may mean well, trying to make a point about how ridiculous such assumptions are, but they also have one thing in common: They are on the defensive. They want to show how broad-minded and liberal they are, but at the same time, they do not wish to be mistaken for homosexuals and need to justify playing a gay role.

When Harry Hamlin hesitated to accept the role of a gay writer in *Making Love*, producer Dan Melnick asked him, "If I came to you with a really great script and asked you to play Hitler, would you consider it?" Hamlin, of course, replied that be would. "So," said Melnick, "you're willing to play a mass murderer but not a homosexual. Think about that."

To his credit, Hamlin did think about it and eventually played the role in *Making Love*. His initial reaction, however, was based not on a legitimate fear but on what I believe is the exploitation of homophobia for political purposes. Distaste for gay people, especially in an image-conscious town like Hollywood, is routinely translated into an economic threat. The stigma of being mistaken for homosexual is used against actors who dare to take chances and refuse to be marketed strictly as heterosexual personalities instead of artists. In the case of gay actors, the threat is used to keep them in the closet. They are warned — falsely, I believe — that playing a gay role may expose their private sexuality. Therefore, many gay films simply don't get made.

The fear that playing a gay character will somehow mark an actor as a gay "type" or, worse, as queer in real life is patently absurd, and yet this myth has become conventional wisdom. When British character actress Beryl Reid came to America in 1968 to promote *The Killing of Sister George*, she was asked point-blank by Johnny Carson on "The Tonight Show" if she was a lesbian. This was the role that Angela Lansbury had turned down because, as she said to a producer in 1967, "Who could play such women? Do you know what they do?"

One might say that abhorrence of lesbians and gay men is marketed in the same way that movies and personalities are sold to the public. Just a few years ago, Lansbury, looking back on her decision not to play Sister George, remarked, "At that time, I just didn't want to play a gay woman. But l think the truth has now filtered down to all of us, over time."

It should be obvious to all concerned that none of this would be a problem if being homosexual wasn't maintained as a nasty, dirty secret. The week Rock Hudson died, I was interviewed by telephone from Atlanta by a radio talk-show host. If Hudson had come out of the closet at the height of his career, the host wanted to know, would he have been able to continue playing heterosexual characters on the screen and retain the love of his audience? I replied that heterosexuals play gay characters all the time and we buy it, so why not? "That's different," he said. "We want to know that our heroes are really heterosexual, no matter what they play."

So it all boils down not to who plays what character on the screen but the tyranny, gossip and suspicion regarding who may be gay in real life.

People are boringly and interminably obsessed with who is and is not queer in Hollywood, and the situation has gotten worse with the advent of AIDS. It has become more important than ever before to maintain the illusion that the entire world is heterosexual, in spite of overwhelming evidence to the contrary. The idea seems to be that we all have a vested interest in helping the general public lie to itself in order to protect it from the ugly truth.

The truth is, playing a gay or lesbian character on the screen has never really hurt the career of a single good actor. The people who have to worry about a homosexual role ruining their careers are not actors, they're personalities — people famous for being heterosexual. When an actor tries to break out of that role and take an artistic chance, he is punished. A recent article by journalist Mary Murphy in *TV Guide* exploited this situation by alleging that playing gay characters has "ruined" the careers of several actors, including Perry King, who played a gay man in Paul Aarons' *A Different Story* in 1978.

The existence of homophobia notwithstanding, King's career was hardly ruined by his role as a homosexual. In a letter to the *Los Angeles Times*, King corrected the impression given by Murphy, saying that he was misquoted. "What I actually said [to Murphy)," wrote King, "was that whether it hurt me or not, I'd do it again in a second, because it's the best film I've ever done and my best work ever.... I'm proud of it."

King maintains that because he played the gay character in *A Different Story* as an average guy instead of a stereotype, he was therefore "too believable" and mistaken for gay in real life. This is the way in which we as a culture preserve our stereotypes. Actors are asked to exaggerate homosexual roles to meet the expectations of a general public that has preconceived ideas of what a homosexual looks like. When those expectations are challenged, people become angry and confused. Both Hollywood and the public want clear definitions of straight and gay behavior. This outlook is adolescent in the extreme. As actor Daniel Day-Lewis has remarked on the subject, "We all expect to play both straight and gay roles eventually — except when we work in Hollywood."

It isn't possible to deny the truth forever. Hollywood's current homophobia is. I think, the last gasp of a society desperately hanging on to its myths. People panic in times of great change, and we are now seeing a revision on the screen of what a gay person looks like and acts like. Hollywood will resist, but it won't be able to stem the truth indefinitely.

Speaking of gay roles, those who have seen an early rough cut of Paul Bogan's film *Torch Song Trilogy* are filled with praise for Harvey Fierstein's performance as Arnold Beckoff. The word of mouth on the film is that it just might reach that crossover market that distinguishes a "gay" film from a mainstream hit. Wouldn't it be a kick if Fierstein becomes the first openly gay person to win an Oscar for playing a gay character? Yes, but then the industry would have to deal with his acceptance speech.

Flaming at Both Ends

January 17, 1989

A film like *Torch Song Trilogy* automatically takes on a significance it should not have to bear. As British film critic Mark Finch commented in a recent London gay journal, it's time we all gave up the fantasy of the "perfect" gay movie. Yet it's difficult if not impossible to avoid judging the just-released film version of Harvey Fierstein's brilliant hit play on whether we think it's "good for the gays or bad for the gays." There are so few films that can truly be called gay that when one this important comes along, we want desperately for it to be successful with a mass audience.

On a political level, *Torch Song Trilogy* is certainly good for the gays. In terms of content, substance and current gay issues, it's brilliant. Fierstein has created an accessible, dramatically powerful, screamingly funny script about gay life before AIDS. It offers us one of the few instances in which the story of one gay man can be said to represent a particular kind of gay life that is fast disappearing. Arnold Beckoff, the leading character, is the last remnant of a literally dying breed of queen. "Once the ERA and the gay rights bills get passed," he says to the audience, "we'll be swept under the carpet."

Fierstein uses the character of Arnold in a way that no film or play has ever attempted. He has made the stereotype into flesh and blood. Queens like Arnold in any medium have traditionally been used as comic relief, stick-figure caricatures with no life outside their limited function as court jesters to straight society. Arnold is defiantly human, and this in itself is a breakthrough.

Torch Song Trilogy covers ten years in the life of a drag queen who seeks love, a home and a family. This premise will upset some so-called radical gays who think Arnold's goals are hetero-imitative and destructive. Yet Arnold is himself radical in concept. He's a pre-Stonewall artifact with a post Stonewall consciousness.

Placing an outrageous character like this in a traditional context is a stroke of genius because as soon as the audience decides that he's a buffoon they can laugh at, he turns on them and becomes one of them. He demands respect and refuses to be something he isn't. He searches for happiness, first in the back rooms of Greenwich Village sex bars; next with a confused bisexual named Ed (Brian Kerwin), who keeps taking a powder; and finally with Alan (Matthew Broderick), the love of his life, who is brutally murdered by teenage fag bashers in a local park. He adopts a gay son. He fights with his mother. He survives. Arnold Beckoff is the best kind of role model, representing the notion that people can be different and yet unexceptional.

At its finest, *Torch Song Trilogy* is so good that its failures are infuriating. The direction is decidedly uninspired. There's nothing cinematically inventive about this film that would make it stand out as an exceptional work of art. The play was riveting. The film is more like an above average television movie of the week. The actors have been directed to play at a fever pitch, and this makes it difficult for audiences to have the same emotional connection with the story that was achieved onstage.

As Arnold's mother, Anne Bancroft is dreadful. It's difficult to know what has happened to this once fine actress, but let's be charitable and say that she needs a strong director and/or a kick in the ass. You have only to look at Shelley Winters's superb performance in Paul Mazursky's *Next Stop, Greenwich Village* to realize that even a monster or a Jewish mother can be played with some subtlety and insight. Bancroft's two crucial arguments with Fierstein are conducted at such a furious level that the issues get lost. She seems to be shouting at the top of her lungs so that she won't have to develop an emotional bond with the material. There's no poignancy in this relationship, and when it should be moving and complex, it's just earsplitting.

Fierstein is at his best in the monologues delivered directly to the audience. He has an endearing quality that makes Arnold's life experiences universal. The nightclub scenes, featuring delightful bits by Charles Pierce, Ken Page and Axel Vera, give Fierstein a chance to paint a portrait of the street queen who made good.

Unfortunately, director Bogart makes some choices in the more dramatic segments that flatten the impact like a pancake. Arnold's first encounter with Alan in the drag club is confusing and poorly plotted. And later, given what we know about him, it's difficult to believe that Arnold would just stand in the street helplessly as an ambulance departs with the body of his dead lover. Worse, his last scene is robbed of significance by an ill-advised cut to a long shot just when we should be watching his face.

Broderick, who has relatively little screen time, proves irresistible. A natural and affecting actor, Broderick creates a counterpoint to Fierstein by playing an "average" gay guy who, miraculously, has none of the traditional gay male hang-ups about drag or effeminacy. Actually, he's a little like Melanie in *Gone with the Wind*--just too good to be true. "If you have an IQ over thirty," Fierstein says to Broderick's sleeping figure, "then there is no God."

Kerwin, as Arnold's perpetually torn bisexual first lover, has a powerful backstage dressing-room scene, in which he confesses thoughts of suicide. He represents the accommodation that gays have made to straight society on a daily basis. The terrible price exacted by his indecision is that he will never be what Arnold Beckoff needs in a lover.

These are all vital issues to the gay community issues that are, in fact, only incidentally universal. *Shoah* can be seen as a universal statement about human suffering, but that's not what it's about; it's about the Holocaust. *Torch Song Trilogy* can be viewed as a universal story about the struggle for fulfillment and respect, but it's really about a gay man and his struggle with life. The film is specific and relentless in its insistence on presenting the gay world in its own terms.

This raises the question of whether a film like *Torch Song Trilogy* can cross over and reach that coveted mainstream audience. I don't think it matters. I think we have to refine our expectations and allow films like this to be what they are. Most of us forget that the famous mass audience out there wants to see very little that's different or offbeat. Most of Middle America did not see the Academy Award-winning *The Last Emperor*, because they didn't want to see a long, arty movie about Chinese people. It isn't even the gay angle that's a problem.

They just don't want to see anything foreign to their experience. They want reinforcement of their own daily lives.

To a certain degree, *Torch Song Trilogy* does reinforce the "normality" of gay emotions. But not enough. As a social and political statement, it's head and shoulders above most films you're likely to see this year. As a work of art, it leaves a lot to be desired. To borrow a phrase from Stephen Sondheim's *Company*, I was sorry/grateful.

Triumphs and Small Favors

A Mixed Bag of New Gay Characters On-Screen

February 14, 1989

It's nice to note, at the beginning of a new year, that in spite of all the gay baiting one reads about in the news and sees on the screen, there are still compensations. Although the AIDS crisis has taken a heavy toll on Hollywood by driving the cowards back into the closets and the homophobes out into the open, people of talent and courage have not stopped making interesting independent films with gay themes.

On the heels of Harvey Fierstein's *Torch Song Trilogy*, a small British film slipped into distribution with little fanfare and even less public attention. Based on Joseph R. Ackerley's novel of the same name, *We Think the World of You* is exactly the kind of film that disappears before you can catch it, and it's definitely worth catching. Set in the 1950s, it tells the short and bittersweet story of a middle-aged English gentleman named Frank (Alan Bates) who is in love with a working-class youth named Johnny (Gary Oldman).

When Johnny is sent to prison for theft, Frank continues his strained and exploitive relationships with Johnny's coldhearted wife and manipulative parents. Eventually, Frank comes to transfer his resentment at their shabby treatment of him to the equally shabby way they treat Johnny's abandoned German shepherd, Evie. He determines that he will take the dog away from them and give it the kind of treatment he cannot lavish on Johnny.

The film becomes a metaphor for the illegitimacy of gay relationships as Frank wages a battle to save Evie from mistreatment. It's also a commentary on the class differences between Frank and Johnny. Johnny's working-class family infuriates Frank precisely because he cannot have what he wants from them and is crushed by their sly condescension toward him.

This is a very funny film. As Frank's fanatical attachment to Evie grows, his life becomes a shambles. He fights for Evie the way, in a different time and place, he would have fought for Johnny. He brings her to the office. He sleeps with her. And, in the end, his relationship with this frisky German shepherd overtakes his love for Johnny completely. As the film comes to a close, Johnny is released from prison and has to face life in a slum with a sour, pregnant wife. Frank, now Evie's master, has gotten the best of the deal after all.

We Think the World of You shouldn't be praised too highly; it's a modest film with modest aspirations that it achieves with grace and intelligence. The performances are lovely, and the direction by Colin Gregg sets just the right tone. And it is further proof that thoughtful, classy work with gay subject matter simply will not disappear in the face of a repressive social climate.

Meanwhile, on the dreary and predictable mainstream homophobia front, that old fuddy-duddy who gave us the witless *On Golden Pond*, screenwriter Ernest Thompson, wrote and directed *1969*. The film deservedly turned out to be one of last year's more spectacular flops. Several mainstream critics noted the gratuitous and offensive fag-baiting sequence that opens the film, in which Kiefer Sutherland and Robert Downey Jr. all but barf when a gay man comes on to one of them.

The actor who played the part of the gay character wrote a letter to *The Village Voice* defending the role, saying that the scene was realistic because in 1969 all those flower children were in fact homophobic. Fair enough. But we have to remind ourselves to ask what that scene was doing in the film in the first place. In a two hour film, ten minutes is a long time, and every scene is meant to tell us something. Why was it necessary for the gay character to be written and played in the cheap, sleazy, stereotypical manner that has constituted the easy way out for a generation of stand-up comics? Not, I think, because Thompson had a desire to illuminate the homophobia of the 1960s for a sophisticated audience. Only, I think, to provide a low-class laugh and reinforce to another generation of teens the idea that fags are disgusting.

CBS's daytime soap opera "As the World Turns" has announced the introduction of a gay character named Hank Eliot, to be played by actor

Brian Starcher. With the blessings of the network and the sponsor (Procter and Gamble), writer Doug Marland has created what seems to be a character out of *Making Love*. Hank has a lover in New York, and their relationship will be strictly monogamous. In the age of AIDS, one would expect this to be the case, but it's difficult to ignore the irony of the situation, considering how monogamous the heterosexual characters are on soap operas.

It's nice to have a gay character on a soap; but it looks as though he'll be so clean and blow-dried that he'll squeak.

The Politics of Abuse

Fag-Bashing is Still a Mean Movie Reality

March 14, 1989

The introduction of verbal and physical fag bashing into a number of recent films marks a departure from the days when gay life was characterized as violent in and of itself. Although violence against lesbians and gay men is as old as homosexuality in our culture, motion pictures have seldom reflected the kind of epidemic fag bashing that goes on in major cities on any given night of the week. Instead, in films like *Windows, Cruising, The Laughing Policeman, Busting, American Gigolo* and *The Detective*, to name a few relics, gays are portrayed as members of a dangerous subculture.

Then there has always been the issue of psychological violence. Lesbians and gay male screen character historically have done damage to themselves as a result of their realization that they are gay. In *The Children's Hour, Advise and Consent, Staircase, The Killing of Sister George* and *The Sergeant,* even the false accusation of homosexuality is enough to ruin a life and/or precipitate suicide. Younger gay people don't remember these films. I think it would be productive for lesbians and gay men who grew up in the 1970s instead of the 1950s to take a look at them in comparison to the current crop of mainstream films that feature gay characters.

Thanks in large part, I think, to the educational efforts of organizations like the Gay and Lesbian Alliance Against Defamation and the Hetrick-Martin Institute for Lesbian and Gay Youth, we have passed into a more enlightened age regarding the reality of gay life on the streets of this country. It used to be that the homosexual killer was a staple of melodrama in the movies. Now, the gay character is more often the target of violence that is increasingly portrayed as perpetrated by heterosexual villains.

Much of the abuse heaped on gay characters in films still comes from the same source as it did in films of the 1950s and 1960s. In Robert Anderson's *Tea and Sympathy*, a student is harassed for not being queer but for being less than masculine in his behavior. In the new release of *The Chocolate War*, the word *faggot* is used generically as the worst accusation one can hurl at a student who bucks the system and is unwilling to go along with the machine. The same is true in *The Year My Voice Broke*, in which adolescent insecurities are the cause of a particularly vicious episode in which a sissy character has his head dunked in a toilet.

Movies for grown-ups have taken a slightly different turn of late. In John Schlesinger's *Madame Sousatzka*, the sympathetic character of an older gay man (played by Geoffrey Bayldon) is brutally fag bashed on a London street by a group of faceless teenage thugs who call him "queer" while punching him out. They are in sharp relief to the gentle, definitively heterosexual piano student played by Navin Chowdhry, who befriends the older man and has no hang-ups about his obviously gay sexuality.

In Oliver Stone's *Talk Radio*, it seems as though everyone is crazy, and the psychological violence that pours through the telephone at the radio station is linked to a sick country being exploited by sick individuals. Yet, for the first time in a major film, homophobia is clearly linked to anti-Semitism, racism and just plain bigotry. It's good for audiences to make these connections.

Probably the most dramatic exploration of anti-gay violence presently on the screen is a scene in Harvey Fierstein's *Torch Song Trilogy* in which Matthew Broderick is murdered when he goes to the aid of a homosexual being beaten in the park. Not only is this the dramatic high point of the film, but Fierstein makes sure to illuminate the issue of fag bashing when his character, Arnold, has a final showdown with his mother. Several of the opening-night benefits thrown around the country for the film were sponsored by organizations concerned with the issue of violence.

I think it's productive that this urgent issue is finally coming out of the closet. In years past, the reason most attacks on gay people were not identified as such was because the victims were reluctant to identify themselves as gay; therefore, the beatings were characterized as "random" violence. People are more likely these days to come forward, and as a result, statistics are beginning to show the extent of the problem.

The problem is also Hollywood, which has always been twenty years behind the times on every social issue it tackles. In the late 1970s, producers thought they were being progressive when *Kramer vs. Kramer* dealt with male parenting. In 1985, they finally got around to the Vietnam War--two decades after the fact.

If, as a colleague recently suggested in these pages, some gay people are "hopping mad," it's because they wish to live free from fear that their very existence will precipitate violence against their person on the streets of this "kindler and gentler nation." It's time we realized and acknowledged that the truly compassionate people among us are those who are willing to express their anger and dissatisfaction with a system of abuse that has now gone on too long and is only tentatively being addressed in the most popular art form of our time.

Down There on a Visit

The Strange Coming-Out Saga of an "Everygay"

April 11, 1989

A new American independent feature, which had its premiere at the Berlin Film Festival in February, is sure to be making the rounds at gay festivals this summer. *Fun Down There*, produced and directed by Roger Stigliano, is described as "a comic coming-of-age drama" about a naive young man from upstate New York who flees to Manhattan and discovers gay life through the eyes of the people he meets in the East Village.

This simple and rather cold coming-out saga was shot for about forty thousand dollars, and it looks it. The low budget feel of the film works both for and against the material at hand. Buddy Fields (Michael Waite) is a blank slate -- a country hick who doesn't seem to have read anything, learned anything, or absorbed anything in his life.

In a depressing sort of way, *Fun Down There* is an accurate reflection of coming out in the age of AIDS. The people in the film observe life from a distance. They have few expectations or passions beyond getting a job and sharing a few laughs with their friends. They don't think much.

They're presented to us as "young," but in truth, they aren't that young; certainly they are old enough to have read a newspaper once or twice. It's difficult to get excited about characters who aren't excited by anything. It's like watching a generation in a holding pattern.

The simplicity of the film gives it a haunting kind of staying power. For days after you've seen it, the images continue to recur. This is because Stigliano has focused on an age-old ritual: the "everygay" leaving home and seeking others of his own kind for solace and spiritual kinship.

The exercise is so lacking in drama that when Kevin Ochs does a wickedly funny impression of Ruth Gordon as Blanche Du Bois, it stands out, along with Paul Saindon's terrific rendition of an old Edith Piaf number, as a high point of the film. The rest of the picture could have used more of this verve.

Considering the recent furor over the lesbian character played by Gail Strickland on "Heartbeat," ABC took a real risk in the chickenshit world of television when it chose to turn Gloria Naylor's novel *The Women of Brewster Place* into a four-hour miniseries for prime time. It also took a chance on *Desert Hearts* director Donna Dietch, and it made the right decision. The presence of Oprah Winfrey, who also co-produced the film, in the leading role practically guaranteed a large audience for this episodic story of the women in a lower-middle-class black neighborhood.

Although I'm sure that Dietch had to make some significant sacrifices in the interests of time and the television mentality, the lesbian relationship between Paula Kelly and Lonette McKee took up most of the second part. It was pretty straightforward — but still daring for network television.

The emotional high point of the film occurred when McKee was brutally gay-bashed by a neighborhood punk. It was a sequence very much like the killing of Matthew Broderick in *Torch Song Trilogy*, but Dietsch made it infinitely more powerful and effective. Kelly's struggle to get into the ambulance to embrace her lover was the catalyst that ultimately brought about the climax of the drama.

As Dietch has pointed out, it was light years away from *Desert Hearts*, but for television, it was still astonishing. I hope they paid her a lot of money and she makes another film immediately.

I recently saw the magnificently restored version of *Lawrence of Arabia*. Despite some claims that the rape-and-torture sequence at Deraa had originally been more explicit, it now seems that no footage was ever shot. In his preliminary notes for the first draft of the screenplay (ultimately credited to Robert Bolt), Michael Wilson wrote:

Much has been made of this scene...as the key to the enigma of Lawrence. It seems to me that it becomes the key only if the question of homosexuality is placed at the center of the riddle...and this I have no desire to do. There is little to be gained by dramatizing the notion that Lawrence finally succumbs to the boy's advances...[T]his does not mean, of course, that we should omit any suggestion of the boy's homosexuality.

So in the end, we are left with Jose Ferrer squeezing Peter O'Toole's tit. Evocative, but bullshit.

Little Wonder in Wonderland

A Schizophrenic Gay Thriller

June 6, 1989

I finally caught up with Philip Saville's *Wonderland* when it opened, like a tired little clam, in New York recently. I was hoping it would be better than the mediocre advance word on it, but no such luck. This slightly wacky tale of two gay teenagers, one black and one white, is too confused about itself to have much going for it. If the film had been a little wittier and less self-consciously offbeat, it could have made a stronger impression, especially with mainstream audiences. As it stands, the enchanting performances of its young stars give the film its only spark of warmth and cohesion.

Eddie and Michael couldn't be a more unlikely pair. Eddie (Emile Charles) is a budding young queen whose mother indulges his devotion to old movie stars and whose father calls him names and tells him to act like a man. Michael (Tony Forsyth) is a runaway, a hustler and a thief, whose friendship for Eddie is his sole emotional bond. When the two boys witness a murder one night at a gay club called The Fruit Machine, they decide they must get out of town to escape their would-be assassin.

Magically, they meet an aging opera star (Robert Stephens) who, that very evening, invites them to stay at his house in Brighton. As if the plot weren't already shaky enough, the Brighton segment of the film seeks to draw a parallel between Eddie's desire for freedom and the plight of some dolphins on display at a local aquarium called Wonderland. The last part of the film chiefly concerns the homophobic killer, who continues to pursue the boys, but there is another subplot about freeing the dolphins from captivity and returning them to the sea.

I don't think screenwriter Frank Clarke (*Letter to Brezhnev*) and director Saville knew which movie they wanted to make. At various times, *Wonderland* is a thriller, a romantic melodrama and a message movie. In the end, it's none of those things. *Wonderland* is painless to watch and far from the hideous bore it might have become in less talented hands. It's been decked out with very classy production values and some genuinely beautiful underwater photography. Unfortunately, the film isn't sufficiently focused on any one subject for us to care about it all that much.

Hollywood on Hudson

Double Vision and the Life of a Closeted Star

February 13, 1990

I had intended to take some time this month to do a wrap-up of gays in film in the 1980s. The recent television broadcast of ABC's Rock Hudson biography, however, made me do some thinking about where the action really is.

Whereas movies are often created for fantasy and seldom have anything to do with the way people really live, television is more of a barometer of public opinion. Television has always been issue oriented. Unlike movies, which can cost a fortune and thus must make a fortune, television has the luxury of year-round programming, so if one week's program doesn't work, there is always another week to try again.

Over the years, television has vacillated between cowardice and courage on the issue of gays. While there has been a remarkable amount of hoopla concerning so-called controversial programs, the small screen has scored more than its share of bull's eyes over the years. A superb example is the 1978 television movie *A Question of Love*, which starred Gena Rowlands in the true story of a lesbian mother in Texas who lost her children in a bitter court battle. Television has also given us *The Naked Civil Servant, Sergeant Matlovich vs. the U.S. Air Force, An Early Frost* and *Consenting Adult*.

Rock Hudson makes me think that more issues vital to a serious debate about gay liberation get raised on television than perhaps in any other medium. Television movies, like the Hudson story, potentially reach more viewers than almost any film. They enable writers and producers to place before the public ideas that it otherwise would never have considered.

In the case of *Rock Hudson*, viewers were presented with a mixed bag of the good, the bad and the decidedly ugly. As Stuart Byron, *The Advocate*'s media columnist said to me, "There were a lot of pro-gay things in it and a lot of things that were ridiculous. You could go through it scene by scene and teach a course on it." If so, the course would be one on internalized homophobia.

For gay viewers, the trouble with *Rock Hudson* was that the only emotion is evoked was pity. It's the story of one of the most tragic and pathetic of all figures, the congenital closet queen. Furthermore, it's the dreary story of a system and a town run by the lowest form of animal life.

Straight and gay audiences react differently to movies such as *Hudson*. Straight Americans' fascination with Hudson's story is really their fascination with their own gullibility and with the American dream, which they want so desperately to believe in and can't resist even when they know it's a sham. Straight Middle America bought Hudson's image in a way that gays never did. Gay viewers know all about the difference between illusion and reality; they've been trained in making this distinction since birth.

Gay people watched two films when they tuned into Rock Hudson. They were sad for him because he was so torn over his sexuality, but they also understood that Hollywood will never allow the truth. They noticed that although every scene seemed accurate in terms of Hudson's feelings about his gayness, the movie was shot and edited in a loaded, stereotypical way.

Gay people read the press interviews and noted where Thomas Ian Griffith (who played Hudson) was quick to mention that he lives with his girlfriend. They read that William Moses (who portrayed Marc Christian) can't understand why they chose him for the role, because "I play football." They wondered what in the hell Moses meant.

Gay viewers observed that the all-boy party at Hudson's pool was just too precious to have anything to do with real life. When Hudson was with his future wife, Phyllis Gates, gay viewers saw all their puppy love and romance. But when he peered longingly out of the window at the gardener, they saw the tragedy of life in the closet. They knew that Gates couldn't possibly have been that naive. And they most certainly noticed that when a man comes home to his lover after a long trip, it would be positively unnatural for them not to kiss hello.

In spite of television's recent openness about gays ("thirtysomething," "Alien Nation," "Heartbeat"), I have never seen two men kiss on a network show. There's an underlying hypocrisy in using homosexuality to attract viewers and then not dealing with the subject. It's particularly offensive in this case. *Rock Hudson* is a cautionary tale about the destructiveness of being in the closet, yet it was made by the very system that demands that people stay in the closet.

Hudson's final speech in the film couldn't have been more misleading to viewers. "All my life I thought if people found out I was gay it would kill me. And now it has," he says to Christian on his deathbed. Hudson confused being gay with having a disease. Being gay didn't kill Hudson, but being in the closet may have hastened his death.

Film Noir

**Marlon Riggs' Dazzling *Tongues Untied*
Explores Black Gay Culture**

March 13, 1990

Every year at this time, the lesbian and gay film community buzzes about the most likely candidates for the lesbian and gay film festivals. The festivals will take place in spring and early summer in New York, Los Angeles, and San Francisco. This year's discovery, which has been getting sensational word-of-mouth praise from coast to coast, is Marlon Riggs' *Tongues Untied*. The excitement is justified.

Usually, politically and socially admirable films fall short of the mark in the aesthetics department. They are praised more for their good intentions and political correctness than for their artistic value. In *Tongues Untied*, Riggs has created that rarest of all birds - a brilliant, innovative work of art that delivers a knockout political punch.

This exploration of racism, homophobia, and black gay male culture is a stunning aesthetic, historical, and social document. The film articulates the mechanisms of oppression and the ecstasies of freedom with a dazzling use of both spoken and visual language.

With *Tongues Untied*, a community has found its voice, and it is one that many of us have waited a long time to hear. The voice is both poetic and rough, angry and soothing, instilled with love and shaped by rage. *Tongues Untied* is an explosion of the feelings held in check for too long by racism and homophobia.

The film has many styles and many messages, all executed with wit and power. It's about an androgynous black man in a yellow headband acting out

Billie Holiday's "Lover Man." It's about the sensitivity and passion of a visual language that transcends masculinity and femininity to allow individual black men to become who they really are. It's about the rap and the finger snap and the endless diversity that has emerged from lifes' joy and sorrow. It's about a drag queen named Star in a zebra dress against a backdrop of Nina Simone's "Black Is the Color of My True Love's Hair." It's about brotherhood in its purest and most positive sense.

The morning after I saw *Tongues Untied*, I read an article in the *Village Voice* about New York City mayor David Dinkins's appointment of a new health commissioner over the objections of the gay community. The mayor was accused of exacerbating conflict between the black community and gays. This statement was made with no acknowledgment that gays are also black and that blacks are also gay. Several times during *Tongues Untied*, the word listen appears against a black screen. Riggs's film has the power to begin to heal our hearts on the issue of racism in the gay community - if we listen.

Riggs recently showed *Tongues Untied* at the Berlin International Film Festival. It's a sure bet that you'll be able to see it at any one of the lesbian and gay film festivals around the country this year. Theaters like San Francisco's Castro will also be running it on a double bill March 16-22 along with last year's *Looking for Langston*. I wish, however, that it could be shown on national television, where it would reach a wide audience and do the most good.

Hot Flashes

Hits and Misses on the Summer Screens

August 1, 1989

The summer has brought a mixed bag of gay characters to the big screen, most of whom are unjustifiably and unconscionably homophobic in their representation. Some of these representations are a job for the Gay and Lesbian Alliance Against Defamation (GLAAD), which now has chapters in six cities and monitors the media for homophobia.

We've needed a national watchdog group for years, and GLAAD seems to have taken off successfully on a national basis, thanks to the efforts of executive director Craig Davidson. If you spot something on radio, on television or in the movies that is homophobic, bring it to the attention of your local GLAAD chapter or the New York office.

You can practically predict which films are going to have offensive and homophobic dialogue and which are more progressive. The gay reference in Patrick Swayze's *Road House* is the classic equation of homosexual men with the feminine role by a character who says, "I used to fuck guys like you in prison." This approach is offensively sexist in terms of gender roles and women and is antigay in the extreme. Taking this theme a little further is the line in Gene Wilder and Richard Pryor's *See No Evil, Hear No Evil*, which goes, "Jail can be fun if you like to take it up the ass." But then you knew to expect this kind of thing from Pryor already.

Heathers is a son of twisted movie that I liked quite well. It's a cross between *Blue Velvet* and *The Breakfast Club* with some gay-positive humor in the form of a sick little murder with a suicide note confessing the gay feelings of one football player for another. It takes off on the face chat the guys could no longer "live a lie" and even has a funeral scene with the jock father proclaiming, "I loved my gay son!"

Incidental characters this summer include two gay police officers in a film I have not yet seen, *Earth Girls Are Easy*. Also, a gay muscle man and his boyfriend have been causing audience titters in my favorite film of the summer thus far, *Miracle Mile*, a literate, intelligent beauty I've seen twice and the best science fiction film I've seen in a long, long while. Run to see it before it disappears. The gay bodybuilder turns out to be something of a hero in this one.

Clearly intended as absurdist exaggeration is a scene in *Cold Feet* in which Tom Waits sarcastically orders Shirley Temples for two butch heterosexual men in a bar, treating the men as if they were homosexual. Waits seems to be underscoring how straight they really are — yet it's symptomatic of how characterizing straight men as gay is used as a put-down whenever it's convenient to deflate the male ego. This is just pure thoughtlessness, especially from Waits, who is my favorite singer and knows better.

The Montreal AIDS Conference, which I attended as a member of ACT UP, a person with AIDS, and a panelist, all in one, told us nothing medically we didn't already know. But the media panels produced by Sidart, a Montreal-based group, were enlightening. The one I was on featured, in addition to myself, actor Tom Hulce, who is openly gay; writer and activist Larry Kramer; former Disney executive vice president Gary Barton; and American Playhouse producer of   *Longtime Companion* and novelist-screenwriter Donald Martin.

Martin co-wrote a Toronto television film called *No Blame*, which no American network will touch, he said, because they all claim they've done their "AIDS show" and nobody wants to see another one. *No Blame* is the story of a pregnant woman (played by Canadian actress Helen Shaver of *Desert Hearts*) who learns that she is HIV-positive. As a result, she is ostracized, and her husband leaves her. Later she discovers that she was falsely diagnosed.

The panel agreed that television has done its AIDS shows and the movies aren't interested in the topic because no AIDS story is box office to the tune of the forty million one needs to break even these days. Kramer went on to discuss his deal with Barbra Streisand, who was to have brought his play *The Normal Heart* to the screen. The project fell apart when it became clear that this timely property was not going to be Streisand's next film and Kramer told her he'd put the word out that she was preventing the movie from being made. Streisand "is terrified of bad publicity," said Kramer, and she eventually relinquished the movie rights.

I also wish to note with great sadness the death by suicide of filmmaker Fred Halsted, whose pioneering *L.A. Plays Itself* and *Sex Garage* have become part of the permanent collection of the film department of New York's Museum of Modern Art, which screened both films in 1973. At one screening I sat behind Salvador Dali, who was mesmerized by Halsted's juxtaposition of sado-masochism and lyrical gay romance. The gentleness that lay just beneath Halsted's rough exterior was beautifully captured in a recent article by Michael Kearns in *Edge*, a Los Angeles gay newspaper. AIDS has claimed many victims, not the least of which is Halsted's generation, a group of men who lived to push sex to its limit in a way that has became an anachronism all too soon.

The Bogus Bogeyman

AIDS Has Become Hollywood's Latest Unseen Monster

September 26, 1989

Recently, a segment of "Entertainment Tonight" rather superficially examined the lack of explicit sexuality in this year's summer movies. Mass-audience films, especially during the summer, have traditionally been known for their high sexual content and frequent use of gratuitous nudity.

With the advent of AIDS, however, the party seems to be over. While independent films with daring or controversial themes are enjoying something of a renaissance, mainstream films seem to be reflecting a definite conservative backlash in the face of the epidemic.

The American screen has always been squeamish and therefore schizophrenic about sex. We're all acquainted with the more celebrated examples of how sexuality in general and homosexuality in particular have been avoided in the movies. Anyone who has seen the screen adaptations of Tennessee Williams' *Cat on a Hot Tin Roof* or *A Streetcar Named Desire* in the 1950s remembers the deletions and distortions perpetrated by an industry trying to make everything palatable to everyone without giving offense.

Truman Capote's Holly Golightly was turned from a worldly call girl into a cuddly, innocent eccentric for the film version of *Breakfast at Tiffany's*. Patrick   Dennis' *Auntie Mame* was sanitized of its more political references to anti-Semitism as well as to Marne's "queer friends on Fire Island." Famous lesbians and gay men of history were (and still are) routinely portrayed as heterosexual.

AIDS has complicated the issue of sexuality onscreen by affecting movies indirectly, creating a climate in which old fashioned values are promoted as some sort of solution to what's perceived to be wrong in the world. Rather than dealing directly with the reality of today, Hollywood has chosen to fall backward, as though a "return" to so-called family values will solve the problem.

Hollywood's "response" to AIDS is, in fact, an inability to respond. On and off the screen, the movie industry is paralyzed by AIDS. The disease is so inextricably bound up with homosexuality in the minds of the public that any film about gays must necessarily have an AIDS angle. Since nobody wants to do that, there are no mainstream films about gays. Having rejected the notion of dealing directly with AIDS as a major plot element, filmmakers don't seem to be able to conceive of a way of dealing with the health crisis except by promoting monogamy and delivering stern warnings about the dangers of promiscuity.

AIDS has become the bogeyman of American film, an unseen but nevertheless ubiquitous monster lurking in the wings of every production. From *Someone to Watch Over Me* to *When Harry Met Sally*, romance has become innocent again. At the other end of the spectrum, films like *Fatal Attraction* and David Cronenberg's remake of *The Fly* have served up subtextual warnings about   what can happen if people engage in "unnatural" pursuits, be they homosexual or heterosexual.

In *Fatal Attraction*, Glenn Close clearly represents the disease. This knife-wielding monster has the potential to destroy the family, and she is what can happen to you if you cheat on your wife. The hideous fate of Jeff Goldblum's character in *The Fly* is presented in terms usually reserved for tabloid descriptions of AIDS. Consider the dialogue in reference to Goldblum's progressive transformation:

"It seems to manifest itself as some rare form of cancer. I won't become some timorous bore crying about his lost lymph nodes."

"Stay away from him. It could be contagious. It could turn into an epidemic."

"I'm sure that Typhoid Mary was a very nice person when you met her socially."

In *The Fly*, Goldblum has inadvertently tempered with the ''natural'' order. Like the mad scientists in earlier horror movies, he presumes beyond human limits and therefore must be punished. In this context, hubris replaces homosexuality as a symbol for unnaturalness and is cast as the cause of AIDS, further confusing a misinformed public about the actual methods of disease transmission and laying the groundwork for a national witch-hunt.

According to a recent column in the *Los Angeles Times*, a full-page ad in the entertainment trade papers recently announced a low-budget film called *The Victims*. The ad shows a bare-chested man flanked on either side by women. The copy reads, "If you don't want to catch AIDS, go see *The Victims!*" The producer, in an interview, termed the film "a cautionary tale" and insisted that AIDS would not be sensationalized.

The danger here advent of AIDS will produce new bigots but that AIDS is becoming the excuse for old bigots to reassert themselves. AIDS is the catalyst that will enable conservatives to seize the moment and push us back to the morality of the 1950s. In such a climate, homosexuality will once again be defined as unspeakable and the phrase "AIDS victim" will take on a new and more ominous meaning.

The Shock of the New

Experimental Gay Films Project Images
from an Evolving History

October 24, 1989

The third annual New York Lesbian and Gay Experimental Film Festival once again played to packed houses at the Anthology Film Archives. Thousands of people showed up last month for more than sixty films billed as "a program that will never be funded by the National Endowment for the Arts."

Festival organizers Sarah Schulman and Jim Hubbard introduced the event by pointing out that in recent years we have seen a dramatic erosion of the rights of gay people as well as the active suppression of homoerotic artwork by the U.S. Senate. As they so eloquently expressed, for lesbian and gay people, silence will always equal death.

Three years ago the festival showed the works of two artists who had died of AIDS — Roger Jacoby and Curt McDowell. This year, the films of seven artists who have died of AIDS were included, plus more work from others who are ill and fighting for their lives. This increasingly insane state of affairs was dramatized on opening night when Schulman announced the death of Jack Smith that afternoon; Schulman dedicated the festival to the pioneering gay filmmaker who made the landmark *Flaming Creatures*.

The majority of films in this year's festival were informed by the lesbian and gay community's increasing commitment to direct action. Collectively viewed, the work presents a vivid call to arms and challenges artists everywhere to become activists.

The festival appropriately opened with a screening of *Gay U.SA.* by the late Arthur Bressan Jr. This captivating and inspiring film, which documents the gay movement's national response to Anita Bryant's hysterical and homophobic crusade, was completed by Bressan in only ten weeks in 1977. It is, as characterized by filmmaker/writer David Lambie, "the parade film to end all parade films." Never has the spirit of those times seemed more relevant to lesbian and gay audiences than now, and never have the film's darker lessons, drawn from the Holocaust, seemed more applicable.

Sol Rubin's 1972 *Gay Parade* is a colorful footnote to gay history and was made by a non-gay Greenwich Village resident who decided to document the 1971 gay pride parade and the gay takeover of his neighborhood. It's wonderful to see such an early parade in retrospect. The film is an outlandish and stirring reminder of how directly connected to the 1960s counterculture gay imagery once was.

Certainly one of the most disturbing films ever made, Lambie's *Bashing* opens with a shocking image of a gay man lying on a sidewalk, blood streaming from his head. Written by Bressan and partially funded by the San Francisco mayor's office, *Bashing* should be required viewing for every senator and member of Congress as well as every lesbian and gay person in America. Documenting the injuries sustained by gay people in violent attacks, the brief film is relentless in its series of devastating photos, re-created footage, and graffiti reading, GAS GAYS and KILL FAGS. The film is difficult to watch, but of course that's the point. It's also got Ella Fitzgerald on the sound track.

Also a bit difficult to watch but equally moving is Carl George's *DHPG Mon Amour*, which covers a day in the life of lovers Joe Walsh and David Conover. Conover, whose sight is threatened by CMV retinitis, must each day inject a drug called DHPG (ganciclovir) into an implanted catheter called a Portacath. A strong attitude of survival runs throughout the film, especially in the statements of Walsh.

"You have to fight everyone about this," he advises," and just fucking do something about it." Calling the trying medical procedure part of "just a regular day," Walsh says simply, "It's not a hassle in our lives. It's keeping David alive."

Several other films reacted politically and emotionally to the AIDS epidemic, including Hubbard's *Elegy in the Streets*, which uses thirty-three minutes of silent footage from a 1987 AIDS memorial march and sequences shot at the Names Project quilt display. Hubbard has colored the footage to give it the look of an eerily beautiful alien landscape. The film provides a commentary on the process of documenting our lives in the 1980s. In one sequence, a police officer at the FDA demonstration in Washington, D.C., takes a snapshot of the demonstrators being photographed by news cameras, all of which is being shot by Hubbard, recording an experience that is both urgent and soothing.

One of the funniest and most accessible films in the festival was Heather McAdams's forty-five-minute gem, *Meet Bradley Harrison Picklesimer*, a portrait of a self-described redneck Kentucky drag queen. The film highlights all the worthwhile things in life: stiletto heels ("I have a very severe shoe fetish"), big hairdos ("a disappearing art, and the fuck-you attitude that has long been the mainstay of drag. Among Picklesimer's heroes is Joan Crawford ("She took those kids out of a fucking orphanage...talk about ingratitude!"). The film also features a terrific song called "Where's the Dress?" which asks the ever-important question, "Do they make a pink pump in a size twelve?"

As in any film festival, you have to sit through a lot of dross to see some really fine work, and this one was no exception. Many of the films were just a little too *Pink Narcissus* for my taste, featuring hippies running around in sheets and pointless strobe effects that can make you as blind as a bat. But the gold was there to be mined if you practiced patience and persevered.

Barbara Hammer's *Still Point* and Jerry Tartaglia's *Ecce Homo* are the kinds of films that make it all worthwhile. *Still Point* is breathtaking filmmaking. Hammer's four-screen multiple images evoke beauty and pain, home and homelessness, and a deep sense of the experience of being caught between several worlds at once yet taking a special joy in each. Her films aren't easy, but they're emotionally and psychically understandable and warm.

Tartaglia's *Ecce Homo* reclaims desire in the age of AIDS by using re-photographed footage of Jean Genet's *Un Chant d'Amour* and male porno films to examine the roots of our completely hypocritical taboos against the seeing of sex. His montages and narration form a dizzying panorama of brilliant associations overwhelming in their primal power. Tartaglia, like Hammer, is an artist at the peak his powers.

At the moment, New York City is inundated with film festivals. In addition to the experimental festival and the New York Film Festival at Lincoln Center, the Collective for Living Cinema is presenting aeries of lesbian and gay video screenings during October.

I think we're all much too close to the reality of gay life in America right now to appreciate it in any meaningful way while it's happening. That's why we have to celebrate the artists in our community who creatively interpret it, allowing us to explore and reexamine reality in new and exciting ways. On opening night of the experimental festival, for instance, filmmaker Phil Zwiegler tossed me a video, a five-minute movie called *Fear of Disclosure*. It wasn't even in the program. I took it home and watched one of the best films I've seen this year.

Schulman and Hubbard, by providing a forum for fresh images and ideas, are helping us to keep our dreams alive.

Who Owns the Past?

Looking for the Truth about Langston Hughes Elsewhere

November 21, 1989

At the press conference following the New York Film Festival screening of Isaac Julien's *Looking for Langston*, a man raised his hand and asked the filmmaker, "What does the homosexuality of Langston Hughes have to do with either his life or his work, and why is it necessary for me to know about it?"

This unfortunate soul (actually one of a multitude of "bananas" who show up regularly for such screenings) articulates perfectly the position of the ostrich school of social history, which says that an artist's homosexuality has, or should have, nothing to do with our perception of his or her work.

New York Times critic Caryn James, reviewing the film, wrote that "Mr. Julien drags Hughes out of the closet, kicking and screaming." Hughes has been dead for quite some time, and under the circumstances, I fail to see how he could possibly kick and scream. It is, rather, those whom filmmaker Julien describes as the "cultural gatekeepers around black history" who are kicking and screaming in their desire to keep the closet door firmly shut against the truth.

In truth, Julien's film is not actually about Hughes. It is, instead, an evocative meditation on the fabled Harlem renaissance, a nostalgic fantasy built around black gay desire and identity. This, apparently, is what caused the executors of Hughes's estate to have a fit when they saw Julien's finished film.

The executors used the fact that several of Hughes's poems are read in their entirety on-screen as an excuse to invoke copyright laws to prevent the film from being screened publicly. "This is a case," commented Julien, "of copyright being used as censorship, an attempt to fix Hughes as a black cultural icon for the black bourgeoisie." At the New York Film Festival screenings, the sound was turned off twice during the proceedings in order to avoid litigation.

Looking for Langston is a relatively short film--only forty-two minutes--but Julien packs it with cultural allusion and political commentary on white racism in the 1930s, the importance of the gay bar as a social anchor for gays and the relevance of AIDS to the black community. It's as though in this one sensual explosion, the issues of a black gay past, homophobia and racism have finally burst out of the confines of "official" history to change forever the nature of the debate on these subjects from a black point of view.

"Talking about black gay identity is very difficult historically," said Julien to a reporter." The censorship exists within our own [black} community. They can't stand the context of the film. In effect, they're saying, 'What you're trying to do is construct him as a gay icon, and he's a black icon.' It's not like whites are doing this."

Mad About the Movies

Apartment Zero's Gay Loner Is Lost
in the Reel World

December 19, 1989

I finally caught up with Martin Donovan's much discussed but little seen *Apartment Zero* at my local cinema recently. This complex, funny, and entertaining psychosexual political thriller deserves a wider audience than it will ever get. Made for only a little over a million and a half dollars, *Apartment Zero* is a perversely twisted yet strangely satisfying exercise, filled with film references both familiar and obscure — a feast for film freaks.

Colin Firth is Adrian, the occupant of apartment zero in a building he owns in Argentina. He also runs a revival cinema that has fallen on hard times. Our first glimpse of him is in the projection booth, where he is watching the final moments of Orson Welles's *Touch of Evil*. Adrian is a prissy, obsessive film lunatic whose pristine apartment is filled with expensively framed photos of James Dean, Montgomery Clift and Charles Laughton. Motion pictures are his life. Repressed, moralistic, absurdly tortured, Adrian is the complete loner, admitting to his solitary world nothing of the realities that swirl around him.

For film aficionados, *Apartment Zero* is occasionally very funny. The screenplay, by twenty-six-year-old David Koepp, is packed with references and homages to Alfred Hitchcock, Pier Paolo Pasolini and Joseph Losey. It's a Pedro Almodovarian experience with a little David Lynch thrown in. When Adrian is asked why he refuses to have anything to do with a particular person, he replies, "I can't tolerate him. He doesn't know who Geraldine Page was." He describes his own mother--with whom he clearly has a Norman Bates-type relationship--as sounding like Erich von Stroheim.

Adrian constantly engages in a game in which one name three actors and asks what film they all made together. Thus, the answer to "Vincent Price, Edward G. Robinson and Yul Brynner" is *The Ten Commandments*. Perhaps the most obscure reference comes when Adrian is walking down a Buenos Aires street called Calle Hernan Weinberg. There is no such street. Herman Weinberg is a film historian who once was connected with the Museum of Modern Art.

Because his cinema is floundering, Adrian must take in a boarder to help with the rent. Enter Jack, a knockout James Dean type who turns out to have the same hypnotic effect on people as Terence Stamp did in *Teorema*. Hart Bochner plays the role brilliantly, with a haunting sensuality reminiscent of Alain Delon in *Purple Noon*. Adrian goes quietly bananas at the sight of Jack. It is here that the film becomes menacing — a psychopathic "buddy film" about murder and obsession.

Adrian initiates Jack into the movie game, makes elaborate breakfasts for him, and begins to do his laundry, clearly wanting to possess him. Jack seemingly has the same effect on the eccentric inhabitants of the apartment house, even coming to the defense of a transvestite being fag-bashed. Yet Jack is not what he seems, and the revelation of his true nature prompts the grisly finale to this complex melodrama.

The performances are uniformly good, and in the case of Bochner, brilliant. British character actresses Liz Smith and Dora Bryan are amusing as two of Adrian's tenants, and James Telfer has some good moments as Vanessa, the transvestite, who says, "I like the dark. The dark is safe. In the dark I seem real. I've been loved in the dark." It's a moving performance.

Apartment Zero is no masterpiece — the direction is relatively uninspired, and it's a little too long — but it's a well-written, unusual film that should not be missed.

Pam Walton's highly professional *Out in Suburbia* won the audience prize for Best Documentary at last year's San Francisco International Lesbian and Gay Film Festival. The twenty-eight-minute film about lesbians in the suburbs is a model of how to make an accessible, honest and life-affirming statement directed toward mainstream viewers. The film profiles a group of women, notable for its racial and generational diversity, who discuss the ramifications of coming out, their relationships with their families and their various attitudes concerning the myths and stereotypes about their lives.

Because the central focus of the film is on lesbians who do not live in large, sophisticated urban centers, the problems are specific to people who must deal with their friends and neighbors in more intimate daily ways. One woman speculates about what the very friendly senior citizens in her neighborhood would think if she came out to them. Lesbian teachers talk about their struggle to come out to their students. There's a charming episode in which a lesbian mother expecting twins shows off the baby bedroom she and her lover have prepared for the new arrivals.

This is the kind of film that should be rented, leased, and bought by high schools, universities, and educational groups wishing to begin the process of raising lesbian issues (and consciousness) for the first time.

Sound and Fury

New Films Focus on the War Waged
by AIDS Activists

April 10, 1990

The media, both straight and gay, have recently focused a lot of negative attention on the activities of the AIDS Coalition to Unleash Power (ACT UP). The subject of all this reporting has been ACT UP's controversial tactics for directing public attention to the AIDS crisis.

The invasion of St. Patrick's Cathedral in New York City last December and the blockade of the Golden Gate Bridge and the disruption of the opera in San Francisco have engendered heated debate about whether AIDS activists have "gone too far" and "turned off" potential supporters.

Certain members of ACT UP, myself included, maintain that the real enemy in this epidemic is the widespread absence of a crisis mentality, the excess of conciliatory rhetoric and the mistaken notion that writing a check constitutes activism. AIDS activism, we maintain, is not a popularity contest but a war, and war is not polite.

For those who are open to learning more about AIDS activism, there are now a number of tough, in formative, and, believe it or not, entertaining videos that chart the course of this militancy.

The films borrow the style of local news broadcasts but transform the format by giving activists a chance to speak on their own terms. The images are backed up by some of the best new rap and New Wave music on the subject of AIDS to emerge in the last decade.

These videos are the products of several new production companies formed in the wake of the AIDS epidemic. They are staffed by AIDS activists whose interest has always been in film and video; in many ways, the companies owe their existence to ACT UP. The most prolific and professional are the Testing the Limits Collective and Damned Interfering Video Activist Television (DIVA TV).

Doctors, Liars, and Women, a film by Jean Carlomusto, grew out of an article published in *Cosmopolitan*. The piece stated, among other things, that heterosexual women cannot get infected with HIV even if they have unprotected sex with an infected male. The film follows the reaction of ACT UP, in particular the women of ACT UP, who first tried to get a response from the magazine's editor and then, when that failed, demonstrated in the streets outside the Cosmopolitan offices.

But the story did not stop there. For some reason, the author of the article, a psychiatrist, allowed himself to be videotaped in his office as he discussed the article with four women from ACT UP. He was demolished by their superior grasp of the issues, and in this sequence the tape comes alive. It is clear that this is a group of people who have done their homework and speak from a position of strength. The tape is also a model of how to build coalition in a democratic structure.

Target City Hall is about the takeover of New York's city hall by ACT UP to secure more city AIDS funding and housing for homeless people with AIDS. It is a powerful, useful work and shows the decision making process involved in planning arrests. It is also emotionally satisfying in its portrait of the reasons why ACT UP members choose to spend their time committing acts of civil disobedience.

A tape in progress, *Voices from the Front*, will be an hour-long documentary on the AIDS-activist movement, told in the voices of the people involved. The film illuminates the issues most vital to the survival of people with AIDS. Few images are more moving than the ones in *Voices from the Front* that show AIDS activists' takeover of the opening session of the Fifth International Conference on AIDS in Montreal last year.

These tapes are indispensable weapons for educating the public about the struggles of people fighting for their lives, are inspiring material for any activist group.

The Loved and the Lost

Private Grief, Public Drama Are
Captured in *Longtime Companion*

May 8, 1990

The American Playhouse production of Craig Lucas's *Longtime Companion* is something of a landmark film for several reasons. It is the first major movie to deal with gay men and AIDS; it doesn't try to explain gay life to a mainstream audience; and it contains more affection and intimacy between men than virtually any other film in recent memory. This is not to say that it's a perfect film or even a film without its share of problems. Yet it's a courageous and powerful statement, and it's something of a miracle that it got financed and distributed at all.

Screenwriter Lucas and director Norman Rene have been very clever in their presentation of the epidemic as seen through the eyes of a group of gay men in New York. The film opens on New York's Fire Island in July 1981 on the day that *The New York Times* published its first story on AIDS ("Rare Cancer Seen in 41 Homosexuals"). It then follows the same group of people on one day each year for the next nine years, showing what happens to them and how they grow and change during the crisis.

The production values are superior, as are the performances, especially those of Bruce Davison and Mark Larnos, who plays Davison's lover. But the major strength of *Longtime Companion* is that it is completely naturalistic and casual in its depiction of gay life. Because gay sexuality is treated as a given, the characters are presented as individuals, and their gayness is just one facet of their lives. Moreover, the script paints a realistic picture of what was happening at various points in history: In July 1981, at a beach house in Fire Island Pines:

"Did you see the *Times* article?"

"Please. Let's not talk about it."

In April 1982, at the emergency room of a New York hospital:

"Have they told you anything more since they called?"

"No."

"Don't worry. It's bronchitis. They give you antibiotics, and it goes away. I'm sure it's not *that*."

"Not what?

In June 1983, in the kitchen of a New York apartment:

"She has all these exercises where you look in the mirror and you say, 'I love my ears. I love my nose. I love myself.'"

A telephone conversation in March 1985:

"We're going to try stopping the sulfa drugs for a week to see if we can raise his white blood count — which is a risk, because he may have another seizure. He can't take this new drug for CMV unless his blood count is at least seven-hundred and fifty, but if he doesn't take it, he'll probably go blind. But if he has another seizure, it may permanently damage his nervous system. So take your pick."

This relentless progression, although punctuated with wit and humor, is the substance of a film that is directed at a group of people who, even after a decade of this horror, still believe that it can't possibly happen to them. The terrible truth this film offers is that many of those in the audience will someday soon make this same inevitable journey from denial to fear to sadness.

Longtime Companion will be criticized on many counts by the same people who always want films like this one to cover all bases and be all things to all people. Aside from the fact that such a thing is impossible, I'm tired of people who demand political correctness in art. Not only isn't it possible, it isn't desirable.

Yes, there are economic reasons why such films have to target an audience as mainstream as is reasonable. After all, look at how many of these films actually get made in the first place. And yes, we're always being put in the position of being grateful for small favors from a system that rarely reflects our lives.

But the only reason people are dissatisfied with films like *Longtime Companion* is that there aren't many movies made about such subjects, so these few films have to bear the burden of reflecting the entire gay community and all the issues surrounding AIDS. There are moments when the film suffers from such compression. In a sequence set in 1984, for example, a character says, "Now that they've found the virus in saliva, I suppose we won't even be able to kiss anymore." This information is not corrected in subsequent sequences.

Virtually all the characters in *Longtime Companion* are white, handsome and upscale professionals — and rightly so, because this is exactly the population first identified with this disease in exactly the setting in which it happened. These are the people whose lives were changed forever when they were rudely shocked out of their "this is our beach house, and these are our cocktails, and these are our magnificent pecs" life-style.

By the end of the film, they're talking about sit-ins outside city hall, wearing ACT UP buttons and T-shirts, and working the phones at the Gay Men's Health Crisis. That's the way it happened, and it's insulting to tell these people that their experience is somehow not valid because they're white.

I am grateful for *Longtime Companion* and appreciate the people who stuck their necks out to see that it reached the screen: executive producer Lindsay Law who financed the film totally through *American Playhouse*; Lucas, who struggled to create a screenplay that is sex-positive and inspirational; Rene, who didn't cave in to the temptation to explain everything to the misinformed and the moronic; and the Samuel Goldwyn Co., which had the guts to pick it up for wide distribution.

Now it's up to the audience to show up and support a film that, by any standards, is a difficult experience. It's time for gays in the audience to follow the lead of the characters in the film and grow up and act like adults who can actually handle life. If you can get your ass out of the house to see *Batman*, you can damn well support work like this. They don't make movies that don't make money. By supporting *Longtime Companion*, you're investing in others like it.

A Friend for the Oscar

Gay documentary filmmaker Rob Epstein now has as many Academy Awards as the late Bette Davis. Epstein, who took home the Best Documentary Feature statuette three years ago for *The Times of Harvey Milk*, has won a second Oscar for *Common Threads: Stories from the Quilt*. An elated Epstein said that he's proud to be bringing home "a gay lover" to keep his first Oscar company and is thinking of dressing them as twins.

In his acceptance speech, Epstein saluted the "courage and dignity of the lesbian and gay community" in leading the nation on the issue of AIDS. After the awards, Epstein was approached by Best Director winner Oliver Stone, who said, "I hope I can make as good a film about Harvey Milk as you did."

Stone is planning to produce — and perhaps direct — the screen version of Randy Shilts' *The Mayor of Castro Street*, with either Dustin Hoffman or Robin Williams in the lead. Epstein's documentary *The Times of Harvey Milk* inspired Stone to pursue a feature on the late San Francisco supervisor.

In the Lower Depths

When I was in high school, Hubert Selby Jr.'s controversial novel *Last Exit to Brooklyn* was the last word in gritty portrayals — here focusing on the denizens of a Brooklyn waterfront neighborhood. Sparing the reader nothing, Selby's six-part episodic chronicle of life's pathetic outcasts offered no hope, no redemption and virtually no tenderness in its portrait of the lower depths. It also prompted a sensational nine-day obscenity trial in England, where the book had been banned since its initial publication.

The hustlers, drag queens and prostitutes of Selby's world were trapped in a hell marked by violence, stupidity and poverty. What was most offensive to some critics was that *Last Exit to Brooklyn* graphically portrayed the kind of loveless sex immortalized in John Rechy's *The Sexual Outlaw*. "What I was trying to portray," said Selby at the time of the book's publication," was the horror of a loveless world. These people wouldn't have known love if they had seen it. It would have been mistaken for something else — weakness and fear."

It is to the credit of German director Uli Edel (*Christiane F.*) that the spirit of Selby's novel has been retained in his relentlessly depressing screen version. I'm not certain that such a faithfully hellish vision of life on the edge will find favor with audiences at the box office, but Edel has certainly been true to Selby's bleak vision.

The film weaves three major plot threads into its tapestry, beginning and ending with the story of Tralala, a pathetic waterfront prostitute who is finally gang-raped into senselessness in an abandoned car. This story stands alongside one of the first literary explorations of effeminate homosexual "trade queens," the tragic Georgette. These born outsiders are held in counterpoint to the "family" life of the neighborhood. With a waterfront strike as a backdrop, the rottenness and corruption of this hopeless world are brought into focus.

The sections of the film dealing with Georgette and his friends are perhaps the most painful for a gay viewer. These lost souls — drag queens, transsexuals and hustlers — are portrayed without any of the humor that saw so many of their kind through the living hell of the 1950s. They constitute a lost world in which gays played the dangerous game of servicing straight studs who were as likely to kill them as tolerate their advances.

The common denominator they share with the other characters in the film is their unrelieved stupidity, an inability to function except in a world of shadow. Clever but not wise, these queens had as much in common with the "tough broads" they parodied as Tralala had with the fractured vision she offered of a deadbeat Marilyn Monroe.

The film itself provides no catharsis, no point, no revelation. It has the look and feel of an exploitation reel in which comfortable middle-class viewers are supposed to be shocked by the grime on the screen and, ultimately, grateful for their own distance from it. The actors' performances are so up-close and played at such a clarion pitch that they cause the film to come across as a Ralph Bakshi cartoon based on *The Amboy Dukes*.

The performance of Zette, a gay nightclub performer, as one of Georgette's world-weary friends brings back a kind of gay life lost to the ages. But what's the point here? I don't know what the motivation would be to sit through this film, but if you want a graphic depiction of just how ugly life can actually be for some people, here it is.

For the Record

I know all of you are on the edge of your seats, wondering if Richard Chamberlain is "officially gay" or not. In a recent story by journalist Rex Wockner in the *Bay Area Reporter*, the actor was reported to have "come out" in the French women's magazine *Nous Deux*, saying that he and his lover of twelve years were building a house in Hawaii and that Chamberlain had "had enough pretending."

The story was picked up widely in both the straight and gay press throughout Europe. Now, of course, all hell has broken loose, with denials and retractions sailing through the air like guided missiles.

According to Wockner, Chamberlain's Los Angeles-based managing agent, Annette Wolf, denies he ever made such a statement. "There is absolutely no truth in this whatsoever," she commented in a telephone interview. "I have worked with Richard Chamberlain for six years, and he is heterosexual...People come up with the most horrifying stories."

Well, I'm certainly horrified, and I hope you are too. We wouldn't want anyone to say such a disgusting, dirty thing about Chamberlain. After all, imagine what a lowlife it would make him if it were actually true. I'm getting absolutely weary of this whole debate about whether or not it'll hurt someone's career to come out of the closet.

As Rita Mae Brown once said, "I've heard all the excuses, honey. And they're all shit."

Malice at the Movies

Mad and Just Plain Fed Up With
Bigots and Spineless Gays

June 5, 1990

It seems like lately I've been turning "bad." I mean bad like a pet who's gotten really nasty all of a sudden or a friend with permanent PMS. I don't have the tolerance I used to have for diversity of opinion. I'm less likely to be gentle with people than I used to be, and I'm often dismissive and sarcastic to them. Part of this, of course, is that these are fearful times and I'm willing to put up with a lot less bullshit than ever before. Also, I'm old. At least I'm older than most gay people I meet socially, and I don't have their fervor about "new" issues anymore.

Take "outing" for example. It seems that I've heard all the tired arguments about outing before, and the debate doesn't excite me. As far as I'm concerned, there's no reason for me to waste my energy defending the rights of closet queens, who as a rule are the lowest form of animal life anyway and don't really give a rat's ass about anything but their own agenda. I no longer want to spend hours pontificating about the right to privacy so they can lie to the rest of the world and inherit Daddy's money someday. Their "right" to lie has become trivial to me over the years.

I've begun to feel the same way about the relationships lesbians and gay men have with their own image on film, which really grates on me. Not only do "average" gay people (I guess I mean non-activist types) not recognize and react to bigotry when they see it on-screen, but they also don't go out of their way to support positive images of themselves.

Let me explain what I mean. I'll meet some guy at a party and because he knows my work, eventually we're talking about movies. It always goes something like this:

He asks, "Did you see *No Way Out*?"

"Yes."

"Wasn't it great?"

"Didn't it bother you that the gay character was the villain, that not only was he hopelessly in love with a straight man but he also committed suicide in the end, and that the Bible is quoted to condemn him in the film?"

"Oh, yeah, there was that one thing, but wasn't it a *great* movie?"

It seems to me that gay people are just crazy in love with the First Amendment to their own detriment. If movies treated other minority groups the way they consistently treat gay people, all hell would break loose. This month two films have opened that do violence to gays. One, *Bird on a Wire*, is a clear-cut case. The other, Sidney Lumet's *Q&A*, apparently is debatable. In *Bird on a Wire*, there are two screaming, flaming hairdressers right out of 1934. Worse, Mel Gibson and Goldie Hawn stand behind their backs and mimic them cruelly. Not only has there been no outcry, but most gays don't even notice it, and most critics (many of whom have gay friends) don't condemn it. Nor has "feminist" Goldie Hawn spoken out against the antigay portrayals in the film.

Lumet's *Q&A* is yet another action film about a bad cop, played by Nick Nolte. The bad-cop film has a long tradition of portraying the "scum" that vice cops have to deal with on a daily basis. Macho cops with a problem have been blowing away fags on-screen for longer than anyone can remember. This seems to make it okay somehow. We've gotten used to it.

In 1973, Stuart Rosenberg's *The Laughing Policeman* was nothing more than a freak show of gay bars containing fat transvestites, go-go boys with glittered eyes and leather killers. The same year, in *Busting*, Elliot Gould and Robert Blake showed their macho credentials by raiding gay bars and beating faggots. In *P.J.* (1968), George Peppard starts a fight in a gay bar and gets his cheeks scratched by a leather number ("That sick faggot scratched my cheek").

In *Q&A* we're supposed to think it's okay that cocksucker and faggot are used over and over again, that Nolte murders two drag queens (of color) and that Nolte is a twisted closet queen whose violence against gays emerges out of his own "problem." We're supposed to think it's okay because he's a racist, a pig and an equal opportunity bigot.

It's not okay. The truth is that I'm tired of films about fat, drunken, bigoted slobs who end up being the hero to an audience of subhuman morons who get their homophobia validated by liberal filmmakers who have a lot of gay friends but never seriously consider the consequences of their films. One out of three gay teenagers will try to commit suicide this year because of homophobia. And gays in the audience just sit there and take it.

Then there's the other side of the coin. I'll be walking down the street, and I'll run into someone I know. The conversation goes like this:

"I saw your review of *Parting Glances*. I heard it was really good. I just never got around to seeing it."

What I used to say:

"It's on video, you know. You should really see it."

What I say now:

"No, but you managed to get your fat ass out of the house to pay seven dollars to see *Batman* twice, didn't you?"

So I've turned bad lately. And I think the real reason is because I've discovered that what I've always known is true. Most gay people have turned out to be nothing but a bunch of Americans who just want to be entertained for two hours and not have any hassles. It stinks. They should be ashamed of themselves.

From Screen to Shining Screen

Richness of Gay Life Is Celebrated
at Film Festivals

July 3, 1990

A long time ago, in the first years of gay liberation, I ran movies once a week at the old Firehouse headquarters of the Gay Activists Alliance (GAA) in New York's Soho district. I was always obsessed with film history, and there was something appealing to me about introducing old Hollywood movies to radical political activists in a gay-positive setting.

There really weren't gay films back then, not in the sense that we know them today. Once in a while I'd show an old dinosaur like *The Killing of Sister George* or *The Children's Hour*, and everyone would be outraged on behalf of their newfound gay pride. But mostly I'd stick to classic gay male favorites like *The Women, Gypsy* and *A Star Is Born*. These caused outrage as well, prompting cries of sexism from lesbians on the verge of a separatist movement of their own and eventually leading to screenings for women only.

But there were also wonderful times when the crowd went wild, when the laughter was genuine, and when the men and women were brought together in shared experience. I vividly remember an entire audience literally jumping out of their seats at the climax of *Wait Until Dark*. And during *Night of the Living Dead*, when the ghouls began to eat their victims, a lesbian in the back row yelled, "Save me a breast!"

This kind of community feeling went to the heart of the necessity for such screenings. Before the gay movement, lesbians and gay men rarely had the opportunity to share such things in a safe space. They were used to hostile audiences in mainstream movie houses, which often featured films with homophobic dialogue and situations. Lesbians and gay men felt trapped and helpless, surrounded by a crowd they perceived to be unsympathetic.

Once I began screenings at the GAA headquarters, lesbians and gay men, for the first time, were in a room with people like themselves who spoke a common language and were able to share their identity freely.

This is the emotional basis for what has evolved into annual lesbian and gay film festivals all over the world. For the past fifteen years, these festivals have been presented in major cities and small towns across America, often as part of gay pride week celebrations. Today they are among the most popular, well attended, and most cherished events in our community, attracting lesbians and gay men who cannot remember a time when such festivals didn't exist.

The sense of community engendered by the gay film festivals is palpable and perhaps even more important than the quality of the films being presented. Film is still a universal language. Apart from the excitement one feels when surrounded by an all-gay audience, there's the wonder of discovering the diversity of gay cultures and communities in different parts of the world. If you spoke of "gay community" in China, they wouldn't know what the hell you were talking about. But now we have Taiwanese gay films, which make us feel connected to another kind of gay experience.

This year, the major festivals are more complex and ambitious than ever before, with New York's and San Francisco's overlapping in June and Los Angeles' scheduled for mid-July. Over the years, these festivals have become truly international in scope, offering world premieres from other countries as well as major retrospectives of American and foreign films.

A measure of their success is that the immutable *New York Times* has finally decided that the gay festivals are legitimate enough to cover. For the first time, the *Times* will review films directly out of festival screenings instead of waiting until they open commercially.

Probably the most talked about feature this year, a popular hit at the Berlin film festival, is Heiner Carow's *Coming Out*, the first gay film from East Germany. It will be screened in New York and is the opening night feature in both San Francisco and Los Angeles. The film provides a last look at gay locations and gay life in East Berlin before the wall came down, an event that coincided with the premiere screening, prompting fanatical partying in the streets after the showing.

Among the many lesbian films being premiered is Joy Chamberlain's *Nocturne*, about two sociopathic lesbian hitchhikers who invade the home of a third woman in a Pinter-esque exercise in power and control. It is being offered on opening night in New York, paired with Stuart Marshall's *Comrades in Arms*, a British documentary in which six lesbians and gay men recall gay life in wartime Britain. A film that the San Francisco festival has been trying to secure for five years is Miguel Picazo's 1985 Spanish feature *Extramurros*, starring Carmen Maura as a Sixteenth-century nun who fakes stigmata with the help of her lesbian lover. It's described as "a lesbian version of the Jim and Tammy Bakker story."

New York instituted a Gay Asia series this year with several lesbian-themed features, including Stanley Kwan's *Full Moon in New York*, which tells the story of three Chinese women immigrants, one of whom is a lesbian. In an entirely different vein, the camp favorite of both festivals promises to be *I Am a Man*, which is a 1988 Thai version of Mart Crowley's *The Boys in the Band*, described as a cross between *Hawaii Five-O* and a Herschell Gordon Lewis epic.

The retrospectives are often audience favorites, and this year they're knockouts. New York is bringing back great 35-millimeter prints of *Walk on the Wild Side*, in which Barbara Stanwyck played the first post-Hays-code lesbian in an American film, and Nicholas Ray's *Johnny Guitar*, in which Joan Crawford and Mercedes McCambridge provide enough butch fireworks to eclipse the gay rodeo.

In its "Lesbians in Prison" series, San Francisco will show Warner Brothers' only 35-millimeter print of the long-unavailable *Caged*, directed in 1950 by John Cromwell. One of the few such films to work equally as camp and serious melodrama, it contains Oscar-nominated performances by Eleanor Parker and Hope Emerson. The film is not available on videotape and is never shown in theaters. *Caged* is one to punch upon with delight. It is also perfectly complemented by a rare screening of *Deathwatch*, directed by Vic Morrow in 1967 from Jean Genet's famous play and starring Leonard Nimoy.

It is impossible to duplicate here the entire festival programs from each city or to do justice to the literally hundreds of films and videos being screened. I could go on for a full page, for example, about the fact that San Francisco is showing the only extant print of Arthur J. Bressan's *Abuse*, one of the finest gay films ever made. There are dozens of moving and informative AIDS films, scores of drag-queen parades, hilarious compilations of coming attractions from older gay films and some of the finest documentaries available today. There's even an intriguing program in the San Francisco festival called "A Woman of Affairs: Greta Garbo's Lesbian Past."

Another gay pride week is upon us, and I can't think of a better way to celebrate our history and our vast diversity than by laughing and crying with our people in the magical comfort of a darkened picture palace.

Here's to passion, politics and popcorn!

A Failure of Image

Why Hollywood Can't Get Past Its Gay Stereotypes

September 25, 1990

I've been thinking more and more lately about the degree to which the representation of lesbians and gay men in popular culture is misunderstood by critics and journalists and therefore misrepresented or ignored. Recently there was an arts piece by Caryn James in *The New York Times* that dealt with the anti-Semitism in Spike Lee's new film, *Mo' Better Blues*. Lee is quoted from a television interview saying, "I couldn't have an anti-Semitic sequence in any of my movies. Jews run Hollywood and would never let me get away with it."

Leaving aside for a moment the astonishing anti-Semitism of that statement, Lee is also plain wrong. Jews in Hollywood have never rocked the boat. They have never taken care of their own. In the 1940s, they wouldn't even make movies attacking the Nazis until Hitler closed off most of their foreign markets. Then I got to thinking how this is true of gay Hollywood executives as well. Gay people in the movie industry don't object to antigay language in film because they don't want to call attention to their homosexuality. Every time I hear some right-wing minister talk about how "gays control Hollywood," I think, *Yeah, right. That's why we have so many positive films about gays.*

In the same *Times* piece, the writer contrasts anti-Semitism with homophobia, and she gets it as wrong as possible, although she still scores points just for bringing up the subject in the first place. Using the example of Mel Gibson's stereotypical hairdresser in *Bird on a Wire*, she says that it's more "callous" than "vicious" and that it stands out as an outrageous "lapse" rather than as a Hollywood rule. Can it be possible that this very sophisticated writer doesn't know that it is certainly Hollywood's rule and that *Bird on a Wire* is only one of dozens of such offensive films that open every week?

Recently, I had occasion to remember a scene from Bill Sherwood's *Parting Glances* in which Nick, the rock star with AIDS, played by Steve Buscemi, says, "Have you ever noticed that straight people are so egotistical that ninety percent of everything you see is about them?" This is true as well of white people in film: Yet there isn't much official complaining these days that most screen characters are white, because black screen visibility is in fact making substantial progress at this moment in history.

Would that we could say the same about lesbians and gay men. While we are still treated to regular denunciations of gay people on-screen and are barraged with antigay epithets, we still do not have even the beginnings of a tradition that would allow characters who are incidentally gay to appear in films. None of this even occurs to journalists like James, nor do most heterosexual critics even notice the extent of homophobia in the art forms they cover. As far as they're concerned, the world is straight the way the world used to be white, and homophobia isn't important enough an issue to make a fuss about.

Some critics will even defend certain language that gay activists find offensive. Whenever the word faggot is used by teenagers in a film and someone complains, there will always be the intellectual philistine who will say, "Oh, faggot doesn't mean 'gay' to these kids. It's a catchall word for wimp or for anyone they don't like."

Well, this week they should take a look at David Lynch's new film *Wild at Heart*. I really thought we were going to get through one entire contemporary film without an antigay slur, but sure enough, just before the end, it arrives.

Nicolas Cage, confronted by a menacing teenage gang on the street, says, "What do you faggots want?" whereupon they beat him senseless. After Glinda the Good Witch appears to him in a bubble (this is a Lynch film), he apologizes to the toughs by saying, "I'm sorry I referred to you gentlemen as homosexuals." So much for the contention that faggot doesn't really mean "homosexual."

I think what's going on these days is that writers, journalists, screenwriters and producers are at a loss to define how to use gay characters incidentally and at the same time don't really care to interfere when they're used stereotypically. Finding ways to portray lesbians and gay men in a casual, incidental manner is an interesting challenge. Actors Equity can insist that Asian actors play Asian roles, but can they insist that a gay role be played by a gay actor? Can we make that demand, ignoring the fact that color is obvious but sexuality is not?

To use gay characters well on-screen or onstage, we have to first change people's perceptions about who we are. We have made many strides in visibility in the last twenty years, but producers and screenwriters simply don't know how to let people know a character is gay without resorting to clichés. They still think their options are either to present gays as sexual or as the obvious stereotype. Sequences using gay people casually are still the exception rather than the rule. There's one currently in *The Two Jakes* in which a gay bar forms the background for a sequence with little or no editorial comment by the filmmakers.

I remember once asking my high school French teacher how one would know which definition a particular word would have if two words were spelled exactly the same but had different meanings. He said, "You should know from context clues. Read the sentence, and you'll know what belongs there." I think that's what's wrong with gay representation on-screen. We have no acceptable context, and it's up to us to create one by being more open about whom we are. Then we will be people and not targets.

On the Horizon

October 23, 1990

There's a lot of screenplay activity involving lesbians and gay men going on at the moment. The most interesting project by far is John Schlesinger's new film, his first with a gay theme since *Midnight Cowboy* and *Sunday Bloody Sunday*, both released approximately two decades ago. Also, the new film is about AIDS.

"I had been mulling over a way to treat AIDS," said Schlesinger recently, "but I realized it was going to be difficult to get off the ground."

After being turned down by Orion Pictures and after Cineplex Odeon showed interest but crashed financially, the project landed at Propaganda Films, which gave us *Twin Peaks* and David Lynch's new film, *Wild at Heart*. The company put up the development money and hired gay writer David Leavitt to write the screenplay, which will have something to do with activist groups like the AIDS Coalition to Unleash Power.

"I thought if John Schlesinger wanted to do an AIDS film," says Leavitt, "and he thought I was the right writer, I ought to give it a try." Leavitt says it will be as positive as possible in spite of the tragic nature of the epidemic. "It will be very much about people living with AIDS," he says, "as opposed to people dying from AIDS. That, to me, is the most important point from both a political and an artistic standpoint."

Another screenplay story, which broke in Liz Smith's nationally syndicated column recently, provides a rare and satisfying insight into how some Hollywood writers have a conscience and a sense of social justice. Joe Eszterhas, who wrote both *The Music Box* and *Betrayed*, has pulled out of his current project, *Basic Instinct*, for Corolco. It seems that Eszterhas and producer Irwin Winkler have been paid off on the film because they object to the way the film is proceeding under the direction of Paul Verhoeven, often characterized as the "bloodthirsty" director of the Arnold Schwarzenegger hit *Total Recall*.

Basic Instinct is an "erotic mystery" about a bisexual woman killer who uses sex to "play" with people. According to Eszterhas, the script was inoffensive, but Corolco wanted to change the basic story to be a very graphic film with a lot of lesbian sex. Eszterhas saw no reason for such sensationalism. He has already had his name removed as executive director.

"I live in San Rafael with my family, right outside San Francisco," Eszterhas said to Smith. "There is a large gay community here, and I respect it. I don't like racism — that's why I made *Betrayed*. And I don't like anti-Semitism —that's why I made *The Music Box*. I despise homophobes. So if Corolco turns this picture into something with ice-pick-wielding lesbians, then I will be the first person out in the street to join the protest against it.

I've often castigated screenwriters for their insensitivity to gay issues, and it's a pleasure this time around to salute the decency and courage of a good man. I hope he wins the battle.

A relatively unknown screenwriter, David Franzoni, has been hired to write the script for the screen version of Randy Shilts' *The Mayor of Castro Street* for Warner Bros. The multimillion-dollar production, scheduled to go before the cameras sometime next year, will have a major star in the role of slain San Francisco supervisor Harvey Milk and a high-powered cast. The film is being produced by Oliver Stone and Craig Zadan and will be the first Hollywood film to focus on the politics of gay liberation.

Hollywood attempts at gay productions have always been personal coming-out stories, such as *Making Love* and *Personal Best*. *The Mayor of Castro Street* will focus on the true story about the antigay assassination of Milk during a turbulent time in San Francisco history. Both Shilts and Milk's former lover, Scott Smith, who is the executor of the Milk estate, have been signed on as consultants to the project. Writer Franzoni's other hot project at the moment is an HBO movie about the life of secretly gay lawyer Roy Cohn.

An anonymous source sent me the screenplay for *Silence of the Lambs*, based on the extraordinarily popular novel of the same name by Thomas Harris. The script is by playwright Ted Tally and follows the novel fairly closely. The film deals with thorny subject matter — the story of a twisted kind of "transsexual" who murders and flays women and saves their skin to make himself a woman "suit" so he can be "reborn" as a female.

The script is not patently offensive, certainly not to lesbians or gay men, but it presents societal problems that are always with us on some level. The dialogue makes it plain that true transsexuals are most often gentle people and that this sick killer is a class apart. Yet he's written and portrayed as a mushy, frightening psychopath (with a dog named Precious) who both hates and envies women at the same time.

What we have to look at here--and this is true of more than one film I've discussed in this column--is the trend in films toward portraying unspeakable violence against women. This trend has persisted throughout the history of the medium, as has the medium's approach to sexual ambiguity.

There's a difference between exploring sexual ambiguity and violence and exploiting it for maximum shock value. Nobody likes a well-written and well-directed action thriller more than I do. It's only a personal matter of taste that I do not care to be frightened out of my wits by disgustingly graphic violence. I am further concerned about the constant generalizations in film about sexual ambiguity. Many films of this nature do not have to be specifically about homosexuals or lesbians to reinforce the idea that "those people" are all a bunch of sickos who are violent and destructive and deserve to die.

I am told by many people that Harris's novel is brilliant. In fact, many of my gay friends say it is the best novel they've ever read. My only moral concern is one that probably has nothing to do with this particular property. It has to do with living in a society in which sexuality and violence are becoming so indistinguishable that it puts any of us who are different in a repellent category and sends a message to people that we live in a sick, twisted world.

Outtakes

Pump Up the Volume, a recent film starring Christian Slater, is about a renegade disc jockey who reaches college students with anarchistic messages that make them want to take action against various injustices. There is a scene in which he receives a call from a student who is probably gay and who has been forced to "service" a group of students. He is confused and troubled.

Slater treats him gently and well and makes the point that we are all more alike than we are different.

It is a small thing but a breath of fresh air in a film designed for young people. Unfortunately, a friend reports to me that director Allan Moyle said that a lot of the gay content was ruthlessly cut.

And, finally, has anybody noticed that in *Postcards from the Edge*, during the homecoming-party sequence, Meryl Streep is wearing a button with a pink triangle on it? It's not an accident. It's an official gay liberation button and it's rather prominently displayed on her denim jacket. We should find the person who thought that one up. Once again, we are grateful for the very smallest of favors.

Buffoons or Villains

November 20, 1990

The current film *Miller's Crossing* is something of a dilemma in terms of its gay content. An intellectual gangster film about Chicago mobsters in the 1920s, the film highlights for me all the contradictions that arise out of the ways in which art attempts to reflect life. Directed by Joel Coen (*Raising Arizona* and *Blood Simple*), the film has two gay characters, both part of the underworld.

My conflicting feelings come both from the casual way in which their sexuality is integrated into the film and the subliminal messages sent out by the ways in which they are used. I have always maintained that that judging the gay content of art should never be a case of whether the presentation is "good for gay people." It's never that simple. I always try to take into account the apparent intent of the artist as well as the context in which lesbians and gay men are presented.

In *Miller's Crossing*, there's nothing stereotypically "queer" about either of the gay characters in gesture, appearance, or attitude. The script tells us they are gay in the most non-judgmental, matter-of-fact terms. One of the most curious and confusing aspects of the script is that the gay character is referred to constantly as "the *schmatta*," a term I always thought was Yiddish for a woman's dress or head kerchief. It's the first time I've ever heard it as a reference for a gay person.

The more significant of the two characters, played brilliantly by John Turturro, is the brother of a gun moll, who spends the movie trying to save him from being bumped off. When someone makes a derogatory comment about Turturro, she says, "That's right, sneer at him like everybody else. Everyone thinks he's a degenerate, but he's not."

We are also provided with the information that she tried to sleep with him at one point to "save him from his friends," which certainly reveals at least one misconception on the part of the screenwriter. Yet people still do believe that the love of a good woman can "save" a homosexual. So is it fair to portray that misconception, or does an artist have an obligation to get the facts?

There are other disturbing aspects to the personality of Turturro's character. Of all the gangsters in the film, he is the only one who, when threatened with being shot to death, begins to bawl like a baby and hysterically pleads for his life. Everyone else in the same situation displays strength and defiance. Is it unreasonable to pin these emotions on the fact that he's gay? I don't think so. He is not killed, and later in the film, he apologizes for falling apart. He says he's sorry for behaving like a "twist." The word *twist* is gangster talk for a woman.

One of Turturro's boyfriends, a character named Mink, is played by Steve Buscemi (*Parting Glances*). He has just one scene. The two gay men have no scenes together in the film. Eventually, the Turturro character emerges as a psychological sadist, but then every character in the film is amoral, like the gangsters in Martin Scorsese's current masterpiece *GoodFellas*. It's difficult, then, to complain that the gays are without redeeming value, because that's true of all the players. Coen has created a world in which we're dealing with vicious killers and immoral slime bags both gay and straight.

Here's where we come to the conflicts. While heterosexual characters in art are routinely presented in a balanced way, this has never been true of gays. Gays have an unbroken tradition of being played as either buffoons or villains. Remember Peter Lorre's Joel Cairo in *The Maltese Falcon*? Or Richard Burton's Vic Dankin in *Villain*? Homophobia is increasingly subtle these days, emerging in ways that remind us of the continuing ignorance about who we are. For example, when one of the producers of David Lynch's *Wild at Heart* was interviewed recently, he said, "I never thought of faggot as a derogatory term. That's just the way we've always talked."

In the end, don't know if I feel comfortable with the endless portrayal of bigots and their language on the screen. *Miller's Crossing* also contains references to "sheenies," "guineas" and "dagos." The usual excuse is that that's the way these people would talk. That excuse is becoming increasingly weak for me.

It always seems that bigots are given First Amendment rights to spew their hatred, whereas we seldom have a public forum to respond in kind. During the scene in which Turturro is about to have his head blown off, an audience member in front of me began to applaud softly. Somehow, I don't think that this represents a step forward for anyone.

A final note: There's a scene I do like in *Postcards from the Edge*, in which Shirley MacLaine's character is approached by a gay man who "does" her in his act. He says effusively, "All my life, I've only wanted to be you." Later she comments, "You know how the queens adore me."

I have been trying to get an interview with MacLaine about *The Children's Hour* for almost ten years. She always says no.

Now I feel like calling her up and saying, "Come on, Shirley, give me a break. You know how the queens adore you."

Acknowledgments

The editors offer our gratitude and acknowledgement to the following individuals who made this project possible: Andrew Ahn, Delia Avila, Carol Contes, Howard Cruse, Trey DeGrassi, Jon Glover, Philip Harrison, John Hoffman, Arnie Kantrowitz, Joy Johnson, Larry Kramer, Michael Musto, Sheila Nevins, Brian Nolan, Michael Oliveira, Michael Schiavi, Michelangelo Signorile, Taryn Teigue, Lily Tomlin, Kieran Turner, and Mark Umbach.

We thank these institutions for their generosity: The Fales Library and Special Collections, New York University, HBO Documentary Films, the Museum of Modern Art (MoMA NY), the New York Public Library, and the One National Gay & Lesbian Archives.

Finally, we would especially like to acknowledge and thank Charles Russo, the Russo Family and the Vito Russo Estate for their support of the project and access to the materials.

CPSIA information can be obtained at www.ICGtesting.com
Printed in the USA
LVOW121317110613

338038LV00002B/44/P